Lady Anne Bacon

/

Lady Anne Bacon

A woman of learning at the Tudor court

DEBORAH SPRING

HERTFORDSHIRE PUBLICATIONS
an imprint of
University of Hertfordshire Press

First published in Great Britain in 2024 by
Hertfordshire Publications
an imprint of
University of Hertfordshire Press
College Lane
Hatfield
Hertfordshire
AL10 9AB

British Library Cataloguing in Publication Data

A catalogue record for this book is available from the British Library

ISBN 978-1-912260-66-9

Design by Arthouse Publishing Solutions
Printed in Great Britain by Henry Ling Ltd

Contents

Illustrations

Acknowledgements

The genesis of this book was my discovery of the existence of Anne Bacon's letters during my research on the Tudor gardens of Gorhambury. The letters were then only available in manuscript in Lambeth Palace Library, and notoriously difficult to decipher (see p. 163). I am grateful to Gemma Allen for her scholarly edition of 2014, which opened the door to this treasure trove of material. My thanks too to my MA tutors at Birkbeck and the University of East Anglia, and the friends from both courses who have given me encouragement and help, especially Ann Kennedy Smith, Alison Baxter, Gill Blanchard and Rob Atkinson for good company and shared writing support and Gwenneth Heyking for Tudor expertise. My membership of the research group of the Hertfordshire Gardens Trust, led by Tom Williamson and Anne Rowe, was the source of discoveries and insights into the history of the houses and designed landscapes of Tudor Hertfordshire. Thanks to the 'Arc and Arc' – the St Albans and Hertfordshire Archaeological and Architectural Society – for the initial publication of some of the material included here on Anne Bacon and Gorhambury. The Gorhambury Estate, Hertfordshire, has kindly assisted me with my research and granted permission for the use of material held in the Hertfordshire Archives. I have further been helped by the Raveningham Estate, Norfolk. When writing and research were difficult during the pandemic, with the loss of access in person to libraries and archives, the London Library's provision of books by post was a lifeline. My thanks to the staff there for their help both then and during easier times. Jane Housham and Sarah Elvins of Hertfordshire University Press have been thorough, patient and attentive. My grateful thanks to them for taking on the book, waiting for it, and putting it into shape.

Particular thanks go to my friends and family for their tolerance and unstinting support through the vicissitudes of life while I pursued Anne Bacon's story. Jane Salvage encouraged me to keep writing during convivial meetings in person and virtually. Stephen Irwin, who willingly embedded himself in the sixteenth century with me, was the first reader of every new chapter, and my companion through the tangles of historical evidence, as well as on expeditions to East Anglia in search of the Bacons, while Rachel, William and Ruth, with their partners and children, have provided much fun and good cheer along the way.

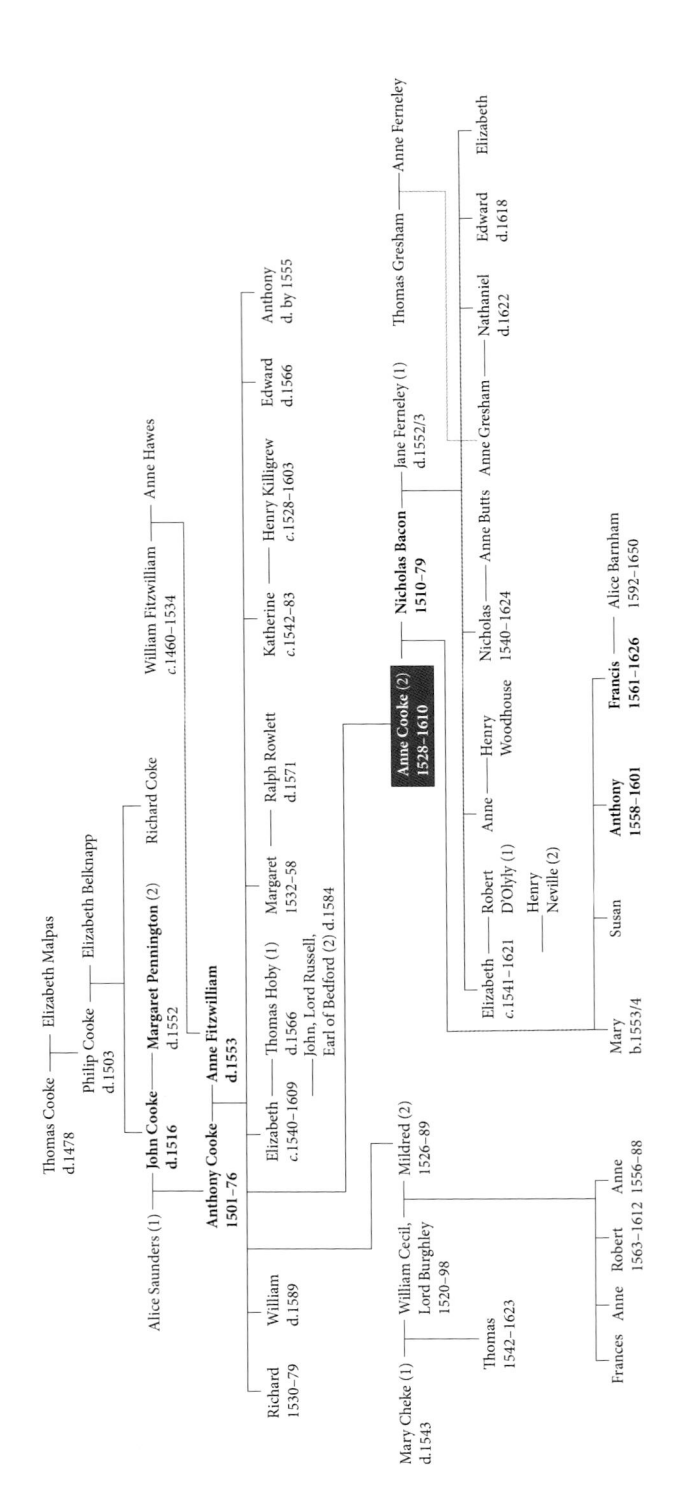

A tree showing the family relationships and connections in *Lady Anne Bacon*.

Introduction

Anne Cooke was the second daughter of Anthony and Anne Cooke. Born in 1528, in the reign of Henry VIII, she was brought up in a well-established gentry family that embraced both the new learning of Renaissance humanism and a new form of religion, ultimately to be known as Protestantism. The Cookes had close connections to the royal family and the intellectual elite at court. Living through the political upheavals and religious reverses of four Tudor reigns, Anne would play a role in events of national significance and serve in the Privy Chambers of both Tudor queens regnant, Mary I and Elizabeth I. A published translator by the age of twenty and ardent supporter of religious reform, who promoted the cause of dissident Puritans in her later years, she saw the end of the Tudor dynasty, dying in her early eighties seven years after James I acceded to the throne of England. She married lawyer and statesman Nicholas Bacon and raised two clever and difficult sons, Anthony and Francis.

History, wrote Hilary Mantel, is 'the record of what's left on the record … what's left in the sieve when the centuries have run through it – a few stones, scraps of writing, scraps of cloth'.[1] We make what we can from the fragments that survive.

The fragments of Anne's life left for historians to piece together include her published translations of Italian and Latin texts, and around a hundred letters by chance preserved with her son Anthony's correspondence in the Lambeth Palace archive. Her face looks out from a handful of portraits. We know where she lived. We can trace her networks of family and fellow religious reformers and contextualise her life in the wider history of the time. This book is my attempt to draw these threads together and put on the record the life of a remarkable woman.

When another young woman was presented to James I, with the information that she knew Latin, Greek and Hebrew, he laughed, 'Ay, but can she spin?' Yet before he came to the throne, England had been ruled for almost half a century by a woman whose preoccupations were not household, husband and family, but knowledge and power. No learned woman would have been treated so dismissively at Elizabeth I's court. Elizabeth was not alone in being a formidably well-educated woman for her time. Other young women of the mid-sixteenth century were taught the classics and humanities, among them the queen's half-sister Mary, her stepmother

Catherine Parr, Lady Jane Grey, the women of the Devereux and Sidney families, and the five Cooke sisters including Anne. The influence of such educated, often politically astute women in the early modern period has been little acknowledged in the past, but for some women – as well as the two queens – life during the reigns of Mary and Elizabeth held more than marriage, household duties and decorative accomplishments.

Four centuries after her death at the Bacon family estate of Gorhambury in Hertfordshire, we can still hear Lady Anne Bacon's distinctive voice through the translations she undertook and the letters that survive from a decade of her widowhood. Thanks to the painstaking work of Dr Gemma Allen in transcribing and editing the letters, and Dr Patricia Demers in editing Anne Bacon's most important works of translation, these sources are now accessible in scholarly editions.[2] Quotations used here are rendered into modern spelling.

Anne Bacon's imprint upon the history of her time was notable, and together with her sisters she has been visible at the margins of historical accounts of the period, but until feminist historians began to open new lines of investigation into the lives and experiences of early modern women, her life was largely absent from the mainstream narrative of Tudor England.[3] This book describes some of the opportunities, achievements and restrictions of Anne Cooke Bacon's life, and the part she played in key events of the reigns of Mary I and Elizabeth I.

Chapter 1
Gidea Hall

Women were taken seriously in the Cooke family. Born five years before the Tudor princess Elizabeth, who would rule England for almost half a century, Anne was the second of five intellectually gifted sisters who were encouraged to develop and school their minds in an age when this was not expected, or for the many women who were denied an education, accepted. Gidea Hall in Essex, where they grew up with their four brothers, became famous for its learned women. Of the five sisters, Margaret, the youngest, died soon after her marriage, aged twenty-six. Two of the brothers also died as young men, with the survivors, Richard and William, leading respectable but undistinguished lives.[1] Of the four remaining sisters, Mildred, Anne, Elizabeth and Katherine, none disappeared into domestic obscurity upon marriage. Over their lifetimes the sisters variously engaged in learned tasks, attendance at court, political influencing, religious reform, estate management and vigorous lawsuits.

While not educated to their level, the competent and forceful woman they knew as their grandmother set an example for them to follow in leading active lives. Margaret Pennington Cooke was the second wife of their grandfather John Cooke.[2] After her husband's early death in 1516 she brought up her stepson Anthony, Anne's father, from the age of eleven. While her brother-in-law Richard Coke acted as head of the family after his brother's death until Anthony was eighteen, Margaret was also closely involved in family affairs. A shrewd manager and businesswoman, she served Catherine of Aragon at court, ran two Cooke family estates and lived into her eighties. Managing her affairs alone as a widow for forty years, she acted as an executor, and ably administered two estates granted her for her lifetime. Her careful handling of property paid off for Anthony and his inheritance was substantial.[3] The Cooke family accrued further wealth when Anthony inherited land in Warwickshire that came from his grandfather's marriage to Elizabeth Belknap, and by his subsequent speculation in monastic land after the Dissolution.[4]

While Anne's mother Anne Fitzwilliam Cooke remains a more shadowy figure, she appears in the historical record in an account of a dramatic incident in August 1534.[5] Travelling to her father's funeral in Northamptonshire, she was escorted by her husband's uncle Richard and accompanied by a group of gentlewomen and servants. As the travellers rode through Hertfordshire, their way was obstructed by a belligerent butcher called Mitchell and his servant, who refused to move their horses aside to allow the family to pass. The pair continued to occupy the full width of the road, kicking dust and dirt over the gentry who were forced to ride behind them. Richard attempted to defuse the situation by offering to buy the butcher a drink at the next town but Mitchell was contemptuous of the courtier class and not to be bought off – the offer seems only to have inflamed his temper. Angry exchanges on the road escalated into a riotous brawl when they reached the Hertfordshire town of Hoddesdon, where Mitchell raised a hue and cry summoning the townsfolk to attack the 'whoreson courtiers', which it seems they did with relish, wielding cudgels and billhooks, staves and swords.

One of the Fitzwilliam women courageously pushed her horse through the melee, calling out 'For the passion of Christ, keep the peace, and save my men, and slay them not', only to be knocked to the ground by Mitchell and beaten. The fight ended in defeat and retreat for the heavily outnumbered Cooke party, with their servants thrown into the town jail, but via a complaint to Thomas Cromwell they pursued justice for the assault in England's highest court, the Star Chamber.[6] The result of the case is not recorded, but Mitchell and the rebellious citizens of Hoddesdon are likely to have received a stern punishment for the 'heinous Riot'.[7] Anne was six years old when the riot brought her mother into such peril. She was being brought up in comfort and security, safe in a prosperous household that was insulated from danger and threats. The assault and its aftermath must have been a shocking intrusion into her family's well-cushioned life.

A prominent Essex family, the Cookes were not aristocrats but owed their wealth and position to a shrewd forebear, Sir Thomas Cooke (d.1478). A successful draper in the City of London, he married an heiress, used his fortune to fund socially upward moves to a country estate and courtly connections, and became Lord Mayor of London in 1462.[8] Securing his position among the Essex gentry, Sir Thomas bought Gidea Hall, Romford in 1452, and enlarged his property with the addition of the manors of Bedfords and Earls in Havering, and Redden Court in Hornchurch. He enclosed 200 acres to form a park and obtained a royal licence to add impressive mock fortifications – turrets, crenellations, battlements and machicolations – to the Hall.[9] While these additions and architectural flourishes enhanced his family's status, Sir Thomas left the house unfinished, distracted by business and political troubles that resulted in two spells of imprisonment, embroiled him in debts and lawsuits and at one point saw his house 'plundered of the furniture, and all that could be carried away; the deer in his park, rabbits, fish etc. destroyed: for which he could not get any recompense.'[10] Despite these setbacks Sir Thomas remained a wealthy man until his death.[11]

Anthony Cooke refashioned and completed Gidea Hall towards the end of his life, during the reign of Elizabeth I, when his daughter Anne was in her forties. He entertained the queen there in 1568. The finished building was arranged round

Detail from John Norden's map of Essex in *Speculi Britanniae Pars: an historical and chorographical description of the county of Essex* (1594), showing the location and extent of Gidea Hall ('Gyddy Hall') and its park to the east of Romford.

LA SORTIE DE LA REYNE ACONPAIGNE DV ROY DE LA GRANDE BRETAIGNE SON BEAV FILS DV CHATEAV DE GIDDE HALLE

This is the only early image of Gidea Hall. Made to commemorate a visit in 1637 of the Queen of France, Marie de Medici, it shows the Hall as Anne would have known it in later life, after her father had extended and updated the house.

three sides of a large courtyard, with an open colonnade on the fourth side, and a moat.[12] His classical learning was displayed in inscriptions on the front of the house. One read: *Aedibus his frontem Proavus Thomas dedit olim, Addidit Antoni caetera sera manus*, 'Thomas the great grandfather raised the front, Anthony long after finished the building'. Other inscriptions in Greek and Hebrew, 'worn out by time', were dated 1568.[13] One of a dozen manor houses within Romford's orbit, the house appears as Giddy Hall on Norden's 1594 map of Essex. It stood north of what is now Main Road in Gidea Park, about 300 yards east of Raphael Park, and was rebuilt 'in an elegant manner ... with plantations of trees, canals and other improvements' in the eighteenth century.[14] No trace of the house remains today: from 1910 the park was gradually developed as a garden suburb, and Gidea Hall was demolished in the 1930s.[15]

Anne's childhood was spent in the manor house, still as it was in her grandfather's time, its courtyards and crenellated walls sprawling across the crest of the wide incline overlooking the town of Romford from the east. The house was surrounded by gardens and set in a park shaded by oak trees, through which the Ravensbourne stream flowed to join the river Rom in the town below. Romford was a busy market town in the sixteenth century, with a population of around 1,300. John Norden, the mapmaker, noted the shire was well wooded, fat and fruitful, and Romford held 'a pretie market on the Wednesday, yielding store of corn and swine'.[16] A changing crowd of traders and travellers was served by the many inns and stables in the town, and at only twelve miles from London, it was conveniently close to the capital.

Anne was named after her mother, Anne Fitzwilliam, the daughter of another well-to-do Essex gentry family: her father Sir William Fitzwilliam was a City of London merchant and Sheriff of London. Lady Fitzwilliam, her maternal grandmother, was a cousin and close friend of Catherine Parr, who would become Henry VIII's sixth and final wife. Gains Park, the Fitzwilliam family estate, was only ten miles from Gidea Hall. The match, made when Anthony and Anne were respectively about seventeen and sixteen, was congenial to both families in terms of money, status and the convenient proximity of the two households.

The couple became parents to five daughters: Mildred (1526–89), Anne (1528–1610), Katherine (1530–83), Margaret (1532–58) and Elizabeth (*c*.1540–1609); and four sons: Richard (*c*.1530–79), William (d.1589), Edward (d.1566) and Anthony (d. by 1555). The present church of St Edward the Confessor, Romford, built in 1849–50, stands on the site in Romford market place once occupied by the medieval parish church of the same name that Anne would have known. It houses the sizeable family monument, designated as of national importance, which was originally placed over the vault in the Lady Chapel of the earlier church. Lengthy epitaphs in Latin and English eulogise the 'worthy knight, whose life in learning led' and his *pulcherrima conjux*, 'most beautiful spouse', Anne.[17] The carved and polished stone image of Anne's mother and father and the children who survived

Details from the tomb of Sir Anthony and Lady Anne Cooke in St Edward's Church, Romford, including their four daughters, Mildred, Anne, Elizabeth and Katherine. Photographs: Deborah Spring.

their parents depicts a row of four serious daughters, with the same long noses and strong profiles, and the two remaining sons. The sculptor must either have seen a genuinely strong family resemblance between the sisters, or he took a guess in their absence and produced a composite face for them all.[18]

Both Anthony's stepmother Margaret and his paternal uncle Richard Coke were attached to the court of Henry VIII, in the service of Catherine of Aragon. Margaret served as one of the queen's gentlewomen from 1514, while Richard Coke was a diplomatic courier, travelling frequently to the continent and carrying messages to and from Charles V in Spain. The connection between the Cooke family and successive royal Tudor households was to be a significant strand in Anne's life.

When Anne was ten years old, her father was appointed to Henry VIII's newly formed personal ceremonial bodyguard, fifty men handpicked from the aristocracy and higher gentry known as the king's 'spears'. Wearing gold chains and bearing gilt poleaxes, they were decoratively positioned in the king's Presence Chamber. Their captain was William Parr, Catherine Parr's brother, and thus a kinsman of Anne's mother.[19] Anthony Cooke took up his post at court in 1539, when he was in his late thirties. This was the final decade of Henry VIII's reign and the king was still alone after the death of his third wife, Jane Seymour, following the birth of their son, Edward. With Catherine of Aragon now also dead, all three of the king's children – Mary aged twenty-three, Elizabeth, six, and Edward, the two-year-old heir – were motherless. Henry was about to marry for the fourth time. When the new queen, Anne of Cleves, arrived in England at the end of 1539, Anthony Cooke was present at her reception in his new role as royal bodyguard. After Henry's death Anthony went on to serve Edward VI. Anne would follow the family pattern as a courtier close to the monarch, in the service of both Mary I and Elizabeth I.

Anne's childhood years spanned a period of increasing religious instability in England, as the king's 'Great Matter', his long campaign to divorce Catherine of Aragon and marry Anne Boleyn, culminated in his break with Rome in 1534. In 1538, Henry VIII was excommunicated by Pope Paul III, after years of papal threats. The Acts of Dissolution, suppressing the monasteries and transferring their assets to the crown, were passed, starting in 1535–6. Anne was twelve years old when Waltham Abbey, fifteen miles from Gidea Hall, became the last religious house in England to be suppressed and demolished. Its organist and choirmaster, composer Thomas Tallis, lost his job when the abbot surrendered to the king's commissioners, lucky to depart with a pay-off of forty shillings and an ancient music manuscript he had managed to salvage.[20]

During Henry's reign, and Anne's childhood, robed priests still celebrated the mass in Latin at altars, churches were furnished with paintings, chalices and candlesticks, and chantry priests said masses for the souls of the dead. Henry VIII saw Lutheranism as a threat and censored the press in England to prevent the printing and circulation of reformist texts. In 1521, before his break with Rome,

Henry wrote his *Assertio Septem Sacramentorum adversus Martinum Lutherum* (*The Defence of the Seven Sacraments against Martin Luther*), attacking Luther as 'this one little Monk weak in Strength, but in Temper more harmful than all Turks, all Saracens, all Infidels anywhere' and condemning his 'impertinent calumnies'.[21] He dedicated his work to the Pope and was rewarded with the title Fidei Defensor, Defender of the Faith, still used by the reigning English monarch.

The movement for reform attracted English sympathisers despite Henry's censorship. Luther's contemporary, William Tyndale, advocated for a simpler, evangelical form of religion. Tyndale left England for Wittenberg in 1524. His translation of the Bible into English was published in Worms and Antwerp and he wrote *The Obedience of a Christian Man*, published in Antwerp in 1528, the year of Anne's birth. Among other reforms, the book proposed that kings should be head of the church in their kingdoms, not the pope.[22]

In 1539 the great wealth of the religious houses was still being systematically plundered and funnelled into the royal coffers, as Henry's programme of dissolution entered its fourth year. In the same year came publication of the 'Six Articles', the agreed doctrine for the new Anglican church headed by the king.[23] The first English language Bible, known as the Great Bible, drew on earlier versions by Miles Coverdale and John Rogers, an associate of Tyndale. It was authorised for use and distributed to every parish church. Although it was based significantly on Tyndale's work, and his views were back in favour after he had initially been condemned as a heretic by Cardinal Wolsey, Tyndale did not survive to see England adopt an English Bible. He had remained in exile and, in 1536, was executed for heresy in the Netherlands.

Although he had been brought up by relations who were closely connected to the Spanish monarchy and who maintained their devout Catholicism, Anthony Cooke and his family would become committed Protestants. However, England was not yet a Protestant country, nor had the practice of the English church under Henry altered so that it was fully 'reformed'. The term 'Protestant' was not yet generally used in England. It arose from the protest made in 1529 by rulers and princes within the Holy Roman Empire against an edict reversing concessions made to Lutherans three years earlier.

While those close to the king dared not openly express Lutheran sympathies, it was safe to praise Henry for his reforms to the English Church and his challenge to papal authority. Accompanying the king on one of his progresses in 1541, Anthony Cooke made a translation from the writings of the early church father St Cyprian which he dedicated to the king, praising him for delivering his subjects from the 'captivity and bondage of Rome'. Such early Christian writings were read and translated by scholars seeking the 'pure' origins of their faith. Anne's parents were among those turning towards the new evangelical faith and away from what Luther and his followers considered to be the excesses and corruption of Roman Catholic practice. Her father was drawn to the company of scholars who both studied the classical humanities and were sympathetic to reforms being promoted by the followers of Luther and Calvin. Luther might have remained a little-known dissident friar, but for the fact that Wittenberg, where in 1517 he posted his first public declaration of the reformers' stand against the sale of indulgences and prayers for the dead, was the town where printers first produced books and broadsheets for a wide readership. Following publication of Luther's *Ninety-Five Theses*, Wittenberg became an important hub for printing in northern Germany and beyond.[24] With printing presses at his service, a flair for publicity, and an outspoken debating style, Luther captured attention across the Christian world and inspired reformist movements across Europe.

Anne's father had matured into a serious and thoughtful man who was known for his love of learning and his thorough approach to educating his children, despite lacking formal academic training himself. He did not attend either Oxford or Cambridge University, though he did enter one of the Inns of Court, then known as England's 'third university', a usual course for young gentlemen who wanted to acquire social polish and suitable connections – not necessarily accompanied by legal studies. His life and character are recorded by seventeenth-century historian David Lloyd, who paints a picture of a sober man: 'Gravity was the ballast of his soul, and general learning its leading'.[25] Although Anthony Cooke took part in public life at various times, sitting as an MP and furthering the religious reforms of Edward VI's reign, according to Lloyd this was contrary to his inclination. He preferred to guide and train others: 'Sir Anthony took more pleasure to breed up statesmen than to be one. Contemplation was his soul, privacy his life, and discourse his element. Business was his purgatory, and publickness his torment'.[26] Although he had not been to university, Anthony was attracted to a scholarly life, and Lloyd tells us he was admired as 'somebody in every art, and eminent in all the whole circle of arts lodging in his soul … His Latin fluent and proper; his Greek critical and exact … his Logic, rational'.[27] As he approached his thirties, Anthony Cooke shifted his attention from the public affairs he disliked to the learning he found more congenial and applied himself to the study of classical languages. This was the time of the English Renaissance, the revival of classical art and learning that had spread across Europe from its beginnings in fourteenth-century Italy to reach England in the early sixteenth century.

The Cooke sisters benefited from their parents' enlightened views on education for girls. Anthony Cooke's view was that 'souls were equal, and that women are as capable of learning as men'.[28] Gidea Hall was an educational hothouse, where the five girls were taught a broad and rich humanist curriculum alongside their brothers. Their father planned and supervised their classical studies, and was reputed to have governed his family by 'prudence and discretion', reason and affection: 'Such the majesty of his looks and gait, that awe governed; such the reason and sweetness, that love obliged all his family'.[29]

Their mother was an important influence, taking responsibility for her children's religious education. Anne recognised her mother's active engagement in the family's spiritual development in a published prefatory letter to her 1551 translation of the sermons of Italian preacher Bernardino Ochino, in which she expresses respect and admiration for the guidance of her 'right worshipful and worthily beloved mother.'[30] She wishes her mother 'increase of spiritual knowledge, with full fruition of the fruits thereof' and writes of her 'godly exhortations and motherly admonitions', her dedication to 'the destroying of man his glory, and exalting wholly the glory of God', and her 'so many worthy sentences' concerning the election and predestination of God.[31] Although the family matriarch Margaret Cooke remained a committed Catholic throughout the religious upheavals of her lifetime, Anne's parents turned decisively away from the traditional church to become leading supporters of the evangelical movement that ultimately led to the Edwardian and Elizabethan religious settlements. The zeal for a simpler and more authentic form of Christian faith that Anne first encountered at Gidea Hall laid the foundation of her lifelong support for the cause of reform, and the Puritanism of her later years. For Anne this vocation to reform entailed active, influential, and sometimes dangerous engagement in the events of Tudor religion and politics across three reigns, not a retreat into the quiet, conventional piety of a gentlewoman.

Old certainties were being held up to the light, shaken out and questioned in young Anne Cooke's world, as religious reformers and scholars alike sought the renewal of ideas relating to faith and philosophy by returning to first principles and 'lost' texts. The Cooke children benefited from an education underpinned by the two great movements that shaped intellectual life in England in the early sixteenth century, overthrowing accepted conventions. The Renaissance brought a revival of classical learning and the adoption of renaissance humanism – the study of the *studia humanitas,* today known as the humanities. The Reformation introduced new perspectives on religious belief, rejection of Roman Catholic rituals and doctrines, and the prospect of throwing over the old order in the Church. What followed for Anne was a lifelong connection with the intellectual and politically elite circles of Protestant Tudor England, founded in her family's evangelical faith and the intellectual framework of an advanced humanist education.

Chapter 2
The schoolroom

The questions of how and how far to educate women were being addressed by Tudor scholars and educators well before Anne and her sisters entered the schoolroom, and the first half of the sixteenth century saw a recognition that non-royal women could benefit from access to learning, both to occupy their minds and to better equip them for their roles as wives and mothers. Access to education had opened up for a small number of elite girls and women by the mid-sixteenth century, the Cooke sisters among them. This was not a uniform dropping of all barriers to learning but arose through a conjunction of scholarly developments, technical advances in the printing and distribution of books, the influence of key individuals, and family support of education for girls. The factors that still circumscribed women's education are unfamiliar to us, based as they are on sixteenth-century interpretations of biblical precedent, religious belief and moral philosophy. To understand Anne's life, it is important to put her learning into context, and before moving on further with her story, this chapter will look at the background to the Cooke sisters' education.

Italian writer Niccolò Machiavelli (1469–1527) delighted in the rediscovery of the ancients. He writes of entering his library each evening:

> I dress myself as though I were about to appear before a royal court as a Florentine envoy. Then decently attired I enter the antique courts of the great men of antiquity. They receive me with friendship; from them I derive the nourishment which alone is mine and for which I was born. Without false shame I talk with them and ask them the causes of the actions; and their humanity is so great they answer me ... I transform myself entirely in their likeness.[1]

The Renaissance scholars reclaiming the art and letters of antiquity were reversing a decline in classical learning during the Middle Ages. Knowledge of classical languages was the key to this renewed familiarity with antiquity and the *studia humanitatis*, then comprising the study of grammar, rhetoric, history, poetry and moral philosophy. Humanists sought to fulfil the principle of a virtuous active life, the *vita activa*. The new learning, as it was called, combined moral and political lessons, drawn from classical sources, with Christian principles, taught through study of the earliest versions of scripture. Guided by such texts, individuals were to build a foundation of personal ethics, spirituality and civic responsibility to inform their management of family and public duty. Of course, for men such a grounding was the logical prelude to a life that was expected to encompass public duties and responsibilities. But how were women to be educated and to what end, when, with rare exceptions, they were excluded from public life?

Some modern scholars suggest that a key motive for families was that an advanced humanist education at this period had become a marker of high social status. While women could never further their families' interests by gaining influential official positions, as men could, if their value on marriage was enhanced by education they could contribute to an upward rise of their families from the gentry into the aristocracy through advantageous marriages. On this view educated women remained passive pawns in the social politics of marriage, with their learning serving principally as added value in the competition to acquire status. In an alternative view, their humanist training gave some women tools to act effectively and with agency – though always within prescribed limits – upon the world around them.[2]

It did not follow that the few women privileged to enjoy an education gained control over their own lives or wider roles in the world. However well educated a woman might be, her learning must never interfere with her most important duties: to be obedient, modest, pious and chaste, and put her family's interests first. She had no place in the public world. William Barker (*fl.*1540–76) translated and adapted an Italian dialogue about the nature of women, Lodovico Domenichi's *La nobilità delle donne* of 1549, adding autobiographical and specifically English material to the text.[3] He sums up women's disadvantaged situation, as men excluded them from the public realm however well fitted they might be for it:

> And now against all justice, the tyranny of men have usurped all things and will not suffer women to do nothing, they may not have any office be they ever so prudent, they may not plead a cause be they ever so wise and eloquent ... They may not teach the word of God which the scripture permitteth saying by the mouth of Joel your daughters shall prophesy.[4]

Despite this gloomy picture, the second half of the sixteenth century would bring two highly educated women into direct power as England's first reigning queens. By the time Barker translated the dialogue in 1559, Mary I had ruled England for five years and been succeeded by Elizabeth I in 1558. Moreover, they were not the first powerful royal women of the Tudor age. Henry VIII's reign was bookended by his connection with two educated, active and determined women, his grandmother Lady Margaret Beaufort and his sixth wife Catherine Parr.

Walter Haddon (1515–72), a lawyer and classical scholar, admired Anthony Cooke, describing him as 'a man of profound knowledge, exquisite literary judgement, varied learning, and truly admirable memory'. When he visited the Cooke family at home in the 1540s he was impressed by the studious atmosphere of the household. Gidea Hall felt to him like a small Tuscan academy of learning, where women as well as men were engaged in scholarship. 'While I stayed there I seemed to be living among the Tusculans, except that the studies of women were flourishing in this Tuscany'.[5]

The Hebrew inscriptions decorating the walls at Gidea Hall demonstrated the family's intellectual aspirations. Anthony Cooke collected books for his extensive library, memorialised after his death: 'Your library was superior to any treasure-house. The mere names of the books would make a book'.[6] The family was dedicated to study, with the five daughters' education taken to the same advanced level as the sons'. Access to such a programme of learning for girls was still unusual in a gentry family, when girls' education was generally limited to basic literacy, decorative accomplishments and the domestic skills they would need to run a household. A clever and ambitious boy, even from a modest background, could rise through school, university and legal training to a position of influence and power – as did Anne's future husband, Nicholas Bacon. For most intelligent young women there was no pathway to higher learning and access to scholarly works. Yet not only did the five Cooke sisters learn alongside their brothers but all four surviving sisters continued to study and apply their learning after their marriages, which were all made with men of similar education and religious outlook – 'distinguished men, who serve Christ by true religion, and whose supreme wisdom is profitable to Britain'.[7]

Would the Cookes have seen their daughters' education as instrumental in improving the family's social status? The evidence does not point to that as a prime motive. Anthony Cooke's early biographer, Lloyd, writes of the care he took over the choice of marriage partners for his children, with the main motive appearing to be the creation of stable and supportive partnerships: 'In their marriage they were guided by his reason, more than his will; and rather directed by his counsel, than led by his authority. ... His care was, that his daughters might have complete men, and that their husbands might be happy in complete women.'[8] However, in the long term, the outcome of the sisters' marriages was to enhance their families' social position. Education was part of the rise to elite status for the Cookes and their circle. Through public service and service at court the Cecils and Bacons moved from the gentry to the aristocracy in one generation. The younger Cooke sisters married diplomats, and Elizabeth Cooke married as her second husband John, Lord Russell, heir to the earl of Bedford. In the next generation both Mildred's and Elizabeth's daughters made aristocratic marriages.

The girls of the family may have shown more aptitude for learning and enjoyed it more than the boys, none of whom seems to have shone in the schoolroom. Historian William Camden described Cooke as 'a man happy in his daughters', whom he 'brought up in learning, both Greek and Latin, above their sex' and married to 'men of good account'.[9] Mildred's husband William Cecil, later Lord Burghley, who became Elizabeth I's most senior minister, wrote after Mildred's death in 1589 that she had a 'singular knowledge of Greek and Latin tongues, which knowledge she received solely at the hands of her father who instructed her'.[10] The Cooke children began their classical education with Latin, and learned modern languages – French, and in Anne's case, Italian – at home as well as Latin and Greek. There is also evidence that Anne probably knew some Hebrew.[11] Princess Elizabeth's tutor Roger Ascham considered Mildred and Lady Jane Grey to be the most learned ladies in England; he reported in 1550 that Mildred spoke fluent Greek and pursued her study of the language with an Oxford scholar, Giles Lawrence.[12] Mildred's husband's biographer, John Clapham, was less enthusiastic about her intellect, voicing what were common suspicions about educated women when he wondered if she was 'as some persons may suppose, of more learning than is necessary for that sex'.[13] He was referencing a general belief that the legacy of Eve's original sin was present in every woman. While young women who were 'apt' for learning should be encouraged, 'I perceive that learned women be suspected of many,' wrote the Spanish educator Juan Luis de Vives, 'as who saith the subtlety of learning should be a nourishment for the maliciousness of their nature'.[14] As the descendants of Eve, all women were characterised as by nature untrustworthy and susceptible to error: 'a woman is a frail thing, and of weak discretion, and that may lightly be deceived, which thing our first mother Eve sheweth, whom the Devil caught with a light argument', Vives warned.[15] A key aim of any education and moral guidance they might receive was to confine and counteract this dangerous tendency.

With few examples of educated gentlewomen to emulate, who and what influenced Anthony and Anne Cooke's choice to educate their daughters to such a high standard, risking the censure of those who held that women should not have more learning than was 'necessary for that sex'? They would have been influenced by the views of humanist scholar Desiderius Erasmus of Rotterdam (1469–1536), who lived in England at various times between 1509 and 1514 and had a far-reaching influence on education.[16] Writing in 1521, he considered the conundrum of educating women:

> It was not always believed that letters are of value to the virtue and general reputation of women. I myself once held this opinion: but More completely converted me. Two things are of the greatest peril to the virtue of young women, idleness and lascivious games, and the love of letters prevents both … there is nothing that more occupies the attention of a young girl than study. Hence this is the occupation that best protects the mind from dangerous idleness, from which the best precepts are derived, the mind trained and attracted to virtue. … Nor do I see why husbands should fear that their wives would be less obedient if they are learned, unless they are such as would require of their wives what

should not be required of proper women. To this end, since the pleasure and durability of a marriage depend more on the pleasure of minds than the love of bodies, they are bound by much stronger chains who are linked in the devotion of their minds.[17]

Thus, for Erasmus, study for women could be a useful diversion from immoral pastimes. It should not alarm a potential husband.

Erasmus refers to his friend Sir Thomas More, father of Margaret More (1505–44). Featuring in her father's story as his amanuensis and support, like many women Margaret remained visible in the historical record because of her association with a prominent man.[18] Famed as a child for her precocious intellect, shown off at court by her father, she was married by sixteen, bore five children and died aged thirty-nine. She began Latin lessons when she was eleven years old and progressed through a thorough grounding in Greek and Latin that included undertaking daily exercises in double translation – from Latin to English and back again to Latin. She practised the skills of letter writing and disputation, and studied a wide range of subjects: grammar, poetry, logic, mathematics, philosophy, theology, medicine and astronomy. When Anthony Cooke set a similar programme of study for his daughters he was compared to More, and Anne Cooke was ranked by John Coke, a sixteenth-century commentator, alongside the learned women of Sir Thomas More's family. Aiming his remarks at French scholars, Coke asserted the superiority of England's learned women: 'We have diverse gentlewomen in England, which be not only well studied in holy scripture, but also in Greek and Latin tongues as mistress More, mistress Anne Cooke, mistress Clement, and others, being a strange thing to you and other nations.'[19]

Influenced by Plato and Italian philosopher Pico de Mirandola, More made no distinction between men's and women's ability to learn, they were both 'equally suited for those studies by which reason is cultivated, and is productive like a ploughed field on which the seed of good lessons has been sown'.[20] He relished setting programmes of study for his own children and others from the wider family who joined the Mores' schoolroom, and he hired tutors to help manage his 'school' of young students.[21] Believing that girls had the same intellectual and moral potential as boys, and deserved to have that potential realised through education, More rejected the notion that girls and women could become corrupted by too much learning. However, he maintained that a woman could never risk her virtue and reputation by taking part in public life. An educated wife and mother would be better equipped to prepare her young children for life, to understand her husband, and support him to fulfil his family and worldly responsibilities. She should demonstrate charity and humility, not personal ambition. He advised his children to remain modest despite their abilities, since 'renown for learning, if you take away moral probity, brings nothing else but notorious and noteworthy infamy, especially in a woman.'[22]

C A deuout treatife vpon the Pater no=
fter / made fyrft in latyn by the mooft fa=
mous doctour mayfter Erafmus
Roterodamus / and tourned
in to englifhe by a yong
vertuous and well
lerned gentylwoman of .xir.
yere of age.

Margaret More seated at a desk with her books. This is the frontispiece from her anonymous translation of Erasmus's *Devout Treatise upon the Paternoster*, 'tourned in to Englishe by a young vertuous and well learned gentylwoman of xix yere of age', edited by Richard Hyrde (1526). British Library c37e6(1) © British Library Board.

More was especially close to Margaret, his 'dearest Meg'. He admired her intellect and warmly encouraged her progress, but would not allow her to write a book, as the aim of her education should be moral virtue, not what he termed the 'gaudy trappings' of renown.[23] With her father's approval Margaret worked on an original religious treatise, 'The Four Last Things', but it was not published, and the manuscript did not survive. However, she became the first non-royal woman to publish a translation. At the age of nineteen, identified on the title page only as an anonymous 'young, virtuous and well learned gentlewoman', she translated from Latin the *Precatio Dominica* by Erasmus as *A Devout Treatise upon the Paternoster* (1524). But her own voice was silenced. As John Guy writes, More 'conformed intransigently to the social convention of his time that it was morally disreputable for a woman to seek recognition as a writer'. Margaret's father advised her to 'regard us – your husband and myself – as a sufficiently large circle of readers for all that you write'.[24]

More saw his daughters' education as innovatory and remarked that erudition in a woman was a new thing.[25] This was not true: scholarly English women may have been thin on the ground at the time, but the 'learned lady' flourished in Italy, France and Spain.[26] The Spanish queen of England, Catherine of Aragon, was well educated and ensured her daughter Mary was tutored to a high level. Erasmus wrote a dialogue in which Margaret More appears thinly disguised in the character of Magdalia, a quick-witted woman running rings around a dull abbot. Magdalia speaks about other learned European women: 'In Spain and Italy there are not a few women of the highest rank who can rival any man. In England there are the More girls, in Germany the Pirckheimer and Blauer girls. If you're not careful … we'll preside in the theological schools, preach in the churches, and wear your mitres'.[27] The more practical advantages to educating girls were not lost on the merchants of Antwerp, the centre of international trade, where girls schooled in modern languages helped to run family businesses. Christophe Plantin, founder of the first great European printing house in that city, had five daughters who were taught Greek and Latin, the most apt of them working as proofreaders of the multilingual publications Plantin printed and distributed throughout Europe.[28]

In declaring there to be a lack of erudite women, More omitted mention of a learned English woman whose influence was felt throughout the century. Lady Margaret Beaufort (1443–1509), grandmother of Henry VIII, founded the professorial chair held by Erasmus at St John's College, Cambridge.[29] Archbishop John Fisher said of her:

> … she was of singular wisdom, far passing the common rate of women … good in remembrance, and of holding memory; a ready wit she had also to conceive all things, albeit they were right dark. Right studious she was in books, which she had in great … number, both in English and in French and Latin and for her exercise, and for the profit of other, she did translate divers matters of devotion out of French into English.[30]

Lady Margaret's endowments to the University of Cambridge, notably to St John's college where she placed men from her own household into key university appointments, established the framework of scholarship that formed the minds of many Tudor statesmen of the next generation and began 'a direct line … from humanist St John's to the heart of the political and religious life of mid-Tudor England'.[31] This 'Cambridge connection' as it became known, came to include Anne's husband, her brother-in-law Cecil and their associates, who would form the nucleus of the reformist and humanist intellectual elite at Edward VI's court. By the 1530s and 40s other families had followed Sir Thomas More's lead, the royal princess Mary was studying a humanist curriculum, and girls' education was the subject of advice for parents and tutors. Princess Mary's near contemporary, the future queen Catherine Parr (b.1512), studied at home in a modest schoolroom at Rye House near Hoddesdon in Hertfordshire. Her mother Maud, widowed at the age of twenty-five after bearing five children, never remarried.

Maud established a schoolroom for her own two daughters and one son and others from the family with the support of her kinsman Cuthbert Tunstall, the Bishop of London. Tunstall shared Sir Thomas More's interest in education, publishing a book on arithmetic that was dedicated to More and used by the More children. It is likely also to have been used by the Parr family. Tunstall encouraged parents to give the book to both boys and girls, writing that nothing was so invigorating to the abilities of young people being trained in liberal studies as mathematics.[32]

Catherine Parr became Henry VIII's sixth wife in 1543. After her marriage she wrote pious books, publishing her *Prayers or Meditations* in 1545 and *Lamentations of a Sinner* in 1547. She also supported university scholarship, writing to the University of Cambridge:

> You seem to have conceived ... a favourable estimation ... of my ... dedication to learning ... showing how agreeable it is to have, being in this worldly estate, not only for mine own part to be studious, but also a maintainer and cherisher of the learned state.[33]

When Henry departed on a military campaign to France in 1544 he appointed Catherine to be Regent General of England in his absence, a far from nominal role. Active and well informed, during her short tenure as regent she engaged in the practical organisation of military resources for the king as well as managing a diverse range of issues at home. Here was an example of an educated woman with a 'quick and decisive mind' ruling England.[34] Her stepdaughters cannot have failed to take note, however remote it might seem that they would ever rule. Catherine remained on good terms with Mary and was an affectionate stepmother to the younger royal children Elizabeth and Edward. She guided their education and religious upbringing, as well as influencing the king to reinstate both his daughters to the line of succession.

Lady Margaret Beaufort, Countess of Richmond and Derby, by an unknown seventeenth-century artist. She holds a book that symbolises both her piety and her patronage of learning. National Portrait Gallery 551 © National Portrait Gallery, London.

Speaking of Catherine of Aragon and other studious women, Erasmus noted, 'We have a queen of England who is a famous learned woman and whose daughter Mary writes very good Latin letters. Thomas More's house is a veritable home of the muses. … The scheme of human affairs is turned topsy-turvy: monks hate books and women love them.'[35] 'It is now a common thing to see young virgins so nousled and trained in the study of letters, that they willingly set all other vain pastimes at naught for learning's sake,' wrote Nicholas Udall, a schoolmaster at Eton College.[36] This development was in reality still limited to a small number of elite girls despite Erasmus's playful declaration about the 'topsy turvy' state of the world and Udall's description of girls' learning as a 'common thing'. It was quite a contrast to the more usual expectation that girls' education should be restricted to conventional accomplishments, exemplified in this account of how two upper-class sisters spent their days:

> Our dancing Master cometh about nine a clocke: our singing Master and he that teacheth us to play on the virginals at ten: he that teacheth us on the Lute and the Viol de Gambo at four a clocke in the after noon: and our French Master cometh commonly betweene seven and eight a clocke in the morning.[37]

For Lady Jane Grey, nine years younger than Anne Cooke, learning was a relief and sanctuary from such banal pastimes and the cruelties of her daily life. Roger Ascham, tutor to the daughters of Henry VIII, recorded finding Jane, then aged about thirteen, in her chamber reading Plato in Greek 'with as much merry delight as some gentlemen would read a merry tale in Boccace [Boccaccio]' while the rest of the household were out hunting in the park.

> And how came you madam', quoth I, 'to this deep knowledge of pleasure, and what did chiefly allure you unto it, seeing not many women, but very few men, have attained thereunto?

To which she replied that her life was full of troubles, and only her tutor was kind to her.

> … whatsoever I do else but learning is full of grief, trouble, fear, and wholly misliking to me. And thus my book hath been so much my pleasure and more, that in respect of it, all other pleasures in very deed be but trifles and troubles unto me.[38]

A description of learned English women, compiled two centuries later by George Ballard, attributes the emergence of a group of scholarly women in England in the sixteenth century to, first, the availability of printed books and, second, the example of More's daughters. He adds that although Henry VIII's daughters' education was often held up as the exemplar, More's daughters were renowned for their learning well before Mary and Elizabeth were born.[39] The advent of the privately owned printed book was key to education for girls. Until the early sixteenth century, most books could only be read in manuscripts or a few early printed copies. The new printing technology gave scholarly girls and women like Anne and her sisters access at home to books that were previously only available to men in university and ecclesiastical libraries.

Along with books came advice about which ones to study, which to avoid and how to balance the benefits and risks of education for women. Catherine of Aragon commissioned Juan Luis de Vives to set out an educational programme for her daughter Mary in the early 1520s. He was another of the European humanist scholars who corresponded with More and stayed with him during visits to London. Vives proposed to expand the limited opportunities for education open to women, so they might be 'fortified with wit and learning'.[40] He nevertheless reinforced the view that the pursuit of learning could only be effective as part of a morally centred approach to life. Women should above all be pious and obedient, accepting that their place would always be secondary to that of their husbands and fathers. While women were as capable of learning as men, their roles remained different. 'I give no licence to a woman to be a teacher nor to have authority of the man but to be in silence,' he wrote, quoting the biblical authority of St Paul.[41] A woman needed goodness and wisdom, not eloquence. Citing the authority of Cicero and Juvenal on the subject, in his work *Office and Duty of a Husband* (1529), Vives advises men:

> But thou shalt number silence among other thy wife's virtues, the which is a great ornament to the whole feminine sex. … Let not thy wife be overmuch eloquent, nor full of her short and quick arguments, nor have the knowledge of all histories, nor understand many things, which are written. She pleaseth not me that giveth herself to poetry, and observing the art and manner of the old eloquence, doth study to speak facundaciously [fluently].[42]

Vives wrote *A Plan of Study for Girls* (1523) for the seven-year-old princess Mary. He followed it up with *The Education of a Christen [Christian] Woman* (1529). This second book, written as a guide to conduct for women, was enormously popular, running to over thirty editions by the end of the century. Richard Hyde, a member of Sir Thomas More's household who translated Vives's original Latin text into English, wrote a dedicatory letter to Catherine of Aragon that was printed in the earlier editions. In it he asks what could be more fruitful than the good education and order of women, 'the one half of all mankind', and wonders at the ignorance and 'unreasonable oversight' of men who complain about women's deficiencies while also denying them the learning 'by which they might have occasions to wax better by them self'.[43]

Though he was supportive of women's education, Vives gave less weight to the value of learning than to the importance of virtue, domestic skills, and womanly restraint. He did not subscribe to the belief that all women were inherently malicious; rather, that they were capable of virtue if properly instructed. He presented Catherine of Aragon as the exemplar of virtue and learning in a woman. Devoting a scant nine pages to education in his guide to conduct, Vives focused mainly on manners and family, especially a woman's duty to respect her husband and his relatives.[44] Women's reading should be supervised and limited, to ensure they only had access to suitable texts. These were mostly religious: the Old Testament, the Acts of the Apostles and the Gospels, and writings by the founding fathers of the church. Plato, Seneca and Cicero were the approved classical works on his reading list.

The list of prohibitions was much longer. Non-royal women should not study works of grammar, logic, history, governance of the commonwealth or mathematics, ruled Vives, they should leave that to men. He excluded the 'filth and viciousness' of Ovid and Boccaccio, writing that 'a woman should beware of these books like as to serpents or snakes'. He further said that non-royal women should not settle down with a book until they had completed all their domestic duties. If a woman did not approach learning in the right frame of mind, or if she resorted to forbidden texts, she should be banned from reading altogether, 'For it is better to lack a good thing than to use it ill.'[45]

The Cooke parents are likely to have read the works of another popular educator, Thomas Elyot, who published his textbook on teaching, *The Governor*, in 1531, following it up with *Defence of Good Women* in 1540. The first book proposed a humanist curriculum for boys that set out a broad base of knowledge and preparation for independent judgement, with the familiar aim of fitting them for public office and the governance of their families. In the second, written in the form of a debate rather than advice, Elyot rehearsed the case for and against educating noble women, cautiously concluding that education brought benefits if it did not get in the way of the wife's obedience to her husband.[46]

When the royal tutor Roger Ascham was teaching the future queen Elizabeth, he wrote, 'There are many honourable ladies now who surpass Thomas More's daughters in all kinds of learning,' singling out Elizabeth, then sixteen, as the brightest star among them. Ascham lists the works she studied, including daily reading of the Greek Testament and Greek orators, 'For I thought that from these sources she might gain purity of style, and her mind derive instruction that could be of value to her to meet every contingency of life.' 'Her mind has no womanly weakness,' he wrote, 'her perseverance is equal to that of a man, and her memory long keeps what it quickly picks up.' Equipped by her education to construct persuasive arguments and shape her ideas, Elizabeth was, as Ascham intended, well armed to meet the vicissitudes of her life. Ascham's own educational treatise, *The Scholemaster*, focused on the teaching of Latin and was published posthumously in 1570.[47]

While Anthony Cooke must have taken account of the views of Erasmus and Thomas More, and Juan de Vives's prescriptions for the conduct and education of daughters, he made his own decisions about his children's programmes of study. The girls and boys of his family were educated together, using the same books. In a textbook in Greek by the classical author Moschopulus, Anne noted 'My father delivered this book to me and my brother Anthony, who was mine elder brother and schoolfellow with me, to follow for writing of Greek'.[48] Evidence about the books they owned and used throughout their lives indicates that, as well as religious works, the Cooke sisters were familiar with an extensive variety of classical and modern texts that went beyond the limits set by Vives. They included books by authors such as the Italian storyteller Boccaccio – forbidden by Vives – and Roman playwright Terence, whose bawdy comedies were often ruled out as inappropriate for women.

Firm evidence about the Cooke sisters' programme of education is limited. They are likely to have worked through exercises in rhetoric and the composition of orations. Such exercises would have taught them to argue both sides of a debate before finding a resolution to the question at issue. They would have worked hard every day making translations in and out of the languages they were studying, which was the accepted way of practising vocabulary, structure and grammar. It is likely that the works of Terence, which were used by grammar school pupils, were the basis of their Latin studies. They were schooled in logic, composition and dialectic, and had access to works on mathematics and medicine. These intellectual tools equipped Anne to address educated men and women throughout her life. Her surviving correspondence includes letters in Latin to French theologians Théodore de Bèze in Geneva and Michel Berault in Montauban. She routinely used Latin and Greek to insert classical and biblical allusions, or on occasion to conceal names and other details from prying eyes. Her letters to senior figures, including Lord Burghley and the earl of Essex, were constructed according to the rules of formal composition, while her translations drew upon all her classical training. During her marriage, Anne and her husband read classical works together. Her preference was for Cicero, his for Seneca, and at their house at Gorhambury quotations from the two authors, known as *sententiae*, were inscribed on the walls.[49] As a widow Anne would embellish her letters to her sons with learned phrases and references to add weight and authority to her advice.

Careful scholarship has led to the identification of some of the books the sisters owned and used throughout their lives, while indications of the content of their reading are found in their letters and other writings. Gemma Allen's discussion of the sisters' books shows they possessed their own works of scripture, including editions of the New Testament and the Bible in Greek and Tyndale's English Bible.

Anne owned Erasmus's *Paraphrase of the Gospel of St John*, inscribed at different times with both her maiden and married names, as well as books of psalms and prayer books. Religious reformers examined the scriptures and other early religious texts to establish what they believed to be the true foundations of their faith. Mildred and Anne are known to have owned, studied and translated books by the early church fathers, including works by St Basil and Chrysotom, which they annotated in Greek.[50] Some of Mildred's books have been traced and identified from her inscriptions in them and records of the copies that she donated to the libraries of Oxford and Cambridge colleges. Seventeen of her books are in the collection at Hatfield House, which is still the home of the Cecil family.[51] They include volumes in Latin, Greek, French and English. Far fewer of Anne's books survive and they are more widely scattered. But they are firmly marked as her property, sometimes more than once – perhaps, as has been suggested, she preferred to keep them as a separate personal collection, apart from her husband's library.[52]

When Anthony Cooke died in 1576 he bequeathed books to his four married daughters, as well as the more conventional bequests of nests of gilt bowls and silver candlesticks. In order of seniority the sisters could choose three valuable volumes each from the classical library he had collected over a lifetime: 'Of my books my daughter Burleigh [Mildred] shall have two volumes in Latin and one in Greek such as she will choose of my gift, and after her choice my daughters Bacon [Anne], Russell [Elizabeth] and Killegrewe [Katherine] shall each successively have two other volumes in Latin and one in Greek.'[53]

Anne's years of shared study with her older sister ended when she was seventeen, with Mildred's marriage in 1545 to William Cecil, the ambitious son of a minor Northamptonshire gentry family. Mildred left Gidea Hall for life in London with her husband, taking her place as mistress of his small household in Cannon Row, Westminster. The marriage probably came about through Anthony Cooke's friendship with John Cheke, a Cambridge scholar and tutor to Prince Edward. Cheke had taught Cecil at Cambridge, and his sister Mary had been Cecil's first wife. That had not been a prudent or ideal marriage for an ambitious young man of nineteen – Mary served in her mother's wine shop – and it earned his father's disapproval.[54] In the event, the love match was short-lived, for Mary died, leaving the young widower with a baby son, Thomas. Within two years Mildred became his second wife. She made a shrewd choice of husband, and for Cecil the marriage was a social step up into the intellectual elite, bringing valuable connections at court.

It may have been hard for Anne to adjust to her sister's absence from their shared hours of study. Nevertheless she continued to apply herself, adding modern Italian to her portfolio of languages. There would have been other demands on her time, as Tudor gentlewomen were rarely idle. Anne must have assisted with the education of her younger brothers and sisters and practised the skills essential for managing a large household. Baking, brewing, preserving and other routine activities of a gentry household were supervised by the mistress of the house, and she had to be well versed in the treatment of illness and injuries. As a married woman Mildred was equipped with the medical textbooks of Galen, while Anne advised on health and administered remedies to her family for long-term conditions including gout and kidney stones, as well as recurrent fevers and other illnesses. The health and welfare of a family depended on women planning and carrying out their many household responsibilities effectively. 'Let no body loathe the name of the kitchen: namely being a thing very necessary, without the which neither sick folks can amend nor whole folks live,' wrote Vives in his instructions on the education of girls: the mistress of the house and her daughters should be prepared to roll up their sleeves and lay 'daintiness' aside to prepare wholesome dishes and sickroom delicacies for the family.[55] Anne's training would have begun early, for when she married, as it was inevitably expected she would, she would need a working knowledge of all household skills.

For most of her female contemporaries, these tasks, together with childbearing, occupied their adult lives. While Anne and her sisters went on to fulfil their conventional domestic duties and responsibilities as wives and mothers, they were not limited to this sphere. Brought up to relish the company of the 'great men of antiquity', as Machiavelli describes them, and married to men who shared their humanist learning, they were, and remained, different.

Chapter 3
The boy king

Obese, constipated, his legs full of suppurating ulcers covered by rosewater-scented bandages, Henry VIII succumbed to his multiple ailments on 28 January 1547, in the winter of his fifty-sixth year. Anne was nineteen. Like most of the population of England, she had known no other ruler. Henry died in misery and pain, but in the knowledge that he would be succeeded by his son, nine-year-old Edward, the outcome for which he had lost or discarded five wives and broken his allegiance to the church of Rome. On the following day, the earl of Hertford, Edward's uncle, broke the news to the prince and his thirteen-year-old half-sister Elizabeth. The earl escorted them from Hertford Castle to Enfield Manor, where 'the death of his father was first showed him,' wrote Edward, speaking of himself in the third person, and marking the moment when the kingly role for which he had been carefully prepared in the schoolroom and at court became a reality.[1] Bells tolled in parish churches across the country as Henry's body lay in state in the chapel at the royal residence, the Palace of Whitehall. Two weeks later, the king's coffin was loaded onto a chariot covered in velvet and cloth of gold for its final journey to Windsor and interment in St George's Chapel, next to Jane Seymour. Edward watched as his father's senior servants ritually broke their staffs of office and cast them into the grave.[2]

Knowing he might die while his son was still a minor, the king had planned a system by which the country would be governed after his death. In his will he revoked Queen Catherine's position as regent. Instead he ordered that a group of sixteen executors, each with equal authority, should rule the country as a regency council until Edward was eighteen. However, Henry's wishes were circumvented. The governing council members decided not to follow his direction to rule as a group of equals voting on decisions. Instead, no doubt encouraged by generous grants of titles, offices and Crown lands distributed under a dubious (possibly forged) clause in the king's will, they chose Edward Seymour, the ambitious earl of Hertford, to lead them.[3] Hertford was the oldest brother of Jane Seymour, who had died after the birth of Edward, her first and only child. Hertford was appointed to the office of governor of the king's person as well as Lord Protector of the realm. He took on the roles of high steward of England for the coronation, as well as lord treasurer and earl marshal. Within a month of the king's death he was advanced to a dukedom, becoming duke of Somerset. The new Lord Protector had accrued to himself the most power exercised by anyone outside the royal family since the Tudor era began.[4]

Henry VIII's reign had been characterised by the king's forceful control of everything and everyone. Now, allegiances shifted as individuals jostled for influence over the child king Edward and his advisers. Anthony Cooke kept his position in the household, later moving to a post in the king's Privy Chamber. At the Lord Protector's side was Anne's brother-in-law William Cecil, who became his secretary and invaluable aide within a year of the accession. He was elected for Stamford to the parliament of late 1547, which repealed statutes that gave Catholic belief the force of law and outlawed the chantry chapels in which priests had prayed for the souls of the dead. Cecil made the most of his position. Cultivating a wide network of contacts, both in England and abroad, especially among Protestant humanists and reformist clergy, he was establishing the foothold in affairs of state that would ultimately lead to his domination of the political fortunes of England as Elizabeth I's chief minister.[5] His humanist education and legal training had prepared him for his future as a senior bureaucrat and his social rise into the aristocracy. Mildred served Seymour's wife Anne and dedicated to her a translation from Greek of one of the church fathers, St Basil, thus underlining the ascendancy of evangelical religion under the new regime, acknowledging her mistress's leading position at court and, not least, furthering her own renown as a pious scholar.

Others around the boy king included John Dudley, the tough soldier who would ultimately oust Seymour and whose son Guildford would later marry the king's cousin Lady Jane Grey, and Jane's father Henry Grey, the earl of Suffolk. Radical religious reform became national policy. Henry's religious reforms had not gone far enough for the evangelicals, who believed that each individual was directly accountable to God, with no priestly or saintly intercession. God's forgiveness for earthly transgressions could not be bought through good works or prayers for souls and salvation was only attainable through individual faith – the central Lutheran doctrine of justification by faith alone. All should be free to read scriptures and prayers in their own language. In England the Archbishop of Canterbury, Thomas Cranmer, was ready to put these principles into practice for the Church of England. Together with Cranmer, the Lord Protector was intent on going further than the partial changes effected by Henry VIII's split with Rome and planned to transform the Church of England into a fully reformed church.[6]

What were the core issues being advanced by the evangelical reformers? Central to their understanding of the Bible, derived from Luther's reading of the Epistle to the Romans, was the understanding that salvation could be achieved by faith alone. A critical development of the reformers' theology was the doctrine of predestination, principally associated with John Calvin. The reformers believed that since God was omnipotent and omniscient he knew, and himself directed, who would be saved – the 'elect' – and who were destined for hell and damnation – the 'reprobates'. How could a God who saw and knew everything not so direct the lives of mortals, they reasoned. It followed that acts of piety and good works, while they might indicate that the individual was one of the elect, could not bring salvation. As the theologian Théodore de Bèze said, while the elect might be open to promptings to good acts and to true belief, the reprobates 'cannot believe, because it is not given to them'.[7] It followed from the understanding that individuals were predestined to salvation or damnation and that salvation was by faith alone, that salvation could not depend on priestly intervention, forms and ceremonies, or prayers of others whether for the living or the dead. These ideas were central to Anne's engagement with church reform and to her activities as a translator.

Strongly influenced by his stepmother Catherine Parr, by Cranmer and by John Cheke, his tutor from the age of six, King Edward was primed to support further religious reform. From 1546 his French tutor Jean Belmaine, a Protestant refugee, used their language studies to reinforce Edward's understanding of the Lutheran doctrine of justification by faith alone and encourage his repudiation of idolatry and papal authority.[8] Edward was quick to conform and took his religious responsibilities seriously, personally as well as in public, in a letter of 1551 urging his absent friend Barnaby to read scripture: 'not doubting but that you would have done so had I not written, but to spur you on'.[9] Clashes with his half-sister Mary over her continuing adherence to the Catholic faith would escalate towards the end of his reign.

Twin constellations of political power and scholarly learning orbited the slight figure of the king. The first group comprised the men appointed to rule during the king's minority. The second group comprised his tutors and religious advisers, a close-knit circle of Cambridge-educated men, who were soon joined by Anthony Cooke. It was said that Cooke had impressed the Lord Protector with his management of his own children. David Lloyd, author of an account of Cooke's life published in the 1660s, records: 'My lord Seymour standing by one day when this gentleman chid his son, said "Some men govern families with more skill than others do kingdoms" and thereupon commended him to the government of his nephew Edward the Sixth'.[10] Though never officially listed as one of the king's tutors, Anthony Cooke was referred to as a tutor in 1550, and in the same year he received an annuity of £100 for life, in return for providing 'training in good letters and manners' to the king. Edward recorded in his journal that his tutors were charged with providing 'learning of tongues … philosophy and all liberal sciences' and instructing Edward in his regal duties.[11]

There are no clues to Anne's whereabouts and thoughts during this time of change and realignment. We might picture her visiting her sister and brother-in-law in Cannon Row, hearing the latest news about the governing regime and comparing ideas about their hopes for the new reign. Later events in Anne's story show that as young women the sisters remained close. Mildred had a troubled path to motherhood, losing a number of pregnancies and young infants. Anne may have joined her sister's household to help and give companionship at such times, as was customary in families. If she was in London in the early months of 1547, she would have seen the city's preparations for the first coronation in four decades, as embroidered banners were paraded in the streets and sumptuous tapestries hung from rich merchants' windows. Londoners crowded to see extravagant displays and entertainments and to cheer the boy king, clothed in white velvet with a fur cape of sable, as he rode in procession from the Tower to Westminster on the afternoon before his coronation.[12] It is very likely that members of the Cooke family were in the city for the king's coronation on 20 February 1547, which proved a doubly momentous day for them. Anne's father attended Westminster Abbey and was knighted during the great feast in Westminster Hall that followed the long coronation ceremony.

Nine-year-old Edward VI was crowned in a ceremony shortened from the usual twelve hours to nine in a concession to his young age. Cushions were piled on the throne to raise him up high enough for the crowning. At the feast that night Sir John Dymoke, the king's champion, rode into Westminster Hall, his horse richly dressed in white gilded harness, to salute the small boy seated alone at a high table with the crown on his head. Flinging a gauntlet to the ground, he challenged any man to battle that would not take Edward for right king of the realm.[13] Nine-year-old Edward drank to his champion, gave him a gold cup, then solemnly attended to the business of dubbing the large cohort of new knights, among them Sir Anthony Cooke of Gidea Hall.

The child king was exhorted to lead further religious change in England. At his coronation Archbishop Cranmer addressed him as a 'second Josiah'. According to biblical texts Josiah became king of Judah at the age of eight and ordered that the word of God should be read to the people, and idols destroyed.[14] Edward was duly charged by Cranmer to see God truly worshipped, idolatry forbidden, the tyranny of Rome banished, and images removed from churches.[15] Religion, monarchy and politics were inextricably interwoven in sixteenth-century England, even for a nine-year-old king. His duties and responsibilities as both king and head of the church were emphasised, although he would not be able to reign alone for years.

The systematic destruction of images in the country's churches began. Under cover of darkness on a winter night in 1547, workmen entered St Paul's cathedral to remove the rood, the crucifix set above the entrance to the chancel, with orders to carry out the work secretly to avoid a public outcry. As the heavy cross was lowered from the rood loft it crashed to the floor, killing two men and leaving others injured. Some saw this as divine retribution. Throughout the country Catholic observances were forbidden, and religious images destroyed under the supervision of officials known as the King's Visitors. Sir Anthony Cooke, a reliable supporter of the new religious and political establishment, was appointed one of the Visitors for London, Westminster, Norwich and Ely.[16]

In London, the Visitors ordered all images in every parish church to be destroyed. St Paul's contained images denounced as 'idols' by Bishop William Barlow when he preached there in November 1547. Trying to save their precious images, cathedral clergy had wrapped up and hidden a statue of the Virgin Mary. Another of their prized possessions was a mechanised Christ that could be 'resurrected' by means of 'vices [possibly levers] which put out his legs of [i.e. his legs out of the] sepulchre, and blessed with his hand, and turned his head'.[17] Following the bishop's sermon against the 'great abomination of idolatry' the boys of the congregation seized these objects and smashed them to pieces, relates a contemporary chronicler.[18]

Cranmer's *Homily of Good Works*, published in July of the coronation year and distributed throughout the country, condemned a list of 'papistical superstitions and abuses' that included 'beads, lady psalters and rosaries ... purgatory ... feigned relics ... bells, bread, water, palms, candles ... superstitious fastings'.[19] Cranmer scorned lay people who ran to the altar to see the sacrament, 'peeping, tooting and gazing at that thing which the priest held up in his hands ... that visible thing which they saw with their eyes and took it for very God'.[20] For the evangelical reformers, the essence of religious faith was a direct, personal experience.

The process of purging practices perceived as corrupt or rooted in superstition had begun in 1538, on Henry VIII's orders. The changes were effected on the authority of Henry's declared royal supremacy as head of the Church. The first Bible in English was published in 1540, with a preface by Thomas Cranmer. The 'Great Bible' was based on Tyndale's translations of 1525 and 1530, modified and extended by Miles Coverdale, later Bishop of Exeter, who had possibly assisted Tyndale in Antwerp.[21] Dedicated to the king, the work had Henry's full approval. However, the king still upheld principles that Lutheran reformers rejected, notably the doctrine of transubstantiation whereby the bread and wine of the sacrament is believed to become the blood and body of Christ. 'After the consecration, there remaineth no substance of bread or wine, nor any other substance, but the substance of Christ, God and man,' he affirmed in the 'Act of Six Articles' of 1539.

Parish churches were at the heart of local life. Before the start of Edward's reign candles burned on the altar, on the rood, and before holy images. Masses were held several times each day in many places, with the priest elevating the Host at the moment of consecration for the congregation to see. Such glimpses of the Host were thought to bring blessing, though most ordinary parishioners only individually received communion at Easter, and on their deathbed. Chantry priests were paid to repeat prayers for the dead to reduce the time that souls would spend in purgatory. Parishioners gathered for feasts, processions and bonfires to mark saints' days and other festivals. Local religious guilds were formed, among other things organising and funding activities and the maintenance of the church fabric, and often supplying churches with 'lights' – candles and torches.

The royal injunction ordering a General Visitation of the Church, proclaimed in May 1547, went a great deal further than Henry's reforms, forbidding all use of beads in prayer, limiting the number of candles in churches to two on the altar, and adding saints in stained-glass windows to the list of idolatrous images to be destroyed.[22] Religious paintings in churches were obliterated with limewash and replaced with written commandments on the walls. Every parish church must have a large Bible in English, and a copy of Erasmus's paraphrases of the gospels. Local parish life unravelled, as the traditional religious festivals and holidays of the liturgical year were abolished and processions were banned by the Visitors, removing long-standing structures of communal religion and local rituals of worship that bound communities together.[23]

Not everyone was committed to the change in religion imposed by the ruling elite or accepted it. In the background to Edward's accession moved the discontented figure of his half-sister Mary, who continued to worship according to the traditions maintained during her father's reign, protesting to Protector Somerset about the changes. Her many supporters believed that Somerset and Archbishop Cranmer should be maintaining the religious life of England as it had been under Henry VIII, not forcing further radical reform.[24] The country faced unrest, conflict and change, with its leadership in the hands of a ruling council whose initial stability soon faltered. The stage was set for Edward's turbulent, politically perilous reign and its disastrous aftermath.

Chapter 4
This godly work

Anne Cooke was studying modern Italian at home, when in the year of Edward's accession the charismatic Italian preacher Bernardino Ochino travelled to England with theologian Pietro Martire Vermigli – known in England as Peter Martyr. Ochino was an important radical figure in church reform. Born in Siena in 1487, he was originally a Franciscan friar, becoming a Capuchin in 1534. In the 1530s he was a leader in the broad reform movement of what were termed *spirituali* [spirituals] in Italy.[1] One of the authors of the Capuchin Constitutions of 1536, the statement of the principles of the Capuchin order which were founded upon close observance of the example and intentions of St Francis of Assisi, Ochino began preaching the Protestant doctrines of faith, justification and predestination. In collaboration with the Spanish evangelical Juan de Valdes he travelled throughout Italy, attracting huge crowds in Naples, Florence, Rome, Ferrara and Venice. Tall and bearded, he was a striking figure who delivered his sermons with such energy and conviction it was said he could make the very stones weep with his oratory.[2] When he reached Ferrara the poet Tullia d'Aragona wrote a sonnet 'To the Preacher Ochino', praising his *dolce dir*, sweet speech.[3] Anne Cooke was one of many learned – and some powerful – women who supported Ochino during his travels and when he settled in England.[4]

Ochino exemplified a new approach to emotions in religious expression: that they should be nurtured, channelled and directed into fervent engagement with faith, disciplined but not repressed. Alec Ryrie examines how in reformation Britain this approach overturned the earlier classical and medieval views that favoured emotional restraint, quoting an early seventeenth-century preacher, Gilbert Primrose: the 'natural affections' are sanctified but not abolished by the Holy Spirit, wrote Primrose, 'God gives them full liberty, when they come from a good cause, and aspire unto a good end'. No excess can be thought 'vicious,' he says, 'in things which are truly good'.[5]

Following the failure of an attempt at reconciling the reformers with the church authorities at the Diet in Regensburg in 1541, the Roman Inquisition was reconstituted in June 1542. In response to the threat this brought, that he might be detained and questioned, Ochino finally broke with the Roman church, evaded a summons to appear in front of the Pope and left Italy for Geneva, where he met

John Calvin. He further travelled to Basel, Strasbourg and Augsburg. In 1547 the Holy Roman Emperor Charles V was besieging Augsburg as part of the religious conflict. The city authorities surrendered: one of the conditions of surrender was that Ochino would be permitted to leave.

This was the point at which Archbishop Cranmer invited Ochino and Vermigli to London. Granted a yearly stipend of 100 marks by the king, Ochino took up a ministry preaching to a congregation consisting mainly of Italians, at the first London Strangers' Church, which used the chapel of the Mercers' Hall in Cheapside. Neither Ochino nor Vermigli spoke English, relying on Italian or Latin to communicate. Nearly sixty years old when he came to England, Ochino's vitality was undiminished and observers noted his vigour in the pulpit, even after days of fasting. His charismatic preaching style earned him a high profile and celebrity status in England. Both he and Vermigli were held in high regard and were awarded prestigious appointments at the universities of Oxford and Cambridge. Through Ochino and Vermigli the Italian approach to reform, which has been characterised as 'enigmatic, evasive and incomplete', met and influenced the English reform movement, which by contrast was political and pragmatic.[6] With the introduction of Vermigli, a renowned theologian, and Ochino the charismatic orator and consummate communicator into the highest circles in England, Cranmer shook up the conservative religious establishment that still looked back to the days of Henry VIII's church. He had successfully acquired two powerful allies to deploy for his project of reform.

Ochino's sermons were attended by leading English reformers, including Catherine Willoughby, duchess of Suffolk, and William Parr, marquess of Northampton.[7] Some of his English audience, including Cranmer and the king, had studied Italian, and many men at court were familiar with Italy through travel, or from study at the university of Padua. Anne was as fluent in Italian as any well-travelled courtier, though as the editor of her translations remarked, she had 'never gadded farther than her father's house to learn the language'.[8] Whether she saw the mesmerising preacher in action or only knew him by his writings and reputation, Ochino's presence in England fuelled Anne's zealous engagement with reform. It is likely that she had read some or all of his *Prediche*, the sermons that were published in Italian from 1543 onwards, either before or soon after Ochino's arrival in England. Patricia Demers suggests that if the volume was not already in the library at Gidea Hall, a copy may have been presented to the family from the stock of books that Ochino and Vermigli brought with them.[9] Given her knowledge of Italian, her family's close engagement with the elite circles in England and Europe through which religious change was being debated and promoted and the ease of travel from Gidea Hall to London, Anne surely sought opportunities to attend the sermons in person. She may have accompanied her father on some of his frequent visits to court, or stayed with her sister, to hear the man everyone in their circle was talking about.

What Anne Overell terms the 'Ochino fever' that spread among the English literati created a demand for the sermons to be available in other languages.[10] Princess Elizabeth translated one into Latin to present to her brother the king in 1547, but it was never published. The first version in general circulation was by Richard Argentine, a schoolmaster and clergyman, who translated six sermons. First published in 1548, they would reappear three years later in a joint edition with Anne's work, as *Certayne Sermons of the ryghte famous and excellent Clerk Master Bernardine Ochine*.[11]

Anne began her translations of Ochino's sermons into English in December 1547. Modestly describing herself as a 'beginner' in Italian, but clearly highly proficient in the language, she translated five sermons dealing with the topics of death and the devil, which were published anonymously in July 1548 as *Sermons of Barnardine Ochine of Sena, godlie, frutefull, and uery necessarye for all true Christians*. The translations are newly available in a scholarly edition edited by Patricia Demers.[12] In choosing these sermons for her first translations Anne took on weighty subjects. Ochino was exhorting his listeners/readers to meditate on and prepare for their own mortality and God's judgement:

> How a Christian ought to make his last will and testament
> How we should answer the devil when he tempteth us and namely in the end of our life
> How answer is to be made at the judgement seat of God
> By what mean [sic] to come to heaven
> How God hath satisfied for our sins and hath purchased Paradise for us.

Anne prefaces the translation with a note 'From the Interpreter to the gentle reader' in which she explains that nothing can be 'a greater stay to the conscience of man' than to know how to go out of earthly life, what to leave behind and what to 'carry with him to his account'. As the devil is 'bragging busily with man' at the time of death, she has translated a sermon that instructs how to answer the devil and achieve a quiet mind.[13] This sermon recounts how the devil, 'using all might, power, slight, deceit and malice', strives to throw the dying soul into the 'assize and pit of desperation'. Just as the godly believer must engage directly with God, with no intermediaries, so it is with the power of evil. The devil is personified as he attempts to sow doubt, fear and despair in a dialogue with the dying: 'he will tell thee how thou art in a maze and perplexity not to be shaken off'. Even on their deathbed, the dying person could not be sure whether they were to be chosen or damned and these final temptations by the devil to give in to despair – temptations which by definition must be predestined by the omniscient God – must be resisted. Ochino offers hope in the form of robust model answers to the devil's malignant attacks on the dying person's faith. The doctrine of salvation by faith alone is central: Ochino instructs the reader, if the devil asks 'where be thy works, whereby thou trusteth to

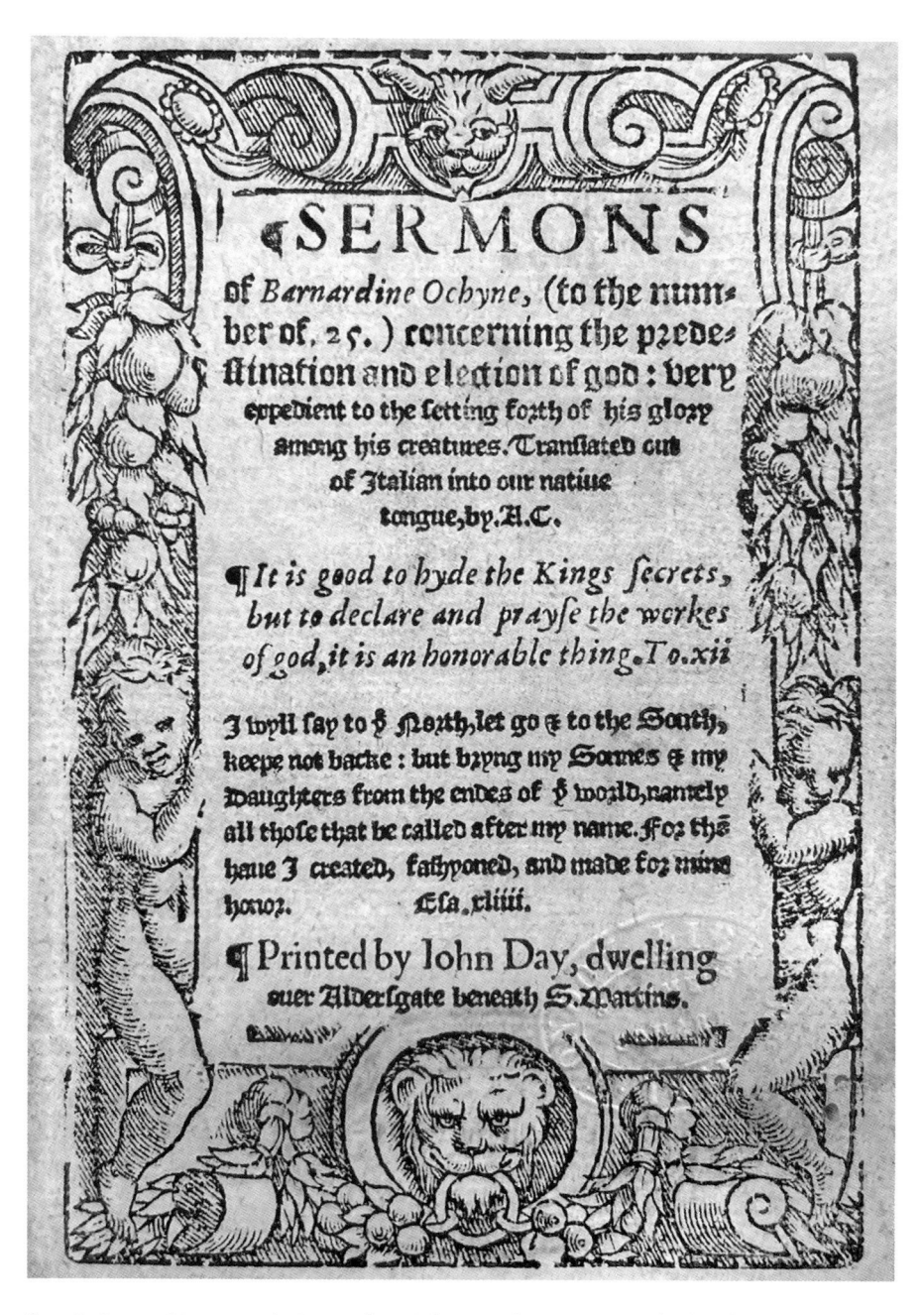

Frontispiece to 25 sermons by Bernardino Ochino crediting Anne Cooke, 'A.C.', as the translator (1570 edition). *Sermons of Barnardine Ochyne (to the number of 25): concerning the predestination and election of God: very expedient to the setting forth of his glory among his creatures. Translated out of Italian into our natiue tongue, by A.C.*

be saved, answer: I trust not to be saved by my works... I hope only to be saved by Christ and his works.'[14]

It takes an effort of imagination, in our secular age, to visualise how the words we read in English on the page in Anne's ardent and imaginative rendering would have stirred the crowds who came to hear Ochino speak them in his own language as well as those who read them in English, or to understand the profound intellectual and emotional shift of religious focus that he articulated. For some who read and listened to such words at the time, the insistence on predestination and the unceasing, lonely work of individual spiritual struggle could lead to what Alec Ryrie terms 'salvation-anxiety', a tendency to paralysing 'dulness' or despair in the face of a terrifying unknown.[15]

A further fourteen sermons translated by Anne were published in 1551, this time with her initials on the title page, for the first time identifying her as Ochino's translator. This second collection of sermons dealt with the topics of election and predestination. They contain a strong evangelical message, drawing on Calvinist ideas and emphasising the doctrine of justification by faith alone. This central plank of Luther's thinking was based on his interpretation of St Paul's Epistle to the Romans, specifically Romans 3:28, which Luther translated in 1522 as 'thus, we hold, then, that man is justified without doing the works of the law, *alone* through faith'.[16]

The theological issues that underlie Ochino's sermons, subjects of urgent debate in the sixteenth century, and Anne's perception of the nature of faith, are not familiar to most modern minds. Anne and her fellow evangelicals believed that a righteous God justified sinful mankind through his grace – which we might call acceptance, or an 'undeserved favour'. As we have seen, they believed individuals could achieve righteousness through faith only, and God elected some to certain salvation. There could be no buying of salvation by intercessionary prayer or gifts to help absolve individuals of sin. The godly person must live their life believing they are one of the elect, but can have no certainty. As Patricia Demers explains, 'While the ungodly perceive only partiality and injustice, the elect, sure of their salvation, know that they are justified through the sacrifice of Christ, their singular judge.'[17] Anne's version of the essence of election, in her translation of the first of fourteen sermons of Ochino, is simple and to the point: 'Yea, it ought to be preached that God hath elected some, and not other some.'[18]

As a woman Anne was not permitted to stand up and preach this doctrine, but she had the intellectual tools and the practical means to reach an English-speaking readership with Ochino's message. For Anne, this was a moral imperative. Demers links the proselytising faith of the sixty-year-old preacher and his young translator: 'Holding firmly to faith as a sure sign of election, Ochino and Cooke heard and experienced the inner call, a conviction that seized them with the determination to evangelize.'[19] In her preface to the first volume of five sermons in 1548, Anne tells her readers that she hopes to publish more of the sermons in English, 'for the information of all that desire to know the truth', and that the sermons 'truly contain much to the defacing of papistry, and hypocrisy, and to the advancement of the glory of God'.[20]

In these translations we read Anne's words and encounter her style for the first time. Her voice is firm and forthright, both in the translation itself and in the dedicatory epistle to her mother that prefaces the 1551 collection. This is no tentative rendition of Italian into English by a pious gentlewoman occupying an idle hour. Anne did not approach translation as a passive act aimed at achieving textbook correctness, but as a platform to urge her readers towards godliness. Commentators have noted her skilful realignment of words and phrases to deliver emphasis and immediacy. Conditional verbs in Ochino's Italian become active in

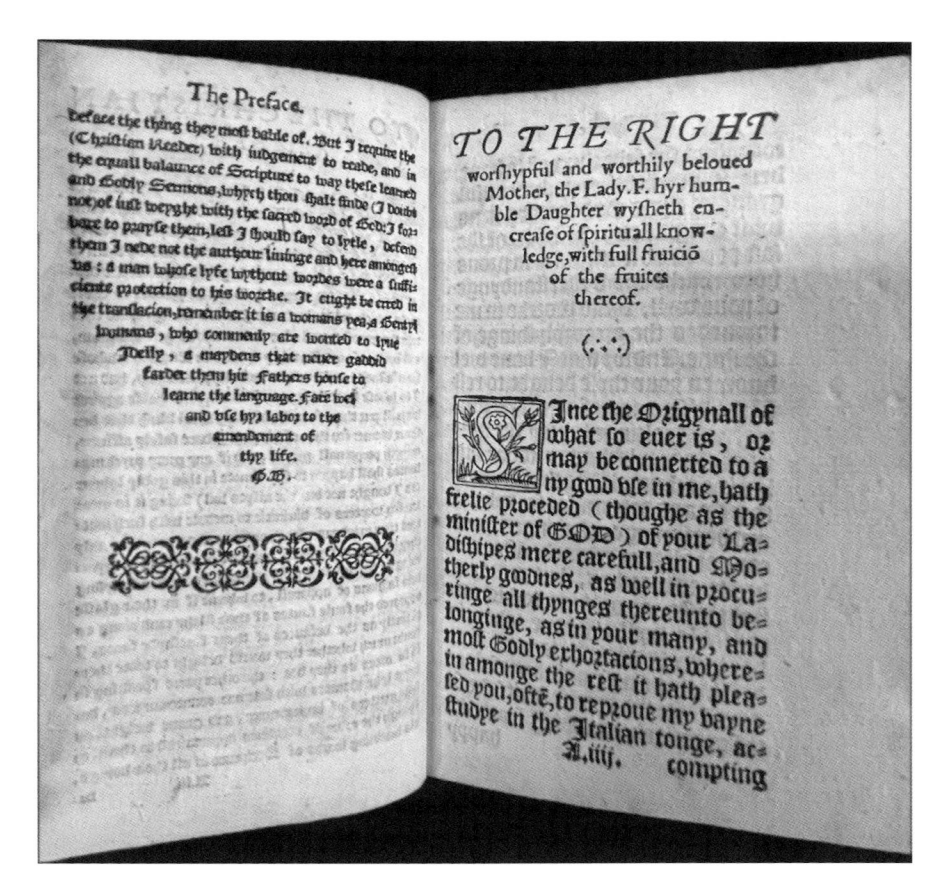

The last page of the preface to the same edition of Ochino's sermons describing Anne as a 'gentylwoman' and 'mayden[s] that never gaddid farder than hir fathers house to learne the language', and the first page of the dedication in which Anne addresses her mother, the Lady F.[Fitzwilliam]: 'it hath pleased you, ofte, to reprove my vayne study in the Italian tongue'.

Anne's English translation – 'would' to 'must' and 'should' to 'ought', for example – and statements become questions that challenge the reader, while the language she employs is forceful and direct.[21]

Anne's dedicatory epistle to the sermons when they were published under her own name in 1551 gives insight into her character and her relationship with her mother, to whom the letter is addressed: 'To the right worshipful and worthily beloved mother, the Lady F. [Fitzwilliam]'. Anne was studying modern Italian at her own wish, having resisted her mother's advice. She reveals that, in her mother's view, she should have confined herself to the study of ancient languages, which she could use to read the scriptures and learned commentaries. Anne's mother had chastised her: all work should have a godly purpose, and learning Italian was wasted labour, seeds sown in barren ground, 'since God thereby is in no whit magnified'. But her study of Italian had borne valuable fruit, Anne reminded her mother, respectfully expressing the hope that she had indeed completed a godly task in translating Ochino's sermons.[22] As Italian Reformation exiles and their writings became better known in England during the reign of Edward VI, Anne's translations were widely read. Her published translations of Ochino's works mark the beginning of her lifelong vocation to the cause of reform.

Anne seems to have encountered no obstacles to reaching a wide readership with her translations. This young unmarried woman became a published author, despite her mother's disapproval that she had strayed from her study of the classics, and the popular prejudice referred to by Anne's editor in the preface to her *Fourteen Sermons*, as he reminds readers that the translator is a woman and that many might think it seems 'meeter for doctors of divinity to meddle with such matters than maidens'.[23] On the contrary, it can fairly be conjectured that she had positive support from her family. The Cookes and Cecils were active in promoting religious reform and embedded in court life. Gemma Allen suggests that the effect of Anne Cooke's anonymity being lifted in the 1551 edition was to draw attention to support for Ochino within the influential court circles in which her family moved.[24]

William Cecil cultivated important patrons, including influential and pious women, publicly aligning himself with those in power who supported religious reform. He often commissioned the printing of reformist works on behalf of the Lord Protector. He not only organised the publication of Catherine Parr's *Lamentation of a Sinner* after Henry VIII's death, but also wrote an introduction to the text. This activity could indicate Cecil's support for the dissemination of pietistic ideas that originated within Catherine Parr's female circle at court, some of whom – Anne Seymour, Mary Fitzroy and Catherine Brandon – were supporters of humanist teaching and patrons of reformist publications.[25] Catherine Parr had been at risk of arrest and prosecution at the end of Henry's reign, for expressing radical religious views. The women close to her at that time were also implicated. Unsurprisingly, for the remainder of the reign Catherine remained cautious. Despite this, she did arrange the publication of a collection of prayers and meditations which she compiled from various uncontroversial sources, including the *Imitation of Christ* by Thomas à Kempis. Unlike earlier writings which circulated only among the courtly elite, this collection was produced in a printed format that could reach a wide readership.[26] It would have been used as a guide to daily prayer by individuals and households. Queen Catherine was also the patron of a translation by Nicholas Udall of Erasmus's *Paraphrases of the New Testament*. Anne Cooke would have been familiar with the efforts of Catherine Parr's circle of pious women to further the Protestant cause through the patronage and dissemination of devotional works, translations and reformist texts. Their names appear as dedicatees in many of the works that were now finding their way into print.[27] Practical arrangements would have had to be made for the publication and distribution of Anne's translations. She could not do this herself. William Cecil could, and he had the necessary contacts.

Anne was one of many translators who benefited from the looser restrictions on print after Henry VIII's death. The 1551 edition of her Ochino translations was printed by John Day, a London master printer with reformist sympathies who produced over thirty books a year during Edward's reign. Day came into prominence during the printing boom that followed Edward's accession, when the production of books and other printed material increased to meet the demand for reformist literature. With most limits on publication removed by the Lord Protector, books that had previously been labelled heretical and banned were openly published and read in England, as well as new reformist works. The influx of literature into England from Europe at the beginning of Edward's reign led to the publication of 157 translations between 1547 and 1549. At least forty per cent of them concerned religious reform.[28] Cecil became one of Day's long-term patrons, employing the printer in London during the reigns of Edward VI and Elizabeth I. The relationship persisted under cover during the dangerous years of Mary I's reign when Cecil continued to commission work from Day, who was then running a clandestine press near Stamford, in the vicinity of Cecil's family estates. It is entirely probable that Cecil, a committed reformer with a godly printer to hand, made the arrangements for Anne's translations to be printed by Day.

However, Cecil had almost been a casualty of conflict over reform, and its political fallout. In 1549, when Cranmer's new prayer book was issued for use in all churches, Mary held an elaborate Latin mass for Pentecost in the chapel of her manor house at Kenninghall, far from London in the Norfolk Brecklands. This public act of defiance spurred the king's Council to order her to obey the Act of Uniformity and stop celebrating the traditional mass. The confrontation was defused to some extent by a concession by the Council that Mary could continue to celebrate mass in private, but Mary was becoming a political liability. The tension between her and Edward over religious observance escalated as the ruling elite attempted to reduce her influence as a focus of conservative opposition to their reforms.

Not only was Mary receiving advice from her cousin Emperor Charles V, via his ambassadors, but she was also the focus of dissent as rebellious uprisings in Somerset, Cornwall and Norfolk against religious change and land enclosures threatened to destabilise the government. John Dudley, the earl of Warwick, led an armed force that summer to put down the Norfolk rebels led by Robert Kett, leaving 2,000 dead after the battle of Dessindale, just outside Norwich. By November 1549 Protector Somerset was accused of incompetence in his handling of the crisis. His adviser William Paget urged Somerset to take control, but Somerset ignored Paget's advice. Increasingly isolated by his opponents on the council, he was removed as Lord Protector and temporarily imprisoned.

William Cecil fell with his master. On 24 November 1549 he was detained in the Tower of London and kept there for eight weeks, paying a large fine on his release. His political career seemed to be over. But in an extraordinary reversal of his dire position, he eased his way into favour with Warwick, assisting him to break a developing alliance between Somerset and Archbishop Gardiner. 'A most witty counsellor,' wrote Warwick, 'as unto the King's Majesty and his proceedings, as was scarce the like within this his realm'.[29] Cecil had come to a market, noted his friend, the duchess of Suffolk, where his skills were 'good and saleable'.[30] He was appointed as a secretary to the king in 1550. In 1551 he was knighted, on the same day that Warwick was elevated to become the duke of Northumberland.

The conflict over religion grew. In late June and early July 1550 Mary was on the point of fleeing the country for the Netherlands but abandoned her plans at the last moment. In early 1551 matters came to a head with Edward, who upbraided her for her defiance. He told her that he had made an exception for her, but insisted he would see his laws obeyed. Drafting her reply with the assistance of Charles V's ambassador, Mary asserted her immunity from the general rules forbidding the celebration of mass. The council responded that the concessions made were only for herself and her personal chamber servants, not her household or friends. Mary did not give in. In March 1551 she arrived in London, openly flouting her brother's laws by riding through Cheapside and Smithfield to her house with an entourage of fifty mounted knights in front of her and a great procession of ladies and gentlemen behind her, all carrying black rosary beads. Mary went to the court at Westminster two days later to dine with the king. Edward delivered an ultimatum, saying he would not tolerate further disobedience if she did not amend her behaviour quickly. Her answer was that she would not change her faith, and her soul was God's.[31]

Unwilling to be drawn into direct conflict with Edward, Emperor Charles suggested the situation might be cooled if the Privy Council allowed Mary to hear mass privately at home. English diplomatic activity was stepped up to reduce political tensions with the emperor and safeguard international trade. But after further hostile exchanges between Mary and the Privy Council, and the arrest and imprisonment of her chaplain and senior household officers, even private ceremonies were forbidden to her. Mary saw off delegations from the council with a repudiation of their authority over her, declaring that she would obey nobody but her brother in matters of conscience – and only when he came of age, not before. She threatened to tell the emperor's ambassador how she was treated and refused to accept a council-appointed controller of her household.[32]

The situation remained at stalemate, with the council turning a blind eye to her continued private celebration of mass in her household, and eventually releasing her officers from prison. In late 1551 and early 1552 her relations with Northumberland improved, and there were no further attempts to force her to conform. In early February 1553 she came to London to visit the king, received outside the city by Northumberland's son, the new earl of Warwick, and Lord William Howard, and with a three-hundred-strong escort of her own forces. She found Edward indisposed, with a chest infection, but not seriously ill. Although she did not know it, this was to be the last time Mary saw her brother.

The religious tension building between Mary and her supporters and the king was the backdrop to a personal turning point in Anne's life. In the summer of 1552, she received a letter from Mildred. The letter was in Latin, concealing the contents from any casual servant's glance, and was informal in tone. '*Mea soror, Cantabrigis fui. Tuum vidi Haddonum, quem amabis, si sapis*', it begins: 'My sister, I have been to Cambridge. I saw your Haddon, whom you will love if you have any sense'. Walter Haddon was the man who had years earlier admired the learned sisters at Gidea Hall. Now, with Mildred's support, he set his sights on marrying Anne. Haddon was by then in his late thirties and a fellow of King's College, Cambridge. Described by the seventeenth-century historian John Strype as a great and eminent light of the reformation in Cambridge, Haddon mixed with other leading humanist reformers, including Matthew Parker and John Cheke.[33]

Mildred encouraged her sister to accept Haddon's offer but acknowledged their father's disapproval: 'your father's will stands in your way. This is a difficult and slippery place, to be sure,' she writes, before urging Anne to make her own decision: 'you should decide to obey yourself. For it is your business which is at stake, and indeed the business of your whole life.'[34] From her comfortable position as the wife of William Cecil, secretary to the king, Mildred brushed aside Haddon's lack of means: 'Haddon is more desirable with these small resources than six hundred from this courtly din, of whom one can only see the external skins of their bodies, as of cattle, while you would swear that their mind has been given as it were to the pigs to serve as preserving salt.' With this florid image, drawn from Cicero, Mildred disparages shallow, worldly courtiers in terms her sister will appreciate. Anne would surely agree that a more elevated mind than displayed by the average member of the 'courtly din' was essential in a suitor.

Mildred had seven years of marriage behind her and a confident grasp of what it took to succeed in the complex mix of religion, patronage and politics that dominated court life. With her own husband sure-footedly climbing the unstable ladder of Tudor political advancement, she recommended Anne to follow her example and marry a man with a future: '[Haddon] lacks nothing but fortune and this indeed cannot long be wanting where there is such a combination of other distinctions and advantages,' she writes, going on to advise her sister to look ahead: 'reflect on this, that hardly anything tends in all cases to pour forth at the very beginning, but that there are certain periods and certain stages of life which usually have to be scaled in order to reach perfection'. Mildred concludes by referring to her own successful choice of a husband: 'Look at me; although I now have an abundant and plentiful fortune, nevertheless at the beginning I followed hope and not actual things.'[35] The only surviving copy of Mildred's letter to Anne urging her to accept Haddon is in Haddon's handwriting. Did he have a hand in drafting it? Or did he ask for sight of Mildred's composition and permission to copy it? Mildred knew her sister well and she would have needed no help to compose her letter in Latin. It does not seem likely that the guiding hand was Haddon's. If Anne answered her sister's letter, her response does not survive.

Why was Anne's father reluctant to welcome Haddon as a son-in-law? Haddon had been seriously ill the previous year, which might have reduced his appeal, and he did lack money. It is also possible that scrupulous Sir Anthony disliked the academic politics that Walter Haddon was playing in 1552. In February Haddon was appointed master of Trinity Hall in Cambridge, displacing Bishop Stephen Gardiner who had refused to agree to an amalgamation with Clare College. Gardiner was a traditionalist, an opponent of the reformers. Then in a further academic coup later in 1552, in breach of college statutes, Haddon was appointed president of Magdalen College, Oxford, replacing the incumbent Owen Oglethorpe, who was also opposed to religious changes. William Cecil had been behind the manoeuvre. Perhaps her husband's recent involvement with Walter Haddon turned Mildred's mind to making a match for her sister. Haddon held the Oxford post for only a short time, but he made his mark on the college, which was described as the most Protestant in the university under his presidency. He was less successful in managing the college's practical affairs, selling off the valuable contents of the chapel for a fraction of their value, money which it was said he 'consumed on alterations, as also nearly £120 of the public money'.[36]

Surely marriage to such an educated, well-regarded man, charged with progressing religious reform at Oxford, and favoured by her sister, would have interested Anne. There is no record of why Sir Anthony Cooke objected to Haddon as a son-in-law, or what his wife's views were. As Mildred's letter shows, lack of fortune had not stopped her marriage to William Cecil. They were emerging as one of the successful couples of Edward's reign, William's political acumen complemented by his wife's keen intellect and her connections at court. Perhaps Sir Anthony thought that Haddon, with his conventional Latin verse writing and stolid expertise in civil law, was too dull a prospect for his clever and forthright daughter.

Whether she gave in to her father's disapproval, disliked being told what to do by her older sister or had doubts of her own about her spendthrift suitor, Anne refused Walter Haddon. He sadly recorded the rejection. Writing in Latin verse, his habit when any special event had to be marked, he told Anne she would always be cherished and admired, regretted and desired.[37]

At the end of 1552 Anne was approaching her mid-twenties as a single woman, with an established public reputation as Ochino's scholarly translator. Fourteen-year-old King Edward was completing his fifth year on the throne of England. His widowed stepmother Catherine Parr had married his uncle Thomas Seymour soon after the death of Henry VIII and both were now dead – Catherine in childbirth in 1548, and Thomas executed for treason the following year – as was the first Lord Protector, Edward Seymour, reprieved after his initial downfall in 1549 but executed in January 1552. After the dispatch of the Seymour brothers the duke of Northumberland seemed to be securely in place as Lord Protector, and Archbishop of Canterbury Thomas Cranmer was steering the English reformation with the full support of the governing elite. The Cooke and Cecil families were in the ascendant in royal service. All seemed set fair for their future in a country that within a few years would be ruled by an independent young king with the intellect and training to make his mark on history as the next Tudor monarch and head of the reformed Church of England.

Chapter 5
Redgrave Hall

Whether the loss of Walter Haddon as a prospective husband was a disappointment or a relief, by early 1553 Anne's attention was engaged by another suitor. He was a widower, eighteen years older than her and the father of six children. Forty-three-year-old Nicholas Bacon was reliable, ambitious, a lawyer with a reputation for hard work and high achievement, and an intellectual heavyweight. Rising from a modest start as a Suffolk yeoman's son via the educational opportunities of school, a scholarship to Cambridge, and a place to study law at Gray's Inn, he had held an influential official appointment as Attorney to the Court of Wards and Liveries since 1547.[1] His wife, Jane, died in the winter of 1552–3.

Jane Ferneley's marriage to Nicholas Bacon had brought him a valuable connection to the East Anglian merchant elite. Her father was a prominent member of the Mercers' Company in London who maintained his Suffolk connections. Marrying her was part of Bacon's move into a social level well above his own family. Their marriage was carefully timed, taking place just after he was confirmed in his first official appointment, as Solicitor to the Court of Augmentations, in 1540. This post was the turning point in Nicholas's career, putting him into the government department responsible for disposing of land confiscated in the dissolution of the monasteries, and giving him inside information about property which he used to begin a lifetime of strategic land acquisition.

Jane bore him six children and helped him establish his first country estate at Redgrave, Suffolk, close to Diss just across the border into Norfolk. She was still alive in October 1552, when Nicholas ordered new gloves for her, the cost of which – 10 shillings – was paid by the household officer controlling expenses for the building work at Redgrave.[2] Did she receive and enjoy his gift? We cannot tell because the date of her death is not recorded and we only know that she must have died some time between October and January, as he had married Anne by February. In 1553 Bacon's accounts record payments to a mason for 'six days work about my Mistress tomb'.[3] Jane's death left him in urgent need of a stepmother for his children and he soon sought to replace her. By now he was associated with the 'Cambridge connection' at court that included William Cecil. It is possible that he met Anne Cooke through the Cecils and the idea for a match came from them. The first document naming Anne Cooke as Nicholas's wife is a licence to grant a manor, dated 9 February 1553.[4]

Their short courtship must have taken place in the winter of 1552–3. It is tantalising to speculate that serious Anne Cooke was also the lively girl who pelted Nicholas Bacon with snowballs in a poem that he wrote about this time. 'Of a Snowball', which contrasts the icy snow with the heat of desire, is undated but thought to have been written after his marriage.

A wanton wench upon a cold day
With snow balls provoked me to play:
But these snow balls so heat my desire
That I may call them balls of wild fire.

It ends after several verses on the theme (including a line about Cupid's 'fierce fiery toe' to rhyme with 'snow'), with the couplet

No snow nor thing this fire can quench
But the like fire of this like wench.[5]

Anne was the oldest daughter at home, with seven younger brothers and sisters. Bacon had six children himself and was known for his easy wit and good humour. It is certainly possible to imagine them caught up in family rough and tumble play on a winter visit, and if the playful 'wanton wench' was indeed Anne the verses show their lives together beginning with ardent physical attraction – at least on his part.

Marriage negotiations were swiftly concluded. At the end of January 1553 an indenture outlining the marriage settlement was drawn up between Nicholas Bacon and Sir Anthony Cooke.[6] It is a piece of evidence of particular significance to our understanding of Anne's earliest role in the interaction of her family with the politics of the court. The document not only details the conventional transfers of money and land involved in a marriage at this level, but also shows that a close tie existed between Anne Cooke and Mary Tudor before the marriage. At the time of his marriage Nicholas Bacon, like Anne a committed religious reformer, knew that through her the Cooke family was nevertheless maintaining an association with Mary, the current heir to the throne – and, of course, still a defiant Catholic. It is a conundrum, to which we will return as Anne's story unfolds.

In the early days of February 1553, twenty-five-year-old Anne Cooke married her heavy-set, jowly bridegroom. It would be easy to see this as one of the marriages of convenience so common at the time, when a wife's death left a gap in the management of household and children that had to be quickly filled, but by now we know enough about Anne to see that this was unlikely. Nor is it probable that she was faced with a match made for her by her parents, though they still had four daughters to find husbands for. She had already refused a suitor and clearly knew her own mind.

For Anne, marriage to Nicholas Bacon was a positive choice, while for him, valuable as Anne's practical skills would be in managing his family, her intelligence, company and connections perhaps interested him more. Anne shared his religion and was at home with the classical authors Nicholas read. She preferred Cicero, while he enjoyed Seneca. She was fluent in Latin, Greek and Italian, had published a well-received translation and had influential contacts among the intellectual elite and at court. While marriage to Jane Ferneley had been Nicholas Bacon's route into advancement in his native area of East Anglia and had provided him with a solid row of male heirs and marriageable daughters, Anne's connections reflected his newer ambitions.

Anne became stepmother to six children aged between thirteen and three, and the mistress of a large household at Redgrave Hall. Far from marrying a Haddon with untested prospects, she was now the wife of one of the acknowledged rising legal stars of the age. Her new husband was politically well placed as a close friend of William Cecil's and secure in his official appointment to the Court of Wards. The marriage went far beyond a convenient arrangement to provide care for Bacon's motherless children. Anne looked for more than a well-appointed home and a kind husband. In this much younger woman, Nicholas found an enduring intellectual partnership he had not known with his first wife. Despite the eighteen-year age difference, they were well matched.

The ninety-mile journey from Essex to Nicholas's house in Suffolk would have been hard going in the winter months, taking up to three days. The Bacons would have travelled either on horseback or in one of the early, clumsy coaches along deeply rutted roads full of icy puddles and heavy with mud. Coaches were only just coming into use and were as heavy and slow as carts. Many people still used wagons as transport. Travel in England was much slower since the monasteries that used to maintain the roads had gone and parishes squabbled about whose responsibility it was to undertake routine roadmending. From Anne's family home just east of London, they could have travelled to Suffolk via Cambridge or taken one of the better highways, the old Roman road to Colchester, then the smaller, emptier roads that led to Ipswich and beyond.

The final day's journey from Ipswich with her new husband took Anne through villages clustered around solid, flint-faced churches with square towers, and past low-lying marshes and fenland. As they turned into the approach that led through a wooded park from the Bury to Diss road, Anne would have seen for the first time the high roofline of Redgrave Hall with its octagonal turret, stepped gables and clustered chimneys. It was very different from Gidea Hall, and quite unlike most other houses she was used to. Nicholas Bacon had bought the estate in the 1540s in the redistribution of property that followed the dissolution of the monasteries. The house, set in a park, was on the site of a derelict former monastic hunting lodge, overlooking a small valley and stream, that had been the property of the Abbey of Bury St Edmunds before the Dissolution. Since he then worked as a lawyer in the government office that oversaw this great plundering of the riches of the Catholic church, was intensely practical, and had a good eye for a bargain, he was in the perfect position to consolidate his career with properties that would add to his prestige and supplement his income with rents and leases. During the 1540s he had bought woods, meadows and arable land centred on the area around Redgrave, that by the time of his marriage to Anne were profitably let to tenants.

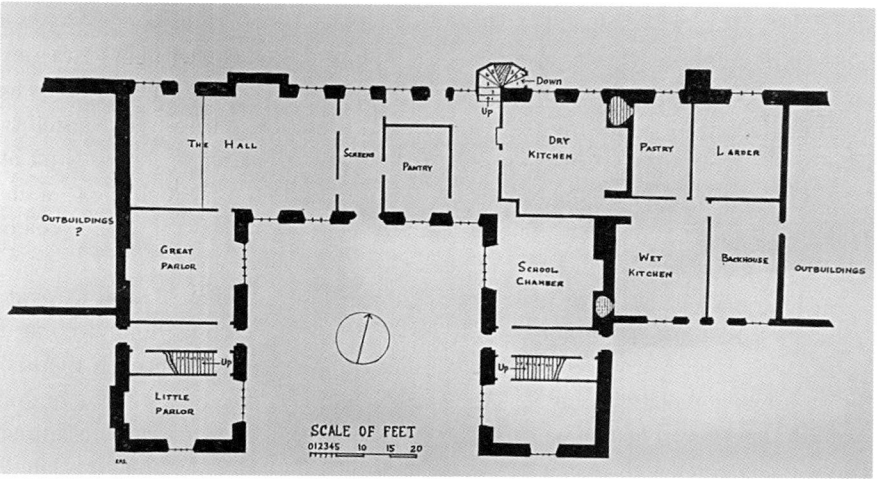

Reconstructed images of the ground-floor plan and front elevation of Redgrave Hall in 1554. Images taken from 'The Building of Redgrave Hall, 1545–1554' by E.R. Sandeen, *Proceedings of the Suffolk Institute of Archaeology and History*, 29/1 (1964) pp. 1–33 (Figs 3 and 4). Reproduced by kind permission of the Suffolk Institute of Archaeology and History.

Bacon designed the house himself, thriftily incorporating parts of the old lodge. Unlike the usual rambling Tudor manor house with stables, workshops and kitchens cluttering the entrance courts, to which Anne was accustomed, Redgrave was of moderate size, elegant and symmetrical, with equal wings, a roof with stepped gables, dormers and a turret, and whitewashed external walls. The graceful façade and open grassy courtyard would have been revealed gradually through the bare crowns of the surrounding oak trees in the park as they crossed a bridge over the stream and followed the slope uphill to the house on its summit. Bacon aspired to renaissance ideals of balance and order, influenced by his education in the classics. He also had a firm grasp of practical matters and installed a piped water supply to the house with stopcocks supplying the kitchens and buttery, courtyard, brewhouse, orchard and pond, an unusual amenity in the sixteenth century. It was Nicholas's first taste of building for himself, and he had a flair for it, closely supervising the work and employing several skilled London craftsmen for specialist work, as well as local labourers.[7] Although he was familiar with the renaissance features that were appearing in fashionable buildings in London, such as Somerset House, he made minimal use of them in this first building project. A decade later he and Anne would create one of the most innovative houses of the age, Gorhambury in Hertfordshire, which publicly marked their place among the Elizabethan political elite. For now, Nicholas brought his new wife home to what Ernest Sandeen, in his account of the building of Redgrave, judges to have been 'a house of which a man of moderate reputation and resources might be proud'.[8]

Owning Redgrave represented a personal triumph for Nicholas, a mark of his social and financial advance. His father had neither owned land nor occupied a position of influence. He was a yeoman, the Abbot of Bury's sheep-reeve, a tenant farmer, in the same part of Suffolk. Now Nicholas owned land himself, and was accumulating more, following the path of other ambitious men of the Tudor era who had risen from obscure origins through ability, education and hard work to become national figures.[9] Nicholas's route to success was not through the Church, as it had been for some of his famous countrymen, but the law, as it was for his friend – and now brother-in-law – William Cecil.

As she walked towards the main door of Redgrave Hall for the first time Anne would have seen the Latin motto newly carved over the porch within a decorated stone panel, *Mediocria firma*, 'Moderate things endure'. She would have recognised the phrase as a quotation from Seneca's *Oedipus*. Anne and Nicholas Bacon shared evangelical reformist beliefs, which in her case would ultimately tend to Puritanism. This was combined with an admiration for the stoic view of life, acquired from their reading of the classics. Moderation was a ruling principle for them both. Nicholas Bacon's chosen motto suited his new wife very well. Their marriage would grow into a supportive alliance in which Anne's engagement with new ideas flourished together with her husband's, reflecting Erasmus's ideal of an educated partnership.

Although externally the house was unconventional, once inside Anne found a more familiar setting, with a traditional layout dividing it into two. The western half was mostly used by the family, with a hall forty feet long, two parlours, a schoolroom and bedchambers; the eastern half was where the servants worked and slept. Above the hall was a minstrels' gallery, and to one side a door opened into the orchard.[10] It was a practical, comfortable family home. The house was full of children, doubtless missing their mother. The oldest of the six was thirteen, the youngest a toddler. We might wonder how Anne began to get on terms with them. She would have felt at home in their schoolroom, a large, light chamber looking over the courtyard, which was in daily use.

As the second of nine children, Anne knew the demands of a large young family and had helped her mother with the tasks of running a household. She was expecting to teach and care for the children but knew that would be only a fraction of her daily work. Anne stepped into the shoes of Nicholas's first wife to take over many domestic duties, applying all the skills expected of a sixteenth-century wife, from brewing, baking and preserving to medical expertise and managing the servants. Did they accept their new young mistress easily – was she welcomed, or resented? No records survive to tell us, but the speed with which Nicholas remarried left a legacy of suspicion from his first wife's family, occasionally surfacing in undercurrents of hostility in later years.

Soon after Anne took on her heavy new responsibilities, and before she had borne a child of her own, her mother died. Her independent-minded grandmother Margaret had died too, shortly before Anne's marriage. With the two senior women of the family gone, Anne and her sisters had lost a significant source of support and advice as they settled and had families of their own.

Back in London, fifteen-year-old King Edward was unwell. The chest infection he was suffering from during Mary's winter visit kept him confined to his bed in the palace of Whitehall with a bad cold and fever during February and March 1553. The planned royal entertainments for Candlemas and Shrovetide – masques, music and 'divers other plays and pastimes' organised by the court Revels Office – were postponed.[11] By April he seemed better, but he was weak and still coughing. In Suffolk, as winter weather softened into spring and the oaks round Redgrave Hall filled with foliage, Anne settled into her new life far from the city. She was expecting her first child. However, within months, fast-moving national events would bring unrest, danger and drama into her life.

Edward's health deteriorated further during May and June. In early May Northumberland reported to William Cecil that the king was on the way to recovery after his initial illness earlier in the year.[12] But the improvement was short-lived. By the end of May, the king's symptoms included swollen legs and fever, and he was coughing up black sputum.[13] Despite attempts to suppress the news of the king's deteriorating health, rumours about it spread from early spring. Northumberland kept Mary informed about her brother's condition during March and April. Traders and diplomats relayed reports throughout Europe, while in England prayers were said for the king. Edward's advisers were deeply alarmed by his deteriorating health and the prospect of Mary taking the throne. As his condition worsened, Edward returned to an idea he had first thought out before his illness, to alter the Act of Succession put in place by Henry VIII, under which the crown would pass to Mary. He also wished to exclude Elizabeth from the succession. Although he and Elizabeth agreed on religion, Elizabeth was in law illegitimate. As for Mary, John Foxe, chronicler of the Protestant martyrs of her reign, recorded:

> The causes laid against Lady Mary, were as well for that it was feared she would marry with a Stranger, and thereby entangle the crown: as also that she would clean alter religion, used both in king Henry her father, and also in king Edward her brothers days, and so bring in the Pope, to the utter destruction of the realm, which in deed afterward came to pass, as by the course and sequel of this story may well appear.[14]

The king put pressure on his ministers to agree a document that he called 'My Devise [Device] for the Succession', setting out his wish to make Lady Jane Grey his heir. She was the granddaughter of Henry VIII's sister and thus his cousin. The Device comprised two pages written and rewritten in his own hand, in which he set out his plans to exclude both his sisters and instead leave the crown to Jane. The document survives, blotched, corrected and with a one-word final amendment that alters his first thought of leaving the crown to 'the Lady Jane's heirs male' to 'the Lady Jane *and* her heirs male'.[15] With a stroke of the pen the alteration presented a living female candidate for the succession, rather than her hypothetical future sons. Edward had been drafting and revising his Device since the previous year, during which he was ill with smallpox. He recovered fully; however, in addition to the escalating hostility between him and Mary during 1551, this illness may have been the catalyst for his decision to set out a new plan for the succession.

In narratives of the Tudor era Edward has often been presented as a sickly child who faded away after years of ill-health. In reality he was a healthy teenager with no long-term health problems. The illness that killed him began with a respiratory infection in February 1553. Modern theories about Edward's illness range from tuberculosis to sepsis following this infection. Modern antibiotics would have saved Edward. As it was, experimental treatments were used that only served to worsen his condition and increase his suffering. At the beginning of June doctors were predicting he would die within days, but he lived for a further month, in agonising pain and discomfort from the final stages of his illness as his body swelled and he was racked with coughing, and the remedies, including dangerous doses of opiates, that were applied as the royal doctors resorted to desperate measures to try to save him.[16] Edward died on 6 July 1553 at the age of fifteen years and eight months.

William Cecil and Nicholas Bacon were government servants, committed to the correct interpretation and application of the law. Anne and Mildred were closely associated with the ruling elite. For all of them, the controversy over the succession opened chasms of risk and uncertainty. Anne's father's position at court ended abruptly, Nicholas's official appointments were threatened, and her brother-in-law Cecil was plunged into a difficult and dangerous political situation. Anne's quiet domestic interlude as the new mistress of Redgrave Hall was brief. As the country fell into turmoil, she found herself centre stage and about to play a part in the most perilous transition of power of the age.

William Cecil's reputation was compromised by the part he played in ratifying Edward's controversial plan. His signature appeared on the king's Device, though he knew the Lord Chief Justice had advised the king it could not lawfully supersede the Act of Succession without a further act of parliament. As the king's secretary he was bound by oath to defend Henry VIII's line of succession. Not to do so amounted to treason.[17] Always alert to consequences, he ensured his name was included as a witness to the document, not a signatory. He was, however, ordered by the duke of Northumberland to rally support for Jane, drawing up lists of the county gentry who could be relied on. When it became clear that many of them were in fact turning to Mary, Cecil was convinced he was facing prison and a charge of treason. He made contingency plans for his arrest, which included how to escape from the Tower if he was imprisoned there again. He wrote a last letter to Mildred, which he entrusted to Nicholas Bacon, asking her to look after his son Thomas, to pray for him and to find a husband of good religion if she wanted to marry again.[18] As well as working directly for the king, Cecil was the principal fixer at court for the duke of Northumberland. Though he had tried to minimise his involvement with the king's Device, inevitably Cecil was at the centre of the conflict that broke out after Edward's death between the supporters of Jane Grey and those loyal to Mary. As he was caught up in Northumberland's attempted *coup d'etat*, Cecil faced the greatest crisis of his life so far. For the first time devoid of any strategy to save himself, he may have felt close to losing his nerve. It was to be his good fortune that his friend and sister-in-law Anne did not lose hers.

Chapter 6
Kenninghall

The royal sisters Mary and Elizabeth knew of their brother's attempt to alter the line of succession through his Device. Mary's property holdings in East Anglia had been significantly increased before his death in 1553, making her the principal landowner in the region and one of the richest individuals in England. This extension of her property holdings, and with them networks of supporters among the region's conservative, Catholic families who had previously supported the Howards, the family of the duke of Norfolk, broadened her power base in East Anglia.[1] With this powerful personal 'affinity'– support network – behind her, as well as her lands, Mary had been handed a local, loyal faction to call upon if she needed to defend herself and her interests. This proved to be a costly mistake for the Council and for Jane Grey's supporters.

In addition to the valuable estate of Kenninghall, which had been confiscated in 1546 from the disgraced duke of Norfolk, and other property that she already held, the king gave Mary two fortified castles, Hertford and Framlingham. What could have been the benefit to the king and his Privy Council of handing over such premium property, apparently in exchange for a string of ordinary manors that Mary held in Essex? Some of the transfers took place years after Henry VIII's death, yet they were presented as fulfilling the requirements of his will. The purpose may have been to move Mary's base away from the Essex coast so she could not so rapidly flee the country for Catholic Europe.[2] Given how adamantly she insisted upon her royal status and rights, it seems unlikely that she would have accepted a settlement of land as a *quid pro quo* for giving way to Jane Grey. Even if we suppose that, to avoid being detained by Northumberland, she did not object to Edward's plan to divert the succession, Mary soon showed she had no intention of giving way.

From the spring into the summer of 1553, Edward's life ebbed away, his body emaciated and discoloured by what was likely to have been septicaemia and renal failure, his hair and nails falling out, his skin covered in scabs.[3] Invited to London by the king's Council, ostensibly to visit the king, neither Mary nor Elizabeth appeared, suspicious of what might lie in store for them. Mary had long mistrusted and disliked Northumberland, describing him in 1550 as 'the most unstable man in England'.[4] They both stayed in their Hertfordshire residences: Elizabeth lay low at Hatfield House, while Mary remained at Hunsdon, fifteen miles away from her sister. On 4 July Mary let it be known that she was leaving Hunsdon to avoid a suspected outbreak of plague there. In fact, probably warned of Edward's impending death by sympathisers at court, she headed to her Norfolk estates by a well-prepared roundabout route, to evade any attempt at interception by Northumberland's agents.

Setting off across the country on horseback, late at night, Mary and a small group of attendants rode at speed, covering some forty miles before staying with supporters, the Huddleston family of Sawston Hall in Cambridgeshire. The next day she pressed on to stay with Lady Burgh at Euston Hall near Thetford in Norfolk. It was there, on 7 July, that she first heard of Edward's death, 'but the cautious princess would not put complete confidence in the messenger and would not let the news be spread abroad', reports her chronicler Robert Wingfield, a loyal Suffolk gentleman.[5] Mary needed to be sure the news was true. She waited for a further two days before publicly claiming the throne. By then she was safely established at her manor house of Kenninghall in Norfolk. Mary assembled the members of her household in the great hall on 9 July and declared herself queen, applauded and cheered to the rafters by her supporters. 'Roused by their mistress's words, everyone, both the gently born and the humbler servants ... proclaimed their dearest princess Mary as Queen of England', Wingfield tells us.[6] Meanwhile, her rival Jane Grey was proclaimed queen in London, with the united support of Northumberland and the Privy Council.

Anne and Nicholas Bacon were at Redgrave Hall when the news came that Mary was defying Northumberland. Jane's supporters had tried to keep Edward's death a secret while they advanced their plans for declaring her queen. When the news became generally known, tensions escalated. The country was alive with rumours and conflicting reports, with stories circulating that Jane Grey's supporters had poisoned Edward. Northumberland, who had never been popular, found it hard to gain public support.

In her flight from Hunsdon Mary had been accompanied by only a small group of attendants: two ladies and six gentlemen. But within a few days of her arrival in East Anglia, she added another gentlewoman to her personal retinue. Anne Bacon became directly involved in the rapidly unfolding drama of Mary's triumph and accession. Kenninghall, just across the border into Norfolk, was only six miles from Redgrave Hall. The news of Mary's arrival spread quickly among the surrounding gentry families. According to Wingfield, her local supporters responded by flocking to 'their rightful Queen, ready to lay out for her in this worthy cause their wealth, their effort, and life itself'.[7] Every connection that might generate support was activated, as Mary and her advisers sent out letters and messengers in all directions.

Whether in response to such a message, or because they had already heard of her arrival from their kinsman in Mary's household – a cousin, George Bacon, was her steward – within days of Mary's arrival Anne and Nicholas Bacon set off to

Kenninghall to see her. The outcome was that Nicholas and Anne Bacon declared for Mary, and that Anne Bacon joined Mary's household in the midst of this crisis. How had it come about that the Bacons so unhesitatingly decided to support Mary, when their sympathies may have been with Protestant Jane Grey? To understand this development, and to grasp the importance of Anne's role in the fate of her new husband and her Cecil relatives, we must look again at the evidence of an earlier relationship between Anne Bacon and Mary Tudor.

A glancing reference to this connection has long been known. Robert Wingfield was a supporter of Mary and chronicler of the succession crisis. He refers to Anne Bacon as having 'once been a waiting woman' of the new queen.[8] This reference gives no indication of what Anne's earlier role had been, how her royal service had begun or ended, or how such a conjunction, on the face of it unlikely, might have come about. No evidence so far pinpoints a date when Anne first served in Mary's household. The household records for 1552 have not survived, which adds to the puzzle. We do know that Anne is first recorded as a gentlewoman of Mary's household in the year 1553, when her name is marked as a person who was in Mary's service before her accession.[9] But on its own, this detail adds little to the chronology. However, the evidence contained in Anne's marriage settlement does help shed light on the apparent conundrum of her service to Mary. A copy of the document survived the scattering of the extensive Bacon archive that was kept for centuries in the Redgrave Hall muniment room. Before the collection was split up and sold in 1921, Edmund Farrer (1848–1945), a Suffolk clergyman and historian, examined it. A miscellaneous collection of papers he left to the Suffolk Archive includes a copy he made of the indenture, which had been preserved in Sir Nicholas Bacon's 'Book of his Lands', now lost. Four foolscap pages contain the transcription in the Reverend Farrer's sloping italic hand of the indenture dated 27 January 1553 between Nicholas Bacon and Sir Anthony Cooke. It details financial and property arrangements to be made for the marriage between Nicholas Bacon and Anne Cooke, specifying the provisions that must be in place by 12 February 1553, thus confirming that the marriage took place in the first half of that month.

From the preamble to the document, we learn that Anne was given in marriage with a portion from her father of 400 marks (the value of a mark was 13s 4d, two-thirds of a pound), and a further £20 towards her apparel. Then follows a further cash present towards the cost of her clothes, detailed as: 'the sum of one hundred marks given by the most excellent princess the Lady Mary's grace of her benevolence to the said Anne being her servant, towards the charge of her apparelling also'.[10] Mary was known for her care and generosity towards members of her household, and it is nothing out of the ordinary to find her paying for wedding clothes – her household accounts record many such payments. But why was Anne in her service, and when did this service begin? So far, what we know tells us that Anne must have been in Mary's service before her marriage in February 1553, and before the onset of fatal ill-health in the young king.

We can unravel some tangled threads by looking back across two generations. When younger, the princess Mary staffed her household with those of high aristocratic rank, but after her father's death it became politically unwise for the elite nobility to serve her. Members of the nobility in the household were replaced by staff recruited from the gentry families living in the areas of her estates.[11] Among the gentlewomen recorded as serving Mary was Mistress Cooke, widow, of Gidea Hall in Essex, who was Anne's step-grandmother. Margaret Cooke had served as a member of the household of Catherine of Aragon, and she transferred to Mary's service after the queen's death in January 1536. In the late 1530s, in a note to Thomas Cromwell asking him to intervene on Margaret's behalf in a property matter, Mary refers to Margaret Cooke as 'my mother's old servant'.[12]

Margaret Cooke's name recurs in Mary's household accounts in the years after Catherine of Aragon's death, when she sent small gifts and treats to the princess: money was given to Mistress Cooke's servant for bringing presents in 1537 and 1544, to her servant for bringing cake and other things at sundry times in 1538, strawberries in 1543, and pudding in October 1544. An elderly woman by the 1540s, Margaret is last recorded as a gentlewoman of Mary's household in the years 1549 and 1550.[13]

As we have seen, after Anthony Cooke's mother died, his stepmother Margaret was a key figure in his upbringing, together with her brother-in-law, his uncle Richard Coke, who became head of the family. Richard Coke too was a devout and conforming Catholic. For twenty years from 1515, he travelled back and forth to Spain as a royal courier and a member of diplomatic retinues, relaying messages and gathering information. He carried letters to the emperor Charles V from Princess Mary and brought home letters to Catherine of Aragon. He may have been a useful go-between when Henry VIII was attempting to keep on friendly terms with Spain.[14] As Anne grew up, particularly given her own convinced engagement with the reforming faith, she must have been aware of how religious differences between generations of Cookes were negotiated and accommodated.

Margaret Cooke died in 1552. Shortly before her marriage in February 1553, Anne received a bequest of 'one old angel' – a sum equivalent at the time to about eight shillings – from Margaret's estate. (This would very roughly equate to around £200 today.) There was another gift in Margaret's will, more valuable than the bequests to her relations. She left a gold and turquoise ring and two gold sovereigns to her former royal mistress, 'my especial good Lady and mistress, my Lady Mary's grace, for a remembrance of my good will and service'.[15]

It is possible that the end of Margaret Cooke's long service, first to Queen Catherine and then to Princess Mary, gave rise to a natural opportunity for Anne to replace her in Mary's household, despite the striking difference in religious position between Anne and her new mistress. After all, such deep religious differences had to be accommodated within the Cooke family, as within other families at the time. There were divided views about religion in many elite families. There is no suggestion of a breach between Anthony Cooke and his stepmother or uncle, despite their continuing devout Catholicism. Within the royal family, Mary had been close to Catherine Parr, who was once her waiting woman, then her stepmother, whose religious views markedly diverged from her own. When Catherine Parr was queen, she asked Mary to assist with her translation into English of Erasmus's *Paraphrases upon the New Testament*, which was clearly a project associated with reform. Mary, who shared her intellectual interest in humanist studies but was the only non-reformer in Catherine's inner circle of ladies, apparently took part willingly. Neither had she openly objected to the prospect of a Lutheran husband in 1539, when Philip, duke of Bavaria asked to marry her. While making it clear that she 'would wish and desire never to enter that kind of religion', as Sir Thomas Wriothesley reported to Thomas Cromwell after a meeting with her at Hertford Castle, she trusted to her father the king's 'goodness and wisdom' and would obey him in the matter of her marriage.[16] The political sands constantly shifted, and Mary's resistance to the demands of King Edward for her household to cease observing mass need not have meant excluding all contact with individuals of the reformist persuasion. It would have been politically inadvisable to isolate herself to that extent.

The sequence of events in the background to Anne's presence in Mary's household before her marriage is still remarkable. The year 1551 saw publication of the full edition of Anne's translations of Ochino's sermons, complete with her initials on the title page and her declarations against 'papistry'. It was in 1551 that Mary was at the peak of her resistance to Edward's orders, the year her supporters rode through London publicly displaying rosaries in a mass act of defiance.[17] After that escalation of hostilities, the Privy Council increased the pressure on Mary to conform, threatening the break-up of her household if she continued to resist. The concession of private worship was confined to Mary and her personal servants, not extending to the whole household. Yet within at the most two years of these events, Anne was serving in the most publicly, unrepentantly, defiantly Catholic household in England. According to Henry Clifford, who was a servant of Jane Dormer, one of Mary's Privy Chamber ladies, at that period Mary's household had been 'the only harbour for honourable young gentlewomen, given any way to [Catholic] piety and devotion'.[18]

Recognising the complexity of relationships across the religious divide, and accepting the potential importance of family connection – grandmother Margaret's long service to Queen Catherine and to her daughter Mary – we must inevitably turn to the possible political importance of this ostensibly unlikely positioning of Anne Cooke, as she still was, within Mary's household, certainly before the young king became seriously ill, certainly before the beginning of 1553 and quite possibly in 1551.

There is no direct evidence on which to draw, and that is perhaps unsurprising. However, we can surmise that after Mary's defiance in 1551, the Council would seek to know as much as possible about how events were progressing in her household. It was a household into which no man could be accepted as fully and as intimately as a woman could be. Yet if the Council and the young reformer king were to rely on information coming from within the household, such a woman would have to be trusted. One basis for trust would be someone who demonstrated convinced and articulate support for the reformed faith. Another would be a direct personal connection to William Cecil.

From the point of view of Mary, whose defiance in 1551 had in the end been sternly met by her brother and his Council, if anyone had to be accepted in her household who was not a believing Catholic, then it may well have been easier to accept the recommended granddaughter of an old and faithful servant. It may also have been easier to accept a well-educated gentlewoman whose views were known and expressed than to live with the prospect of seeming religious allies being suborned, the suspicion of traitors in the camp.

These conjectures cannot be conclusive. There is no definitive evidence establishing the detailed chronology or the motivations of the parties involved in organising Anne's service to Mary. The puzzle is only partially solved through the evidence we have to date. However, whenever precisely Anne began to serve Mary, the marriage indenture at least opens the prospect that, when he married Anne Cooke, Nicholas Bacon was fully aware not only of her incisive intellect and her reforming convictions, but of her political value, placed so close to Mary. And this political value potentially cut two ways.

While Anne and Nicholas's marriage came shortly before Edward's fatal illness took hold, the king had been ill the previous year with smallpox. He was already tinkering with his plans to alter the succession. That was certainly known to Cecil, and very likely to his ally Bacon. There was always the risk that Edward would not survive or, if he did, that he might not produce an heir. Nicholas would have been fully alive to the advantages of a wife who was intellectually able, committed to religious reform, sister to Cecil's wife and had a position in Mary's household: indeed, who quite possibly had the confidence of Mary or might gain that confidence despite their religious differences. The potential political gain from such an alliance must surely have been clear, however fate might deal with both Edward and Mary. In this context, it is interesting to recall that Nicholas Bacon's first wife died some time after October 1552, and he married Anne Bacon in early February 1553.

As best it can be teased out from the evidence we have, this was the situation that existed in the background to the Bacons' short journey to Kenninghall, to declare their loyalty to Mary as she defied the threat to oust her from the succession. It is still possible to reconstruct their journey across the county border from Suffolk to Norfolk. They would have passed by the shady stands of old oak trees that surrounded Redgrave Hall and a scatter of buildings by the Redgrave village green. Beyond the trees rose the tower of the great church of St Mary. Once a symbol of the Abbot of Bury's prosperity and power, it had been stripped of its ornaments on the order of the king's Visitors. Its roodscreen and statues were broken and the carved angels that had soared beneath the roof beams had been roughly hacked off. Elaborate medieval wall paintings had been plastered over and whitewashed. As they left the village behind them, the Bacons' horses would have carried them uphill for a mile through birch woods, before the road dipped to run beside the marshes of Lopham Fen. They crossed the narrow river, where the countryside opened into the flat expanse of Low Common, wide acres grazed by cattle and sheep and scattered with oak and willow trees, as fen and grassland merged. Then there was a climb up the long, slow hill to South Lopham, its square church tower a landmark ahead. The final miles crossed what was then a lonely heath, empty of settlement, as they drew closer to the sprawling, seventy-roomed palace of Kenninghall, surrounded by gardens and parkland.

Mary had acquired the house six years earlier, after it was confiscated from the disgraced duke of Norfolk, though she returned it to the family after her accession. The site of Kenninghall's park is a disused wartime airfield and only a fragment of the vast house survives after demolition in the seventeenth century. A full inventory taken at the time of Norfolk's detention in 1547 does survive, describing the lavishly appointed private and public rooms that Mary now occupied, including the great hall in which her supporters acclaimed her.[19]

Despite their earlier connection, how might Anne have felt as she approached the house and a meeting with Mary? She had previously known Mary as an isolated figure excluded from power. Now she had to contemplate life in a country with Mary as queen, where her own family and friends might at best be diminished in standing and at worst imprisoned or executed. Mary might be giving assurances now, when she needed support, but what of later? Could Anne be sure her father was safe and what would become of him, a prominent supporter of the Reformation, if Mary was queen?

Nicholas Bacon was doubtless anxious to gain information and take any opportunity he could to influence events. He was well aware of William Cecil's situation. By appearing at Kenninghall at that moment Nicholas and Anne Bacon publicly demonstrated their support for Mary as the legitimate heir to the throne, as well as identifying themselves closely with the East Anglian landed elite they had so recently joined. They also publicly stepped away from Northumberland and the Council, at a time when the outcome of the crisis must have been unknown and uncertain. Every move must have been made in ready contemplation of civil war. Mary was co-opting loyalty. During the crisis that followed Edward's death her defiant identification with traditional religious observance was moderated, secondary to the urgency of rallying support. She seemed inclined to reduce, not inflame, religious conflict, exhorting her subjects to live peacefully without disputing with or reviling each other.

Despite their close connections with the Council, and Nicholas Bacon's significant official role under the Edwardian regime, the Bacons were relatively lowly figures among the stream of nobility and long-established landed gentry coming from all corners of East Anglia to declare allegiance. Yet despite their comparatively low rank, and Anne's known antipathy to 'papistry', Mary immediately brought Anne into her reduced entourage. Anne would remain close to her throughout that tumultuous summer and beyond.

Questions surface about motives on both sides. Why did Nicholas and Anne take the risk of declaring allegiance to Mary at the earliest opportunity, when her rival Jane Grey and the Northumberland faction might prevail? Why did Mary bring the daughter of the prominent Protestant courtier Anthony Cooke into her most intimate circle just at that moment? No-one knew whether Jane Grey or Mary would gain the throne. Supporters were changing sides and their motives were complex. It seems that some changes of allegiance from Jane to Mary owed more to local circumstances and personal grievances than to the recognition of Tudor legitimacy or support for the return of a Catholic monarch. Nevertheless, Anne and Nicholas Bacon did not hesitate.

One factor must surely have been William Cecil's fear as to the likely outcome, reflected in his letter to Mildred, and consequently the family's concern for his and Nicholas's safety. In his letter, Cecil had indicated that he would follow his conscience to support the lawful heir to the throne, whose authority was derived from God, wherever that might lead: 'seeing great perils threatened upon us by the likeness of the time, I do make choice to avoid the peril of God's displeasure'.[20] The Bacons now had every motive to soften Mary's view of William Cecil and to ensure that a representative of the Bacon and Cecil families was positioned close to the legitimate heir. Cecil was in a critically dangerous position, whoever won the struggle for the throne. If Jane's faction defeated Mary, Northumberland would not forget his principal secretary's reluctance to sign Edward's document. If Mary came to the throne, how could she ignore the fact of his signature and his work to raise support for Jane among the county elites? Either side could brand him a traitor. While William Cecil continued his work in London for Northumberland and for Jane Grey, Anne took up her post at Kenninghall, in the innermost circle of Edward's legitimate successor.

Constructing a court around a woman reigning in her own right was to be a new challenge for those who wanted influence. At any royal court, access to the monarch is key. In previous reigns there would always have been men around a king to assess his mood, hear his thoughts on issues of the day, and be first in line for orders. None of this could happen with a woman reigning alone, encircled in her private hours by female attendants and inaccessible to the men of the court. As new power structures emerged, together with the threats to the Cookes, Bacons and Cecils that would likely come with Mary's reign, it might prove a huge advantage for the women of the family to have access to the queen. The call to support Mary's legitimacy, to safeguard her husband and brother-in-law, and to maintain the family connection with Tudor political life surely overrode Anne's profound differences with Mary over religion.

Whether she offered her renewed service to Mary voluntarily, seeing an opportunity, was persuaded to stay by her husband or even ordered to do so as a pledge of good faith from the Bacons and Cecils, whose position was so compromised by their close association with Edward VI, Anne proved a trusted attendant to Mary in the midst of the crisis and well beyond. Support from across the politico-religious divide would obviously be a benefit from Mary's point of view. If her throne was to be stable, particularly at the outset of her reign and in the face of a potential war of succession, Mary would need well-connected allies and supporters who were not committed Catholics. She needed to broaden her base. Although publicly immovable in her adherence to traditional observance during Edward's reign, Mary attempted to minimise religious conflict as she sought to control events and gain the advantage in the early days of July. In addition, we should not overlook a simple personal, human factor. It is surely conceivable that Mary, with only two women in attendance after the flight from Hunsdon, wanted to gain the company of an intelligent young woman already known to her, in addition to Anne's useful information and connections.

Once these pieces of the jigsaw are slotted together, it is less surprising to find the Bacons hastening to Kenninghall to declare their fealty in the face of civil war, and Anne Bacon remaining and continuing to serve the woman who, within a few days, would be the acknowledged queen of England.

Chapter 7
The crown is not my right

At the beginning of July, Lady Jane Grey had the support of senior political figures in London. The studious girl, whose chief desire was to be left alone with her books, was instead at the centre of an insurrection, the political pawn of her father the duke of Suffolk and her father-in-law the duke of Northumberland. Now remembered as the powerless victim of a failed political manoeuvre, as we have seen she was then recognised and admired for her intelligence and scholarship. John Foxe, who would include Jane in his chronicle of Protestant martyrs, described the learned young woman who was blossoming under the guidance of skilled teachers:

> Between this young damosel and king Edward, there was little difference in age, though in learning and knowledge of the tongues she was not only equal, but also superior unto him, being instructed of a Master right notably learned. If her fortune had been as good, as was her bringing up, joined with fineness of wit: undoubtedly she might have seemed comparable not only … to any other women that deserved high praise for their singular learning: but also to the University men, which have taken many degrees of the Schools.[1]

Jane was not ignorant of the idea that she might become queen, but she had no wish to take the throne from Mary. Earlier that year, as it became clear to Edward's inner circle that he was seriously ill, sixteen-year-old Jane was in the midst of wedding plans. The duke of Northumberland had made a successful bid for her marriage to his son Guildford Dudley. In April 1553 rich fabrics of cloth of gold and silver were delivered to the Northumberland household at Durham House in London, as elaborate preparations got under way for a triple wedding: Jane to Guildford, Jane's sister Katherine to Henry Herbert, son of the earl of Pembroke, and Guildford's sister, also Katherine, to Francis Hastings, son of the earl of Huntingdon.

The wedding celebrations on 25 May at the duke of Northumberland's house on the Strand in London were ostentatious and splendid. Durham House was a former bishop's palace, one of the important residences built along the north bank of the river. An imposing two-storey house set round a courtyard, its main façade, flanked by three-storey towers, faced the Thames. The river was London's busiest thoroughfare, crowded with boats crossing back and forth between the north and south banks or ferrying passengers between the City and Whitehall. The wedding guests would have arrived by boat and strolled around walled gardens with open views across the wide river towards Lambeth and its low-lying marshes. Northumberland, granted his dukedom by Edward, had recently acquired the house, and seized the opportunity to showcase his wealth and importance. 'The French ambassador was present, and most of the English nobility dignified the ceremony with their attendance', records a contemporary chronicler.[2] The feasting and entertainments lasted for two days. Guests took part in jousts, games and masques, and the brides' and grooms' families paraded in magnificent clothes and jewels. For Northumberland, it was a triumph.

After the wedding, Guildford remained at Durham House, with Jane visiting him while remaining based with her own parents. Her marriage was to last no longer than nine weeks.[3] She continued to live between the two families, harried by the commands and demands of a mother-in-law who, as the king grew weaker, was eager to see Jane inherit the throne and her son made king. On 9 July, after becoming unwell, Jane was having a brief respite from the pressures of her new life at another riverside house at Chelsea when a cryptic message was brought from the Privy Council by Mary Sidney, her sister-in-law. She must immediately go upriver to Syon House, another of Northumberland's residences, 'to receive that which had been ordered by the king'.[4]

At Syon, Northumberland and four other noblemen knelt to her. They told her Edward was dead and had named her his heir. Jane collapsed, weeping, and tried to refuse: 'The crown is not my right and pleases me not. The Lady Mary is the rightful heir.'[5] Finally persuaded, next day she was taken in a barge down the Thames to be received at the Tower with a great company of attendants. She wore a gown of green velvet, the Tudor colour, and her mother held her train. Trumpets sounded, and heralds proclaimed her the legitimate queen, declaring the Lady Mary to be 'unlawfully begotten'.[6] As the heralds marched through Cheapside and down Fleet Street repeating the proclamation, a dissenting voice called out from the crowd: Queen Mary had the right to the title, shouted one Gilbert Potter. The young man who dared support Mary in public was hustled away. Early next day he was brought out and locked into the pillory. A trumpet sounded, a herald denounced him and Potter's ears were cut off before he was released.[7]

Although Jane had the support of the religious establishment and the City of London, the ordinary population of London were less certain. Bishop Ridley's sermon preached at Paul's Cross in support of Jane's right to the throne was received without enthusiasm by the crowd. While Mary was free, and gathering support, Jane's position as queen was not secure. Caught without a plan to contain Mary, the Council hastily sent letters to the Crown's county representatives, the Lords Lieutenant, warning them that Mary might invoke the help of 'some foreign power' and exhorting them to suppress any 'stir or uproar' in their localities.

Jane and her Council debated who should lead the force needed to capture Mary. The commander had to be a senior nobleman with the experience and authority to control a volatile situation. Northumberland was the most outstanding military commander of the time, but he wanted to remain in London to manage events and set a strategy, rather than lead Jane's troops from the front. Though Jane had accepted the crown for herself, she had infuriated her husband and his family by refusing to make him king. She now perceived their true colours. 'Thus in truth,' she wrote, 'was I deceived by the duke [of Northumberland] and the council and ill-treated by my husband and his mother'.[8] The slight, scholarly sixteen-year-old now once more asserted her authority over the assembled council of men, all closer to her father's age than her own. She did not want her father to be given the task of leading an armed force against Mary, and no-one else but Northumberland had the experience and seniority to take it on. By default, it fell to Northumberland to command her troops. Some accounts say Jane wept and begged for her father to be kept at home, others that she was firm and clear in her resolve he should remain. Jane's mother, who had been close to Mary, may have been keen to avoid her husband being appointed Mary's captor.

In practical terms, whatever Jane's views or her mother's, the duke of Suffolk would not have been an ideal choice to lead the troops. He had a lacklustre history of opting out of military command and preferring life at home. By accepting the command of the troops in the field, Northumberland took the step that would finish him. Instead of remaining a key figure managing the crisis, he left London and the council, taking efficient practical command of the military force but distancing himself from the crucial decisions that would be made over the next seven days. Jane's father-in-law was suddenly on his own, initially confident in the force he led from London and the prospect of reinforcements, unaware that he was now on the course to downfall and death.

Mary and her supporters, still at Kenninghall, were also making plans for a military confrontation. Swept along in the intense activity around Mary, Anne continued as one of the small group of gentlewomen in attendance. She would have helped with many practical tasks – organising Mary's clothes and other possessions, packing, directing servants – as the household prepared for a rapid move to the fortified castle of Framlingham in Suffolk. There was no time for the niceties of leisured meals and days spent in conversation, reading or fine sewing. Kenninghall, a sprawling brick palace with some seventy rooms, was situated in a 700-acre park, 'well stocked with deer, the north side guarded with woods and groves, being distant at least a mile from the town, which lies westward'.[9] It already felt like a military headquarters, with encamped soldiers surrounding it, messengers coming and going at all hours of the day and night and urgent meetings between Mary and her advisers and supporters. Intelligence reached Mary daily, both about unfolding events in London and the progress being made in marshalling support and troops to her cause. As well as calling on prominent East Anglian families to bring troops and arms, Mary was also securing support in Middlesex, Buckinghamshire, Berkshire, Oxfordshire and Northamptonshire.[10] Momentum was building behind her, but even in East Anglia she was not secure. The town of King's Lynn opposed her, and in Ipswich both Jane and Mary were proclaimed queen on the same day.

As she watched the situation develop at Kenninghall, Anne must have known that as secretary to Northumberland, William Cecil was heavily involved in the plans and activities of the opposing faction. We do not know how much contact Anne had with her husband Nicholas once she was in Mary's household, or what messages passed between them. Perhaps Nicholas's kinsman the Kenninghall steward was helpful in keeping her informed about the family. From whatever sources were available, she must have tried to glean as much as she could about what was happening, seeking news of her family amid the tumult of fact and rumour.

After leaving Hunsdon in Hertfordshire in time to evade the first attempt to detain her after Edward's death, Mary had continued to act with speed and decision. She dispatched Thomas Hungate, a long-serving and trusted servant with a defiant and uncompromising message for the Council. After at least two days on the road, Hungate arrived in London while the Council was in urgent session, to a hostile reception. Northumberland told him a man his age should have more sense and had him locked up.[11] But Hungate had completed his mission, safely delivering the letter from Mary. In her message to the Council Mary asserted her right to the succession and demanded that they accept her as queen. Her tone was regal but reasonable. While she knew they were consulting 'to undo the provisions made for our preferment', and knew of the 'great bands, and provisions forcible' they were preparing, when established as queen she would nevertheless pardon the Council members and take their actions 'in gracious part, being also right ready to remit and fully pardon the same, with that freely to eschew bloodshed and vengeance against all those that can or will intend the same'.[12]

Mary's speed of action and her resolve surprised everyone. Previously when under pressure, her reaction had been first to flee then to prevaricate.[13] The Council expected her to try and escape by sea from one of the east-coast ports to the protection of Charles V in the Netherlands or call on him to come to her aid by invading England. Ships were positioned along the coast in readiness for either outcome. The French were keeping a close watch as events unfolded, offering support if a conflict escalated. The men who had confirmed Jane as queen did not expect a challenge to their decision about the succession. Neither did they expect Mary's well-organised call to action, clearly pre-planned, with followers rallying to her at Kenninghall within twenty-four hours of her arrival.

The Council replied to Mary the same day, sweeping aside both her claim and her offer. Her letter had elements of conciliation, theirs was menacing. The Council's letter was drafted by Anthony Cooke's friend John Cheke, installed as principal secretary to Jane. In it the Council advised Mary to keep quiet. She should 'surcease by any pretence to vex and molest any of our sovereign Lady Queen Jane her subjects from their true faith and allegiance due unto her grace'. If Mary will 'for respect show your self quiet and obedient (as you ought)' she will find them 'all and several ready to do you any service that we with duty may, and be glad with your quietness to preserve the common state of this Realm'.[14]

On receiving this reply, Mary knew that there was no more room for conciliatory offers. She prepared for a military confrontation. By 15 July she had moved from Kenninghall and was holding her first council at Framlingham. Anne would have accompanied her on the journey to Framlingham, a fortified medieval castle some twenty-eight miles south-east of Kenninghall, and nearer to the coast. Updated and improved by the earl of Norfolk, who owned it before it came into Mary's possession, Framlingham was a huge, uncompromising stone fortress: moated, massive, enclosed by high curtain walls punctuated by thirteen towers. How did Anne feel as she rode in over the drawbridge and through the heavy gates? She had spent her whole life in cultivated surroundings and company. Now duty had brought her to a fortress on the front line of what was increasingly looking like civil war. The road to Framlingham would have taken Anne close to Redgrave, her home for the brief few months of her early married life before she re-entered Mary's service. We do not know if she had time to see her family and household.

Meanwhile, in London, the duke of Northumberland was gathering his forces. The citizens watched carts piled with weapons and ammunition rumble through the streets to the Tower of London. England had no standing army: men, horses and weaponry had to be brought together at short notice. Northumberland's troops left London in stages over the next two days. On 13 July after eating dinner at the Tower, he held a muster of armed men at Durham House and Whitehall. Earlier in the day, he had addressed the Council, his tone cautious rather than optimistic. The next morning, he led his mounted troops through the city and out through Bishopsgate towards Cambridge. The crowds of Londoners who turned out to see the cavalry seemed motivated more by curiosity at the spectacle than encouragement of his mission to capture Mary. There was no warmth to the send-off:

> The Duke of Northumberland prepared his power at London for his expedition against the Rebels in Norfolk, and making hast away, appointed the rest of his forces to meet him at New-Market-Heath: of whom this saying is reported, that passing through Shoreditch … seeing the people in great numbers came to see him, he said, The people press to see us, but none bid God speed us.[15]

If the lack of popular support seemed ominous, it did not deter him. The most successful and experienced military commander in England was now engaged in a well-planned operation. At short notice he had pulled together an effective fighting force that was superior to anything Mary had at her disposal. His aims were to intimidate the opposition, secure the east of England against threat from both Mary's supporters at home and her overseas allies in France and Spain, seize Mary, and shed as little blood as possible.[16] Meanwhile, at Framlingham Mary announced a substantial reward for the capture of Northumberland, and spent three hours inspecting her troops. The opposing forces were, it seemed, ready for each other.

Only a week later, London saw an entire reversal. After Northumberland left, reaching Cambridge on 16 July, rumours reached London that a massive force of Mary's supporters was ready to invade the capital. The collective nerve of the Council broke and key members decided to switch sides and support Mary. In Northumberland's absence William Cecil was among the dissenting councillors who resolved to proclaim Mary queen and hope to be granted her pardon. Late in the afternoon of 19 July, Mary was proclaimed queen at the cross in Cheapside in the City of London, though Londoners would not see her in person for another two weeks. Still in Cambridge, deserted by most of his troops, Northumberland knew the game was up. According to Robert Wingfield, the university and town authorities resolved to detain Northumberland and hand him over to the queen, 'so that they might by this fair deed amend and entirely obliterate the fault which they had previously committed by giving the enemy such a splendid welcome'.[17] It was the end of Lady Jane Grey's brief time on the throne, leaving her poignant mark on history as the 'Nine Days Queen'. Two senior Council members, Lord Paget and the earl of Arundel, had already set off to tell Mary of the reversal and ask her pardon, reaching her on 21 July. Cecil, who had orchestrated the Council's about-turn, delayed his own departure from London to see Mary, sending his secretary in advance to prepare the ground.[18] Finally, Cecil was delegated to find Mary on behalf of some other Council members and declare his and their allegiance, a dangerous task with no guarantee of a safe outcome.

Robert Wingfield was the owner of the house where Mary was staying in Ipswich. A previously obscure and undistinguished local gentleman with a fine house, he suddenly found himself at the epicentre of events, the queen's host at her hour of triumph.[19] Later rewarded for his service with a life annuity of twenty pounds, Wingfield wrote a first-hand account of the events that unfolded. When Cecil caught up with Mary – according to Wingfield, in the company of Nicholas Bacon – he found that his sister-in-law Anne had smoothed the path for him, despite his connection to what Wingfield calls the 'factious conspiracy' to put Jane on the throne. Wingfield describes what happened.

There also arrived Sir William Cecil, lately one of the secretaries to Edward VI, and Nicholas Bacon, attorney of the court called Wards; these men had married two sisters of remarkable education, daughters of Sir Anthony Cooke. They were not strangers to this factious conspiracy, and Bacon's wife, who had once been a waiting woman of Queen Mary's, was their chief aid in beseeching pardon for them.[20]

Anne passed on reassurances to her brother-in-law about the queen's view of him. For now, at least, he was safe: Mary had told Anne she thought well of Cecil and believed him to be an honest man. This account suggests Anne's presence at the queen's side was critical in deflecting the threat of prison and worse from her husband and brother-in-law. Her courageous intervention on their behalf must have taken intelligence and nerve. Yet despite Anne's help, Cecil was not yet in the clear. He had stayed with the collapsing government until its final days. He would need to construct a persuasive account of his own actions to confirm his loyalty to the legitimate queen.

In London the trumpeters and heralds of arms turned out again to attend a throng of the great and good for the latest proclamation before the crowd moved into St Paul's, where the men and boys of the choir sang the solemn hymn of deliverance *Te Deum Laudamus*, with the organ playing, 'and all the bells ringing through London, and bonfires, and tables in every street, and wine and beer and ale, and there was money cast a-way'.[21] Amid the celebrations another outspoken lad was consigned to the pillory, this time for speaking against Queen Mary. While Londoners revelled, the unlucky backers of Lady Jane Grey's claim to the throne were rounded up and confined. Now labelled traitors, they passed through the decorated streets on their journey to the Tower of London. In a dark mirror image of the celebratory processions that would follow, the prisoners were flanked by trumpeters, massed horsemen and foot soldiers armed with spears and guns. Chief among the accused was the duke of Northumberland. Arrested in Cambridge on 21 July and brought to London, he was taken to the Tower together with other members of his family four days later.

On 27 July four more men were arrested and taken to the Tower, relates Henry Machyn in his diary.[22] The best known of them was the duke of Suffolk, Jane Grey's father. Just over two weeks earlier, Machyn had recorded a very different episode in the Suffolk family's fortunes, describing the triumphant entry of Jane Grey to the Tower as queen, 'with a great company of lords and nobles . . . and the duchess of Suffolk her mother, bearing her train, with many ladies'.[23] Now Suffolk's ambitions, which had begun with a failed attempt to marry Jane to Edward when she was in the household of Catherine Parr, and ended with a failed attempt to put her on the throne in her own right, were over.[24]

While Anne had succeeded in making the delicate case to Mary for pardoning her husband and brother-in-law, and was still in place as one of Mary's attendants, her father was in danger. Both 'Master Cheke, the king's schoolmaster, and Master Cooke' were consigned to the Tower together with the duke of Suffolk. Known to be close to the king and influential in their advice to him, Cheke and Cooke were arrested on suspicion of being complicit in Edward's attempt to alter the succession. News travelled slowly to Suffolk where Mary and her retinue were still based. Ordinarily it was three days' ride from London, and even the fastest messengers, riding non-stop and changing horses along the way, could not cover the distance in a day. Anne would not have known straight away of her father's arrest.

John Cheke had been an influential figure in the inner circle of some thirty-five men surrounding Edward in the Privy Chamber. His outlook shaped the king's worldview and strongly influenced Edward's Protestantism.[25] Mary knew that it was Cheke who had drafted the council's reply to her letter of 9 July. He was placed under house arrest on 26 July before being sent to the Tower. On 12 August, with the vice-chamberlain and captain of the guard, Sir John Gates, he was indicted and found guilty of treason. They were jointly accused of attempting to bestow the royal title on Jane, recognising her as queen, and writing and publishing letters and proclamations. However, at that stage the new regime was lenient towards Cheke. His only punishment was to be left in the Tower until the following spring, when he was granted a licence to go abroad, leaving his wife and family behind. Never himself charged with any misdemeanour, and detained for only a short time, Anthony Cooke nevertheless joined Cheke, choosing voluntary exile with his friend nine months after his own release from the Tower.[26] His absence was to be another heavy loss for Anne. Less than a year after her mother's death, her father was also removed from her life and she would not have known if she would ever see him again. Cheke and Cooke reached Strasbourg on 14 April 1554 and then travelled to Basel. Cooke remained safely abroad for the whole of Mary's reign, in the company of fellow religious reformers and financially supported by his family in England.

As Anne continued her attendance on the queen, Cecil sought to consolidate his precarious restoration to favour by composing a statement casting a loyal light on his actions and motives during the insurrection. For the youthful William Cecil, the upward trajectory that retrospectively seems so secure was far from certain that summer. Trapped on the losing side as the country fell into crisis and dissent, he was not yet out of danger, but he was a political survivor and applied his wits to making the best of his position. By the end of July, he had presented in person a 'defence' to the queen, culminating in a plea that he might 'feel some difference from others that have more plainly offended'.[27] It seems his declaration was believed, or at least accepted, as he was the first of the former Council members to kiss the queen's hand, on 31 July at Ingatestone Hall in Essex, during her slow progress from Framlingham via Ipswich to London.[28] Ingatestone was the home of a senior Council member, Sir William Petre, a veteran administrator who, despite his involvement in installing Lady Jane Grey as queen, had also been quick to declare allegiance to Mary after the coup failed. Unlike Cecil, he retained a government post, sworn in as the queen's secretary at Ingatestone at the same time as Cecil's visit. His wife joined Anne as one of the queen's attendants as Mary continued her journey towards London.

Two other petitioners closely associated with the failed attempt to put Jane on the throne sought the queen's pardon at Ingatestone. One was Jane Grey's mother Frances, the duchess of Suffolk. Mary kept her waiting until two in the morning but granted pardons to both Frances and her husband. The duke was released from the Tower the same day, though Sir Thomas Wyatt's rebellion early the following year, in which he took a leading part, was to seal his fate and Jane's. Both were executed, together with Jane's husband Guildford Dudley, but the duchess and her remaining two daughters remained in favour with the queen throughout her reign.[29] Jane Dudley, the duchess of Northumberland, was refused an audience with Mary at Ingatestone. Nevertheless, she was permitted to remain free, later pursuing a determined campaign for the release of her sons from detention in the Tower.[30]

On 29 July Princess Elizabeth rode into London escorted through the city by trumpeters, standard bearers and colourful ranks of courtiers dressed in velvet, satin, taffeta and lace, their horses equally resplendent. On 31 July Mary set off again from Ingatestone, accompanied by five thousand soldiers on horseback, to be greeted by wild scenes of public rejoicing: even 'men of authority and years could not refrain from casting away their garments, leaping and dancing as though beside themselves'.[31] On 3 August the queen triumphantly entered the city through Aldgate, which was fluttering with bright streamers. Trumpet fanfares blared as her vast procession advanced through streets laid with gravel to even out the dusty, rutted surfaces. Along the route stood representatives of the craftsmen of London, beneath their banners and streamers. A thousand men in velvet coats and embroidered cloaks preceded the queen, followed by the Lord Mayor bearing the mace, and the earl of Arundel with the ceremonial sword. Behind the queen rode Princess Elizabeth, who had ridden out to meet her at Wanstead, and a crowd of ladies, followed by aldermen, and finally guards dressed in the royal liveries of green and white, red and white, and blue and green.

Queen Mary took up residence in the Tower of London with a hundred ladies. As with so much of Anne's life at this period, evidence about her whereabouts and activity is scant. Given her established position in the household it must be likely that Anne came to London with Mary. Did she assist in preparing the queen for her entry into London, and ride in the procession? Anne had been with Mary throughout the weeks of crisis. Without firm evidence we can only surmise the high likelihood that she was there and saw at first hand the scenes of celebration as Mary made her way to the Tower. The royal apartments so recently occupied by Jane were now Mary's. She would stay there until her coronation, as was customary.

Jane had arrived at the Tower of London on 10 July 1553 as queen, and on 19 July she became a prisoner there.

While we can set the scene of Mary's triumphant entry into London, we cannot conclusively place Anne in it, but it must be probable that she came to London, riding with the queen as one of her attendant ladies. If so, her feelings must have been mixed and she needed all the courage she could muster. The Tower of London, crowded with the queen's retinue, was also accommodating many prisoners. By then Anne must have known that her father was one of them, detained there for a short time on suspicion of treason.

Edward VI's funeral finally took place on 8 August. Mary wanted a full requiem mass for her brother, complete with prayers for the dead, but was persuaded that this could stir up serious trouble with religious reformers. There had already been violent disturbances in London by objectors to the reintroduction of the mass in churches. A compromise was agreed. The king was buried in Westminster Abbey with Protestant rites, the service conducted by Thomas Cranmer using the English Book of Common Prayer – the first time it was used for the funeral of a monarch. Mary did not attend the funeral, instead holding a private mass for her brother in the Tower. In what must have felt like a suspension of current reality, Edward's funeral was attended by those who had served him. Assuming their old official posts for the last time were William Cecil, who stayed at Nicholas and Anne Bacon's London house for the occasion, and Anthony Cooke.

On 29 September, the day before her coronation, Mary rode from the Tower of London to Westminster 'in a rich chariot of cloth of gold', followed by 'a flock of peeresses, gentlewomen and ladies in waiting, never before seen in such numbers'.[32] Anne must surely have been there. She remained with the queen and was still recorded as one of seven gentlewomen of the Privy Chamber two years later.[33]

Anne had played a crucial part in deflecting the threat to her family. It is arguable that, without the wit and nerve of twenty-five-year-old Anne Bacon, the future Lord Burghley might never have returned to favour after the events of July 1553. He might have chosen exile with his father-in-law, or if not, may not have survived to see Elizabeth I take the throne. As it was, William Cecil and Nicholas Bacon survived to continue their voyage through the choppy waters of Tudor politics. When Anne's first daughter was born, later in 1553, she named the baby Mary, and as the record shows, Anne remained close to the queen for at least the next two years.

In December 1553, diarist Machyn records a proclamation, made 'through London and all England', forbidding any English service or communion after 20 December. Married priests were banned. Services must be said in Latin and every parish church must have an altar, a cross and staff. The steady progress of English religious reform during Edward's reign, to which Anne had publicly contributed with her translations of Ochino, was reversed. Before her marriage, Anne's world was encompassed by learning, faith, and a cultured, well-ordered life with her family at Gidea Hall. By the end of 1553 she had been caught up in events that brought the country to the brink of civil war. Her mother and grandmother were dead. Her father, together with others of their faith, was contemplating exile, while Anne was in the ambiguous position of demonstrating service and loyalty to Mary. Family life would henceforth take second place to her duties at court, and if she and those close to her were to survive, her cherished religious faith would have to be hidden beneath surface conformity. It must have seemed that Mary's accession signalled the indefinite postponement of any return to reformed religion in England. If the new queen married and produced an heir – she was thirty-seven, and this was still a possibility – the country's Catholic future would be sealed.

Chapter 8
A new reign

The accession of Mary I was a historic turning point, the start of what was to be fifty years of rule by two queens regnant. Mary reigned alone for five years from 1553 to 1558, followed by Elizabeth from 1558 to 1603. Mary began to appoint her new Privy Council as soon as she had prevailed in the struggle for the throne. Initially an unwieldy group of forty-four men, the Council resolved into a core of around twenty regular active members, with others attending less frequently. Mary could not rely solely on her close supporters, as most of them did not have experience in national government. Some members were reappointed from Edward's Council: Mary needed people to provide continuity from the previous reign, and she needed people who knew how to run the country. There was friction between the two groups, as those who had served Mary loyally through the crisis found they had to govern alongside men who had tried to deprive her of the throne. William Cecil did not acquire a post close to the queen nor did he join the new Privy Council. Some sources say he was invited, but declined, others that he was deliberately kept at arm's length.

Nicholas Bacon retained his official post as Attorney to the Court of Wards. The Bacons and Cecils neither joined the exodus of Marian exiles to the continental countries where Protestantism flourished, nor put themselves at risk by continuing to advocate for reform at home. The Bacons' proximity to Kenninghall in the crucial days of early July, their speedy declaration of loyalty and Anne's timely aid in placating Mary had helped ensure their freedom. William Cecil felt secure enough to return to his home and family in Wimbledon. During Mary's reign he lived relatively quietly, yet still took opportunities to remain connected politically, becoming a member of parliament, and even joining a diplomatic mission to France, though with no official role.[1]

Ten days after her brother's funeral Mary issued a pronouncement that emphasised her personal religious preference. She qualified this, making it clear that while she would be glad if her subjects followed her example, she would not enforce change for the time being and her aim was for everyone 'to live in quiet sort and Christian charity'.[2] A letter she sent to her cousin Cardinal Pole, who had spent twenty years in Rome following a charge of treason during the reign of Henry VIII, reveals that she would have liked to go further, confiding, 'what pain the queen feels from being as yet unable by any fitting means to manifest the whole intent of her heart in this matter'.[3] Nevertheless Mary was setting in motion religious change. In a series of proclamations and injunctions she banned the printing and circulation of controversial religious treatises, and many Protestant books were publicly burned.[4] Mary initiated a correspondence with Pope Julius III suggesting the re-establishment of papal authority. She never countenanced the radical evangelism of Edward's reign but had appeared to accept Henry VIII's reforms. However, on taking the throne she made it clear that she would not follow her father's and brother's lead as head of the Church of England.

Northumberland was tried and convicted of treason. His execution, set for the morning of 21 August, was halted at the last moment, in front of the 10,000 people who had turned out to watch. It was not a reprieve but a postponement, to make the most of the prisoner's recantation of his Protestant beliefs by gaining the maximum publicity for his words. On the scaffold that day, Northumberland received the sacrament and spoke of the 'false and erroneous preaching of the new preachers'. He was executed next day, after a speech in which he quoted from the creed, 'I believe in the holy catholic church.'

Many prominent supporters of the Protestant doctrine were quietly encouraged to leave the country. Mary did not want to prosecute everyone; even Lady Jane Grey survived, living on in the Tower until there was no alternative but a trial and execution following her father's part in the Wyatt uprising against Mary of 1554.[5] Letting her live, to be the potential focus of further insurrection, had become impossible. On 12 February 1554, Jane Grey and her husband were beheaded within the Tower walls. Jane was buried there in the Chapel of St Peter ad Vincula.

During Mary's reign the Bacon household moved between Redgrave, Bedfords – a house on the Cookes' Gidea Hall estate in Essex – and Thames Street in the centre of London. In London, Nicholas attended to business at Gray's Inn and Anne fulfilled her duties at court. Mildred Cecil gave a home to her unmarried younger sister Elizabeth and brother Richard in Wimbledon. The Cecils did not entirely disappear from public life. William Cecil was playing his usual wily political hand, remaining visible and useful although not actively engaged in government. When Philip of Spain arrived in England for his marriage to Mary in 1554, his secretary Gonzalo Pérez lodged at Cecil's house. When Cardinal Pole was granted the manor of Wimbledon by the queen on his return to England in the same year, Cecil became his high steward.

Pole was appointed papal legate in August 1553. His return marked the revival of Roman Catholicism in England. Mary married the Catholic Philip of Spain in the summer of 1554. At Philip's first meeting with her after his arrival in England, in Winchester on a drenching wet day in July, she was accompanied by her ladies – who were numerous, but not, according to a member of his entourage, beautiful.[6] Once again, with no positive evidence to place her at the scene, we can only speculate that Anne was among them and that it is highly likely she attended the magnificent wedding in Winchester cathedral on 25 July, at which the queen was surrounded by a great company of richly dressed ladies and gentlewomen, and the feasting and dancing that followed.[7]

The royal couple made an appearance in London then spent the autumn at Hampton Court before returning to the capital, where Philip was installed in apartments in Whitehall palace formerly occupied by queens consort. Despite some spats between his Spanish servants and the English household officials assigned to him, Philip was settling into his new role.[8] The serious business of Mary's reign began. In an emotional ceremony attended by Mary, Philip and the assembled Lords and Commons in November 1554, Pole formally restored the realm to the Catholic faith under the authority of Pope Julius III. He was conciliatory to begin with, saying that he came not to destroy but to build, and that the past should be forgotten. However, it was by now clear that Mary would never return to the course steered by her father: in her vision of England the Church would resume full engagement with Catholic practices.

Aged thirty-eight when she married Philip, Mary finally seemed happy after her years alone and numerous marriage plans that had come to nothing. However, no heir was conceived. In 1555, Philip left for the Netherlands, not to return for two years. During his time in England the Catholic restoration had been achieved. Now enforcement began. Early promises of tolerance were forgotten as Protestants who refused to conform were tried and publicly burned in towns across England. In 1555 alone, seventy-eight Protestants were burned for the crime of heresy. The joy that had greeted Mary on her accession was over. By 1556 the country was disturbed by dissent and rebellion fuelled by Mary's marriage to Philip and the prospect that he might be crowned king of England.

Three years into Mary's reign, the persecutions were coming close to home for the Bacons and the Cecils. In May 1556 John Cheke, the Marian exile who had left the country in the company of Anne's father, was captured near Antwerp on the orders of Mary's husband Philip. He was taken to England and imprisoned in the Tower of London. In October he made a full public recantation before Mary's court to avoid being burned at the stake. His Protestant friends were deeply shocked. What can Anne have made of this humiliating betrayal of principle by a man she had known since childhood, so respected by her family and prominent in the reformist cause? His recantation was a triumph for the Catholic regime. Released from prison, and with some of his estates and income restored, Cheke did not long survive. He died in London in September 1557, probably of influenza (not, more dramatically, of grief, as chronicler Strype suggests). Anne's former suitor Walter Haddon wrote a Latin epitaph for his monument.[9]

Earlier in the year another of the Bacons' and Cecils' old friends, the reforming Archbishop of Canterbury Thomas Cranmer, was burned for heresy in the town ditch at Oxford after spending two and half years in prison. Mary hated Cranmer for the part he had played in the end of her parents' marriage and the triumph of Anne Boleyn, as well as his influence over her brother Edward. Now in his mid-sixties, Cranmer was put under relentless pressure to recant. Although he initially complied and signed documents denying his beliefs, unlike Northumberland, Cranmer did not make a public recantation before his execution.

'I shall therefore declare unto you my very faith, how I believe, without colour or dissimulation. For now is no time to dissemble, whatsoever I have written in times past,' he said in his final speech to the crowd, denying the government the propaganda coup they were expecting, and famously thrusting into the flames the hand that had signed the earlier documents.[10]

Only days later, Mildred Cecil made a conspicuous appearance at a grand Catholic church service in London. Cardinal Pole preached, having been appointed Archbishop of Canterbury immediately after Cranmer's death. At Easter the whole Cecil household received the sacrament of the mass and made confessions to a priest. The Cecils remained safe by outwardly conforming and keeping their political and religious views to themselves, but they had not abandoned their true beliefs. Cecil was hedging his position, quietly keeping in touch via intermediaries with the Princess Elizabeth and managing property for her.

John Day's printing press was operating out of an obscure Lincolnshire village, Barholm, on land Cecil owned.[11] During 1553 and 1554 the press turned out reformist tracts under the name of 'Michael Wood of Rouen'.[12] It was a dangerous game for Cecil, and for Anne's brother William Cooke, a member of Cecil's household, who was also involved with Day's clandestine press and who was briefly committed to prison for his part in commissioning work from Day. The secret of the printer's identity and location does not appear to have been particularly well kept: Day himself was detained in the Tower of London in 1554 for printing 'naughty' books, according to diarist Machyn, and spent some months in Newgate prison in 1555.[13]

Cecil continued to sit in parliament. Although he stood by his exiled friends by opposing a parliamentary bill to confiscate their lands, Cecil was a pragmatist: he was not prepared to go to the stake for his beliefs, nor to be forced to recant, like his old friends Cranmer and Cheke.[14] While he kept quiet about his views, Cecil privately kept a diary in which he recorded the numbers of Protestants burned for heresy.

It seems that Nicholas Bacon chose a lower profile than Cecil during Mary's reign, marking time in his non-political post of Attorney of the Court of Wards and serving as Treasurer of Gray's Inn. He was also apparently slow to conform with the revival of traditional Catholic religious rites. After his appointment as Treasurer in 1552, he had begun to sell off the vestments and objects associated with Catholic worship belonging to the Inn's chapel. He was in no haste to replace them after

Mary's accession: 'the reluctance with which the vestments of the old rite were restored ... bear[s] the clear imprint of Bacon's incumbency', in his biographer's view.[15] Both men corresponded with their father-in-law Anthony Cooke during his years of exile and administered financial affairs on his behalf. They kept in contact with other exiled reformists, and both were said to have attended secret prayer meetings at the house of Richard Morison, a godly layman who had been a committed evangelical since the reign of Henry VIII.[16]

The evangelicals who had left England labelled those who had been practising Protestants but now stayed put and conformed 'Nicodemites', after the biblical figure Nicodemus, a Pharisee who concealed his interest in Jesus' teachings by only visiting him at night. An uneasy dialogue unfolded between the Protestants in exile and those who remained. The exiles called on those who had stayed to declare their faith openly – true Protestants should choose martyrdom or exile, not dissemble. In turn those in England who risked persecution accused the exiles of leaving behind their other obligations. Of course, the real picture was more complicated and nuanced. Around 1,000 Protestants went into exile and few of those who remained risked persecution or sought martyrdom by declaring their faith openly.

The Nicodemite strategy that the Bacons and Cecils, among many others, practised during Mary's reign meant they stayed in control of their interests, in touch with other sympathisers, and ready for whatever might come next. The exiles relied on their contacts in England to watch over their interests and channel funds to them. Cecil's position was particularly useful to them. There was no noise from the exiles regarding his commitment to their cause, and his part in the parliamentary victory of December 1555 on the question of allowing them to draw on their assets and funds at home enabled them to remain well supplied and well organised, ready to return home when the time was right. In some parishes Protestant ministers outwardly conformed to ensure their congregations had continuity of religious guidance, rather than risk a new incumbent more committed to Catholic practices.[17]

It is not easy to picture Anne conforming to Catholic religious observance, accompanying her sister to hear Cardinal Pole preach, or tolerating life at court while Protestant 'heretics' were being burned at Smithfield. Yet like the rest of the family who remained in England, she accepted a life of outward conformity during Mary's reign. After Elizabeth I's accession, she would play a vital role in the revival of the Protestant faith and its wider dissemination throughout England. But from 1553 until Mary's death in 1558, she continued to serve at Mary's court, where she was joined by her younger sister Margaret who served as a maid of honour. Mildred was also often in attendance both alone and with her husband.[18]

Whatever accommodations the family had reached over religious observance, it did not damage the close ties between the two older Cooke sisters and their husbands. Mildred and Anne were both by now mothers, but for each of them maternity was a troubled path. Anne's and Nicholas's first daughter, Mary, died in infancy. After nine childless years of marriage Mildred Cecil gave birth to and lost a daughter, Frances. The sisters each had another child, and Anne looked forward to seeing her second daughter, Susan, playing with Mildred's baby, Anne. In August 1557 a letter from the Bacons to the Cecils records that Susan was ill with a 'double tertian' ague, a recurrent fever, but she was nevertheless 'somewhat amended, her fits being more easy'. Anne added a hasty but cheerful postscript as the messenger waited to take the letter, asking after the Cecil's baby Anne, known as Nan to the family:

> We at Bedfords are no less glad of Wimbledon's welfare, and specially of little Nan's, trusting for all this shrewd fever to see her and mine play fellows many times. Thus wishing continuance of all good things to you all at once because your man hasteth away and my husband to dinner. Your loving sister,
>
> A Bacon.[19]

Although Susan lived longer than Mary, she did not survive to be her cousin's playmate and Anne suffered the loss of this second daughter. There is no record of the baptisms or burials of Mary and Susan at Redgrave or in Essex. They may have died in London. Not all deaths of infants at the time were recorded, but it has been estimated that up to a fifth of children born in sixteenth-century England did not live beyond their tenth birthday.[20] The two lost Bacon daughters are portrayed on the family tree (Plate 1) in their dresses and caps, Mary with a feeding bottle in her hand, and Susan holding a doll.

Nicholas's partial retreat from public life allowed him more time with Anne. Following a period of illness in the last year of Mary's reign, he wrote a poem to her, naming their favourite writers and recording his pleasure in her company as she took care of him and they shared their thoughts. Headed 'Made at Wimbledon in his Lordship's great sickness in the last year of Queen Mary', it shows how close their marriage had become and reflects their sadness over the lost children.

> Calling to mind my wife most dear
> How oft you have in sorrows sad
> With words full wise and full of cheer
> My drooping looks turned into glad,
> How oft you have my moods too bad
> Borne patiently with a mild mind
> Assuaging them with words right kind.
>
> Thinking also with how good will
> The idle times which irksome be
> You have made short through your good skill

In reading pleasant things to me.
Whereof profit we both did see,
As witness can if they could speak
Both your Tully and my Senecke [Cicero and Seneca].

Calling to mind these your kind deeds
And herewithal wishing there might
Such fruit spring out of these your sides
As you might reap store due of right
Strait want of power appeared in sight
Affirming that I sought in vain
Just recompense for so great gain.[21]

By the fifth year of Mary's reign, the great advance of the English reformation during Edward's reign must have seemed distant to everyone who had supported it. There was little hope of change, as Mary was only in her early forties. The safest path for the Bacons and Cecils was to conform, serve, and wait. One of a few chosen gentlewomen in Mary's service and maintaining that role through all the cruelty and anguish of those years, Anne must have schooled herself to propriety and circumspection.

Chapter 9
Women in waiting

What does it mean when we say that Anne Bacon served the queen 'at court'? The Tudor royal court was neither a fixed place, nor a permanent collection of people. The most useful working description seems to be that the court was wider than the royal household, with a fluctuating attendance of those who were permitted to be there, that it was located anywhere that the reigning monarch was living, and it comprised those people with access to the monarch.[1] Anne, appointed a Gentlewoman of the Privy Chamber, would have spent her time wherever the royal household was based, moving between palaces including the palace of Whitehall by the Thames at Westminster, Greenwich down-river to the east and Hampton Court to the west. The Privy Chamber was simultaneously the political and domestic centre of both court and household.

In earlier reigns the king's private living quarters had been a male preserve. The monarch's body servants were men, with privileged access to his private apartments, day and night. Some of the titles held by men of the Privy Chamber sound menial but became politically significant positions during the reign of Henry VIII, when, in what has been called an 'institutionalisation of intimacy', the Privy Chamber took on the functions of a central administrative department of the royal court as well as organising the monarch's domestic life. Those who were in intimate attendance on the king had to be of high rank and had two roles reflecting the dual aspects of the existence of the king. As domestic servants they took care of the king's personal needs and his physical body, while as men of rank and distinction they served the ruler and embodiment of the state, the 'body politic'.[2] The job of Groom of the Stool might appear unappetising to modern eyes: to be the receiver and keeper of the close stools used as lavatories by the king and attend the monarch while they were used. But in Henry VIII's reign the holder of this post became the head of the Privy Chamber, in charge of all the other staff. He held the Privy purse strings and was keeper of the dry stamp of the sign manual – the king's signature, essential for any government decision to be formalised. Constantly in attendance on the king, with intimate knowledge of his moods and health, he was responsible for arranging details of royal daily life.

With Mary's accession, for the first time women took over the roles closest to the sovereign's person, while powerful men at court were largely excluded from access to the queen when she was off duty. While Mary might spend much of her day engaged in official business with her male councillors, her private hours were passed with her female attendants, behind the closed door of the Privy Chamber. The Tudor court was a world of intense competition for favour and preferment, where the sovereign was not a symbolic figurehead, but the focus of political life, wielding direct, personal power. Ambitious individuals could open the door to social advancement and lucrative royal patronage, including promotions to office and the allocation of valuable wardships, lands and annuities, by cultivating connections with the monarch and establishing influence with them.[3] Direct access to the ruler was essential to pursue these aims: the actors in these political transactions were 'deploying the power of intimacy on the public stage'.[4]

There was little recognition of women's agency in early biographies of the Tudor queens regnant, when historians highlighted the statesmen and noblemen who influenced events and dominated the political scene. Apart from the queen, women would enter the narrative as extras, in relation to men and families or noticed for their decorative qualities. In a biography of Mary I published as recently as 2007, Anne Bacon earns a brief mention, in which her appearance is given as much weight as any other characteristic: she is 'comely as well as learned'.[5] The same biographer speculates that the queen's ladies would have talked to her about intimate and personal topics and the 'lighter aspects of court life' – clothes and entertainments – and suggests that it is not possible to assume any level of influence on weightier matters.[6] Yet there is evidence, now more widely acknowledged, not only that the women of the Privy Chamber exercised considerable influence, but also that it was recognised at the time.

'In 1553, Mary and her servants … moved without any difficulty into both the actual living space in the palaces, and their proper place at the top of the country's political and social structures,' writes Charlotte Merton, the author of a detailed study of the women who served the Tudor queens regnant.[7] Feminist historians have been reinforcing the importance of recognising the role played by upper-class women as power brokers, showing that their goals and behaviour, and their identification with their families' interests, were the same as those of men from their own class. After Mary's accession, each woman serving in the Privy Chamber was a point of contact with the queen, the conduit through which their relatives and friends could seek political power and influence. Their roles went far beyond fixing pins and stitching fine embroidery: the women around the queen were political assets. Historian Barbara Harris concludes that instead of consigning women to the background of political history, political historians should acknowledge informal channels of power in their analysis of political processes of the late fifteenth and early sixteenth centuries in England, while Charlotte Merton stresses that Privy Chamber women were not pawns, but active participants in the political game of marriage, money and power.[8]

Mary's Privy Chamber appointments were highly sought after and almost all were made from families who had supported her and to whom she was connected by faith. Many of the women in Mary's Privy Chamber were the wives of men who had declared themselves her supporters in July 1553, or whose mothers had attended her own mother. Families would lobby hard to gain posts in the Privy Chamber for their female relations. Once at court the women operated within close networks of kin, supporting and promoting their interests. Anne's class position as a gentlewoman was typical of this group, as Charlotte Merton describes it:

> The Privy Chamber staff did not grind axes identical to those of the powerful landed nobles who frequented the Court, simply because none of them were major landowners in their own right. Because of their sex and class most of them were at one remove from the immediate difficulties of managing large estates, and did not have their own pressing interests to promote. They were therefore a more useful means for those outside the Privy Chamber to extract land, promises, offices and pardons than a group acting in their own self-interest. Their concerns were those of their families and friends, and to an extent their own personal gain.[9]

Physically close to the monarch, Privy Chamber women in both reigns were besieged by applicants for the queen's attention and favour. They were not slow to take full advantage of the opportunities this brought. They exchanged news and information through wide networks of connections. They could recommend favoured candidates for appointments, and both defend and promote their families' and allies' social and political ambitions. As well as directly lobbying for favours, they would take the temperature of the queen's likely response to an approach. Advising political suitors for Elizabeth I's favour, Robert Beale, the Clerk to her Privy Council, counselled them to make sure they had the right contacts: 'Learn before your access her Majesty's disposition by some of the Privy Chamber with whom you must keep credit for that will stand you in much stead.'[10]

Before Mary's marriage to Philip, Charles V's ambassador Simon Renard complained that Mary was not paying attention to him and was too much influenced by the advice of her attendant ladies. He was alarmed by their campaigns on behalf of different contenders for her hand in marriage, and their incessant 'chatter of marriage' to her.[11] In Elizabeth's reign, Anne's sister Mildred's access at court was recognised as a source of information and means of influencing her husband and, through him, the queen. When the Spanish ambassador, Diego Guzmán de Silva, wanted information about Cecil's attitude to Elizabeth's potential marriage suitors, he referred to Mildred, commenting, 'Certainly if anybody has information on the matter it is Cecil's wife, and she is clever and greatly influences him.'[12]

Despite having direct access to the queen, and the other privileges of a position in the Privy Chamber, Anne's freedom and her choices were constrained by her post. She could not spend her time in studious exercises or managing the home and family she had only just acquired. In addition to suppressing her private beliefs while she was in Mary's pious Catholic household, we can surmise she drew heavily on reserves of tact and forbearance to fulfil her role. As part of the inner circle of royal attendants who saw to the queen's every private need from early morning until last thing at night, she was charged with a miscellany of duties that ranged from intimate to formal, and from menial to grand: 'The Privy Chamber staff made the queen's clothes, distilled, nursed, cooked … Tractability was a prized virtue,' writes Merton.[13] The highly educated queen must have valued Anne's erudition and intellect, and Anne experienced unequalled access to the ebb and flow of events and ideas at the highest levels of the royal court. Nevertheless, many aspects of her role would have been mundane and tedious.

The lessons that Anne learned from life as a courtier surface in advice to her adult sons about their dealings with those in power. She was surely speaking from experience when many years later she counselled her older son Anthony about the dangers of joining the household of the earl of Essex: 'crede mihi fili [believe me, son], you shall find many inconveniences not light. Envy, emulation, many pains, great urging for suits [petitions for favours]'; 'Everything you do shall be spoken and noted abroad and yourself brought as it were into a kind of bondage where now yet free.'[14]

When Anne was offered the opportunity to be a gentlewoman of Mary's household, there would have been no option to decline the position. The posts close to the monarch were filled according to the queen's personal choice. They were formally offered and regulated, with prescribed duties and rewards. Anne would have taken an oath of loyalty and service before the Lord Chamberlain. Being a member of the queen's personal staff was not a token role. It involved living at court, away from family life. Even heavily pregnant women were expected to be on duty, and to return soon after the birth. This was possible because the babies of noble and gentry families were usually sent to wet-nurses who undertook all their care as infants. Very few women of wealthy families breast-fed their babies, though it was not unheard of, and influential educators including de Vives, Elyot and Cranmer encouraged women to follow the natural order and nourish their own babies. London families would often choose to send babies to wet nurses in the country, where there was less risk of infection.[15] As Anne gave birth to two babies during Mary's reign this is likely to have been the case for her in the latter part of 1553 or early 1554, and again when her second daughter was born.

Though there were gradations of religious belief, the proportion of non-Catholics among Mary's personal staff would have been far smaller than in the court as a whole, and Anne would have been conspicuous for her adherence to Protestantism if she maintained it publicly during this time. The established presence of Anne, the ardent reformer, even if she appeared to conform to the prescribed state religion during Mary's reign, is a continuing enigma in her story. Enough of the factors that led Mary to appoint Anne to her service before her marriage to Nicholas Bacon – the Cooke family connection, combined with the political wisdom of keeping a line of communication open with those who had supported her brother in the previous reign – must still have applied once Mary gained the throne. At this stage in Anne's history, we can no longer speculate that she was in her post because of pressure on Mary from a Protestant regime.

Some families steadily supplied women to serve in such posts, from one generation to the next.[16] As the Cookes had been in royal service for at least three generations, Mary had long known members of the Cooke family who served at court. Mary appears to have remained favourably disposed to Anne when she married Nicholas Bacon: she contributed to her marriage expenses, listened to what Anne had to say on behalf of her husband and brother-in-law, retained Nicholas Bacon as Attorney to the Court of Wards, and kept Anne in her service for the duration of her reign. We might conclude from this that the events of July 1553 confirmed Mary's trust in Anne and her value as a reliable companion and servant. However, for some women, it has been suggested, 'service in the Privy Chamber could be looked on as a form of protective custody'.[17] It is possible that, though in part a reward to the Bacons for their prompt identification with Mary's cause, Anne's presence was also a surety for the rest of her family.

The queen's female attendants fulfilled daily domestic tasks that included serving food and drink in her private apartments, the care of her clothes and jewels and the work of dressing and undressing her. Clothes were put on in layers and sections, fastened by laces and pins. Mary took an interest in clothes and jewellery. She favoured relatively plain gowns for daily wear but when she wanted to impress jewellery, jewelled buttons, starched ruffs, elaborate girdles and 'attires' – head dresses – added to the impact of the regal outfit. Elizabeth, of course, went further when she was queen, presenting a magnificent appearance as part of her public persona. Constructing the queen's appearance, carefully taking it all apart again late at night, and keeping track of every valuable item were serious responsibilities and the process could take hours. Some women remained on duty all night, as neither queen ever slept alone. A member of her staff would either sleep with her as her bedfellow, or in a small bed in her room.

The hierarchy within the queen's Privy Chamber, formalised in Mary's reign, followed the structure set up for earlier queens consort rather than for reigning kings. In the early years of Henry VIII's reign, Mary's mother Catherine of Aragon was served by eight ladies in waiting and eight ladies of the bedchamber and maids of honour, many of whom were the wives, sisters and daughters of the king's friends or favourite servants. In 1540, the year that Anne of Cleves was replaced by Catherine Howard, the queen's household included eight 'great ladies', nine ladies and gentlewomen attendants, five maids in waiting, four gentlewomen of the Privy

Chamber and four chamberers. In 1546, when Catherine Parr was queen, there were twenty-five women plus the queen's maids.[18]

The complement of staff in Mary's Privy Chamber remained similar to that of earlier times for queens consort. She employed three or four ladies of the bedchamber, who were her most senior attendants. They included her close friend Lady Susan Clarencieux, who acted as a vigilant gatekeeper to the queen. The post of Groom of the Stool did not feature in the queen's staff. The duties it had encompassed were split between the senior women, and a male courtier, the Lord Chamberlain, became the administrative head of the Privy Chamber. During Elizabeth's reign his responsibilities were extended to the entire royal household. Of Elizabeth's four senior ladies of the bedchamber, Catherine Asteley took on the position of Chief Gentlewoman, and kept the queen's close stools. Blanche Parry also served her turn as Chief Gentlewoman.[19]

Next in line were twelve ladies, gentlewomen and maids of the Privy Chamber. As a Gentlewoman of the Privy Chamber, Anne Bacon belonged to this group and she was entitled to payment of £33 6s 8d per annum for her service (equivalent in purchasing power to around £16,500 today).[20] Then there were six maids of honour supervised by an older woman, the Mother of the Maids. These were young girls from good families for whom living at court centred on the possibility of making a good marriage. Despite the reputation of Mary's household for piety and sobriety, the maids could be troublesome, falling for unsuitable young men, and playing games, shrieking and laughing in their shared rooms late at night, which annoyed the more staid members of the household. The Mother of the Maids often had her hands full. Three or four chamberers, paid £20 a year, did the more basic domestic work such as making the queen's bed daily to a prescribed ritual, maintaining bed linen and storing it. A small group of men: five gentlemen and seven grooms of the Privy Chamber, whose tasks included cleaning, setting up tables and carrying food and other provisions from the kitchens and buttery, completed the list of servants nearest to the queen. Elizabeth reduced the number of men to two gentlemen and a maximum of eight grooms during her reign. One of the grooms handled small financial outlays for Queen Elizabeth while her chief minister William Cecil – who was acting as both her private secretary and her Secretary of State – took over the queen's coffers and control of more significant items of expenditure.

After long public days at court, the queen could look forward to respite from duty and formality in her privy lodgings. The bed chamber, privy chamber and a private chapel comprised the lodgings' inner sanctum where the queen ate, slept, was entertained, and prayed with her closest attendants. The presence chamber was the lodgings' more public area, containing a throne beneath a canopy of state. Here the queen received visitors and larger scale royal meals and entertainments took place. Elizabeth added a withdrawing chamber to the privy lodgings. She was not keen on eating in public and often ate alone in private, while the ceremony of formal service continued in the presence chamber. Beyond the most private rooms was a Great Chamber, which was a guardroom. The private apartments were richly decorated, with scented rushes strewn across painted oak floors, panelled walls hung with tapestries and elaborately patterned ceilings. The queen had a privy garden, a secluded area where she could walk on gravel paths between beds of flowers and fruits.

The privy kitchen supplied choice food for the queen whenever she wanted to eat, while the rest of the court kept to fixed mealtimes. In addition to the food delivered from kitchen and buttery, the queen's attendants made extra treats, ordering in substantial quantities of expensive spices and other supplies to brew up comforting drinks and desserts: 'Sundry kinds of spices, as sugar, cinnamon, zinzer [ginger], cloves, mace, nutmegs etc., commanded into the Privy Chamber by Ladies and others for possets, caudles, etc.', reads an entry in the accounts – a caudle was a thick, sweet hot drink, and a posset was made from wine, eggs and spices.[21]

The relatively private world of the Privy Chamber was the closest thing that Mary had to a family life. When Elizabeth succeeded her in 1558, the Privy Chamber became even more of a family unit. Where Mary had been linked to most of her supporters and personal servants by faith, Elizabeth was more often connected to hers by family ties, though she also took on some of Mary's own Privy Chamber staff. Anne Bacon was one of those who moved straight from Mary's service to Elizabeth's.[22]

As one of Mary's personal staff, Anne would have been provided with livery, rooms, and 'bouge (or bouche) of court' – a daily food, lighting and fuel allowance for herself and her own servants. Status determined the extent of the allowances and perquisites for different categories of royal attendant. A 'warrant dormant' issued for Anne Bacon's livery is dated 15 December 1553 in the queen's household accounts.[23] This kind of warrant provided for livery to be supplied year after year and is an indication that Anne's position in the household was expected to be long-term. Livery was supplied as cloth to be made up for each individual, allowing a choice of style. Women's livery gowns for everyday wear would usually be fairly plain, and royal livery was often of russet-coloured cloth.

Mary continued to favour women of the Cooke family. Anne's younger sister Margaret – no doubt named for her formidable step-grandmother – is recorded as one of the maids of honour in January 1557. Meanwhile Mildred Cecil, like her husband, remained visible and involved in court life, even if only on the sidelines. More women of the family had positions at court after the accession of Elizabeth I. Anne would stay on into the new reign, and Mildred would receive a formal appointment as a Gentlewoman of the Household.[24] Mildred's daughter Anne Cecil, countess of Oxford, lived at court for a year in 1584 as an attendant to Elizabeth.

By the time she married Philip the queen was thirty-eight, and desperate to conceive a child. When she stopped menstruating in September 1554 she was overjoyed – her belly swelled and it seemed that a pregnancy was progressing. The date of delivery was estimated to be sometime in May 1555. In April, apartments at Hampton Court were prepared for Mary's lying-in, and the queen withdrew to an all-female world to await the birth. Pregnancy and birth were high-risk events. Great care was taken of aristocratic and royal women who might be on track to produce a much-anticipated male heir. They went into seclusion well before the birth, sheltered from the shocks, accidents and infections of the world in a birth chamber hung with rich fabrics and carpets, the windows and keyholes covered. Special luxury clothes were supplied for the expectant mother, which must have been a lucrative trade for tailors and seamstresses. Lady Lisle was advised in the 1530s that she would need a selection of nightgowns in damask, velvet and satin, and ermine bonnets among other expensive items.[25]

Anne would have taken part in the flurry of preparations building up to the confinement, as the chamber at Hampton Court was fitted out, wet-nurses and 'rockers' – teams of women to rock and soothe the baby – were put on standby for the birth, and prayers were said for the queen's safe delivery. At the end of April a rumour that an heir had been born set off feasts and celebrations around the country, soon curtailed. Optimism turned to puzzlement and the due date was revised. May and June came and went, as the queen insisted the dates must be wrong. The women around the queen must by now have known that the supposed pregnancy was questionable. One of them, Frideswide Strelley, never believed in the pregnancy and told the queen as much; others encouraged Mary, maintaining the fiction of a healthy outcome.[26] As the weeks went by the atmosphere in Mary's closed, darkened chamber at Hampton Court must have become increasingly stifling and desperate. Finally, in the intimacy of the lying-in chamber with its empty crib, Anne may have witnessed at first hand the queen's misery and despair as the truth could no longer be avoided: there was no baby.

What had produced such persuasive evidence of a pregnancy in Mary? Modern medicine can resolve such issues early with tests and ultrasound examinations, but in the sixteenth century doctors relied on visible symptoms. The reasons for phantom pregnancy, a condition still recognised by modern doctors, are various and can include psychological elements. Mary desperately wanted a child and eagerly interpreted any positive signs. Apart from no-nonsense Frideswide, her medical advisers and attendants were deferential, and reluctant to contradict the queen's belief in her pregnancy. But she had a history of menstrual problems and, at thirty-eight, the likelihood of conceiving was reduced, the risk of complications high. In early August the chamber was dismantled, the nurses were sent away and Mary left Hampton Court for her house at Oatlands in Surrey. Nothing more was said about a baby.

Already grief-stricken after the false pregnancy, the queen became even more distraught when her husband slipped away at the end of August to join his father in Brussels. Philip stalled endlessly about a possible return in response to her passionate entreaties for him to come back to her, in which she trailed the possibility of elevating him to become king of England. Elizabeth, who had been under suspicion of colluding with rebels and under effective house arrest, had been summoned to join Mary at Hampton Court during the 'pregnancy' and would stay with her until October 1555 before returning to Hatfield and her own loyal servants.

On 8 March 1555, in consideration of her service to the queen, Anne Bacon and her husband were granted rents and lands in Tutbury, Stafford.[27] Anne was still recorded as a member of the Privy Chamber staff on 1 January 1557. By then Mary was forty-one, and there was little hope of a further pregnancy, but that year Philip did finally return to England and Mary again became convinced that she was pregnant. Once again, it was a false alarm. A year later, her reign would be over, and there would be no child to take her place.

Mary took to her bed feeling unwell at the end of August 1558. Over the following months her health deteriorated until it was clear to everyone, including the queen, that she would not recover. There was not only a devastating influenza epidemic sweeping the country, but also typhus – the combination doubled the average number of deaths in many English parishes.[28] There is evidence that Mary became ill after Jane Dormer, a favoured member of her staff, was infected with influenza – but recovered – in July.

Although she is still recorded in the service of the queen at the beginning of 1557, evidence suggests that Anne was absent from court for at least some time in the final year of the reign. We have seen that in 1557 she wrote to her sister and brother-in-law from Bedfords, the house on the Gidea Hall estate that the Bacons used, and she refers in her letter to the health of her baby, Susan. It is possible that this was the period of her lying-in and she was at Bedfords to be near her family home for the birth, or that she was temporarily away from court to visit her baby and family in the country. The heading of the poem, quoted earlier, that Nicholas wrote to her the following year refers to 'his Lordship's great sickness in the last year of Queen Mary'. In it he thanks Anne for her care of him at this time, and their losses are referred to in the poem, together with his hope that she may bear other children.[29] It could be that Anne had leave of absence from court to look after sick members of her family during the epidemic, that the 'great sickness' afflicting Nicholas was influenza, and that he survived when their baby daughter had not. Wimbledon, where the poem was written, was the Cecils' home. It is likely that Anne and Nicholas were staying with or near Mildred and William, not in their own house in central London, as people with the means to do so always tried to get away from the city at times of mass infection.

At some time in 1558 Anne gave birth to the first of her babies who would survive infancy. She named her son Anthony, after her father. A further unknown in Anne's life during that year is where and when the birth took place, a time when she would again have been away from court. Thus we do not know whether Anne was still in attendance at court as the autumn passed with the queen confined to her chamber. As Mary's illness worsened, she finally named Elizabeth as her heir. Eyes turned from the queen to her successor. By the time she died on 17 November 1558, an exodus of courtiers to Hatfield House, the home of twenty-five-year-old Elizabeth, had begun.

Chapter 10
Accession

The day after she was proclaimed queen, Elizabeth set out from Hatfield towards London, and 'was on the way encountered and entertained in all places with such a concourse of people, with so lively representations of love, joy and hope, that it far exceeded her expectations,' writes John Hayward, an early historian of her reign.[1] For the Protestants who had survived Mary's reign, the years of watchfulness and retreat ended with her death. Unlike the turmoil and fear of the succession crisis of 1553, this time the process was smooth. As Elizabeth entered the Tower of London, according to Hayward, she contrasted her past and present circumstances: 'Some have fallen from being Princes of this land, to be prisoners in this place; I am raised from being prisoner in this place, to be Prince of this land.'[2] The transition from one monarch to the next brought relief and optimism for Anne Bacon's family. The new queen was young, highly intelligent and educated and she shared their faith. Once Elizabeth I took the throne the Protestant exiles began to return and Anne was reunited with her father after his years abroad.

After their careful navigation of the Marian period, Nicholas Bacon and William Cecil resumed the careers that had been dormant for five years. Plenty of other hopefuls sought favour and office from Elizabeth: 'when she came to London … many great persons, either for birth, or worthiness [or place in the State,] resorted unto her; and now, rising from dejected fears to ambitious hopes, contended who should catch the first hold of her favour'.[3] Neither Nicholas Bacon nor William Cecil, the consummate politician, needed to join the crowd of contenders. Within days they were at the centre of the political stage. Master political operator Cecil, already trusted and well regarded by the young queen after maintaining channels of communication with her throughout Mary's reign, moved into the position of supreme power and influence as Elizabeth's senior minister that he kept for the rest of his life. Nicholas Bacon became the chief spokesman for the crown in parliament and before the law, a post which also lasted for his lifetime.[4]

The queen decided against appointing a Lord Chancellor. The list of candidates had included Sir Anthony Cooke, whom she possibly regarded as too dogmatic in his Protestantism for her taste. While she was a convinced Protestant, Elizabeth shocked some reformists when she retained religious images in the Chapel Royal and permitted the continuance of choral music both there and in cathedrals throughout England. In place of a Lord Chancellor she appointed Nicholas Bacon to be Lord Keeper of the Great Seal. She had confidence in him as Cecil's close associate, an experienced government lawyer with proven loyalty to the principle of legal succession. She knew him to be hard-working and congenial to her intellectual and religious outlook. This post made Bacon the chief legal spokesman for the crown. He was knighted, but not rewarded with the title of Lord Chancellor despite effectively being given by letters patent all the rights and responsibilities associated with the office.[5] Bacon's lowly social origins may have been a reason for the queen withholding the most prestigious title.

The Spanish ambassador, Count de Feria, would later that year secretly marry the devoutly Catholic Jane Dormer – the former lady in waiting who had been a possible source of the queen's fatal infection. With Mary's death the count had suddenly lost all his access and influence at court. He wrote an ill-tempered account of Bacon's appointment, to the widowed Philip, now king of Spain: 'They have not … appointed a Chancellor but they have given the seals to guard to Mr Bacon, who is married to a sister of the wife of secretary Cecil, a tiresome bluestocking, who belonged to the bedchamber of the late Queen who is in heaven. He is a man who is not worth much.'[6] The dismissive label he gives to Anne Bacon suggests that the count finds her too learned and capable as well as suspiciously Protestant in her leanings. He knew Anne to be influential and believed her connections had a significant bearing on her husband's appointment.

Nicholas Bacon was neither aristocratic nor ostentatiously rich, and he had not been appointed to the most senior law office of Lord Chancellor: for these reasons, in the count's view, he lacked worth. However, those who knew Nicholas Bacon recognised his formidable intelligence and learning, underlying firmness of purpose, a brisk and practical approach to business and a lively wit. Bacon's everyday conversation and his expertly polished rhetoric were leavened with a rustic turn of phrase and epigrams drawn from his early life in rural Suffolk, an element of his oratory enjoyed by those who heard him speak. He was described by contemporaries as 'a most eloquent man, and of rare learning and wisdom' and one of the 'chief pillars of our English speech'.[7]

The Nicodemites' wait-and-see strategy had paid off as Elizabeth could immediately make the appointments that ensured her government was swiftly established. As the exiles gradually returned, they were integrated into the new regime. The publication in 1563 of Foxe's *Acts and Monuments*, better known as *Foxe's Book of Martyrs*, put the Protestant sufferings of Mary's reign permanently on the record, including key Protestant texts written before Elizabeth's accession and showing how Protestant heroes and martyrs had tested their faith. Foxe collaborated with John Day, newly reinstated as London printer of choice for the English Protestant elite, in the compilation and production of this massive work.[8] To present the new queen in the most favourable light, deflecting any criticism of her observance of the Catholic faith during her sister's reign, Foxe appended an account of her dangers and tribulations. It allowed recognition of and reflection on the moral challenges and ambiguities that had been faced by Protestants such as the Bacons and Cecils who, along with their new queen, had chosen to conform rather than defy the regime or flee.[9]

Reporting back to Philip, Feria painted a picture of the court at the point of transition from one reign to the next. The new queen, he says, seems 'incomparably more feared than her sister and gives her orders and has her way as absolutely as her father did'.[10] From his point of view much was in disorder, with the most urgent questions being who the new queen would marry and what would happen to religion:

> what can be expected from a country governed by a Queen, and she a young lass, who, although sharp, is without prudence, and is every day standing up against religion more openly? The kingdom is entirely in the hands of young folks, heretics and traitors, and the Queen does not favour a single man whom Her Majesty, who is now in heaven, would have received.[11]

In a final twining of their fates, the Archbishop of Canterbury, Cardinal Pole, had died on the same day as Mary. The preferred candidate to replace him, who was not formally appointed until a year later, was Matthew Parker, one of the remaining members of the close-knit 'Cambridge connection' that included Cecil and Bacon. Once a chaplain in the household of Anne Boleyn, Parker had flourished in the reign of Edward VI. During Mary's reign he retired to a hidden, quiet literary life where, according to an account written in 1574, he reportedly 'lurked secretly … within the house of one of his friends leading a poor life without any man's aide or succour'.[12] Within weeks of Mary's death, he was invited to London by his old friends Nicholas Bacon and William Cecil and offered the position of archbishop. However, it took months to settle the succession. Parker demurred, not travelling to London until February, after two further summonses from Bacon and Cecil. Once he did accept, after nine months of discussion, there were more lengthy delays as bishops appointed in the Marian era refused to officiate at his consecration.

Feria reported other trouble between the old and new religious regimes at the outset of Elizabeth's reign. 'Some of the heretics from Germany have come hither,' he wrote at the end of December 1558. The godly men wanted to preach in the church of St Augustine, which had been given to the Italians in London. 'They first sent to the Italian Consul to ask for the keys. He is a Florentine, and refused to give them up so they went and broke the door in, and preached four sermons during the day.' Further,

> On the Sunday of Christmas-tide the Queen before going to Mass sent for the bishop of Carlisle, who was to officiate, and told him that he need not elevate the Host for adoration.

The Bishop answered that Her Majesty was mistress of his body and life, but not of his conscience, and accordingly she heard the Mass until after the gospel, when she rose and left, so as not to be present at the canon and adoration of the Host which the Bishop elevated as usual. They tell me that yesterday she heard Mass said by another bishop who was requested not to elevate the Host and acted accordingly, and she heard it to the end. I should like in these affairs to animate and encourage the Catholics so that she may find difficulties in the way of doing the wicked things she is beginning, but I am doing it with the utmost caution in order that she may not be offended or quarrel with me more than need be.[13]

Feria received short shrift from Elizabeth. He refused to attend her coronation and returned to Spain, where his English wife Jane Dormer, the former favourite of Queen Mary, continued actively to support the Catholic cause and give refuge to exiled English Catholics.

Religious change was again under way in England as Elizabeth's new administration began reversing the changes made by Mary. Elizabeth knew that she had to take formal steps to alter national religious policy but may have wished to delay implementing change until the most senior and powerful Catholic members of the clergy had been replaced and other pressing matters – including the country's financial instability, the legacy of war with France, and insecurity on the Scottish border – were under control.[14] The important religious business of Elizabeth's first parliament in 1558/9 was largely managed by Nicholas Bacon, who as Lord Keeper presided in the House of Lords. He also organised theological debates in Westminster Hall as preparation for the changes that were being introduced.[15] Sir Anthony Cooke, who on his return to England sat in parliament as a knight of the shire for Essex, was, along with other prominent Marian exiles, impatient to see an immediate reformation of the church: 'We are moving far too slowly,' he complained in February 1559.[16]

Forming congregations in Protestant enclaves such as Zurich, Basle and Geneva during the Marian years, some of the exiles had departed from the prayer books of Edward VI's reign, which for them were still too close to the old Catholic rites, and further reformed Cranmer's liturgies. They returned to find Elizabeth requiring Catholic observances such as the wearing of vestments to continue, with the aim of reconciling old and new doctrines to establish the Anglican *via media* of religious moderation.[17] The Church of England's independence from Rome was re-established by the Act of Supremacy of 1558, while the Act of Uniformity that followed in 1559 reintroduced Cranmer's Book of Common Prayer (a copy of the 1559 edition with Bacon's name in it still survives), reinstated ten Acts revoked by Mary, and conferred on Elizabeth the title of Supreme Governor of the Church of England. This was intended to placate those who did not believe a woman could lead the church as 'Supreme Head on Earth of the Church of England', the title held by her father and brother.

The Act of Supremacy reinstated an Oath of Supremacy to be taken by individuals in local public or church office. When it was later extended to include members of parliament and those with university posts, many resigned rather than take the oath. Most of the bishops as well as many fellows of Oxford colleges lost their positions. This left the way clear for the appointment of bishops who were sympathetic to reform. However, the religious settlement did not put an end to religious dissent during Elizabeth's reign. Catholic recusants and radical Protestants alike would, in different ways and for different reasons, continue to resist and disobey the doctrines of the national church.

Elizabeth's coronation combined splendour and display with clear messages about the future direction of the church. On 14 January 1559, the day before the coronation, the queen was carried through London from the Tower to Westminster on a golden litter. She was presented *en route* with a series of pageants that emphasised her descent from English kings and queens (in implied contrast to Mary's Spanish geneaology), portrayed her as the Biblical prophet Deborah who ruled the House of Israel for forty years, and signalled the virtues of a healthy commonwealth and 'true religion' as opposed to superstition and ignorance. The figure of Truth presented the queen with a Bible written in English, which she theatrically kissed and laid next to her heart as the crowds cheered.

At the coronation next day, some parts of the service were read twice: first in Latin then in English, heralding the religious settlement to come. It proved difficult to find a suitable bishop to crown the queen. Archbishop Pole was dead; the archbishop of York said he would attend but declined to officiate because of reforms that Elizabeth had made at the Chapel Royal; the bishop of London had been a leading figure in the burning of Protestant 'heretics' and was unacceptable to Elizabeth; and others were out of contention through illness or because they were under arrest. Finally, the bishop of Carlisle, who was a long way down the episcopal pecking order, accepted the role.

Anne, now Lady Bacon, appears in the first list of ladies of Elizabeth's Privy Chamber of January 1559. Mildred, Lady Cecil, makes her appearance as a Gentlewoman of the Household in the same list. While some of the queen's most senior attendant ladies were supplied with livery for the coronation, neither Anne nor Mildred is included in that category.[18] However, even if they were not given clothing for the occasion, their status as the wives of senior government officials and their own Privy Chamber appointments meant both were there, splendidly dressed, and they would have been involved in the court's detailed preparation for three days of religious ritual, conspicuous display and feasting.

Once the coronation was over Anne would have seen little of her husband. Her baby Anthony would have been sent to a wet-nurse for his first year, Anne was in attendance on the queen, and Nicholas was immersed in his new responsibilities. The Supremacy Bill was presented to the House of Commons at the beginning of

February, but little was resolved as the Puritan faction, led by Sir Anthony Cooke among others, sought to drive through more radical reform than the moderate members would accept. The parliamentary debate was adjourned until after the Easter recess, and a religious debate or disputation took place in the adjournment period, chaired by the Lord Keeper. The Westminster Disputation, as it was known, allowed eight spokesmen from each side to debate three different issues: the use of English in services, the English Church's right to decide on its own rituals and practices, and the question of the Mass. While the Disputation descended into an acrimonious row over procedure on the second day, with Bacon's evident partiality for the Puritan faction decried by the Marians, the Supremacy Bill was approved by both houses of parliament after Easter.[19]

Alongside the consuming public demands of court and politics, the Bacon and Cecil families privately flourished in the early years of Elizabeth's reign. Anne's second son Francis was born at York House in the Strand, the Lord Keeper's official London residence, on 22 January 1561 and was baptised in the church of St Martin in the Fields. Mildred and William's surviving daughter, Anne, was joined by a son, Robert, born at Westminster in 1563. The following year work began on the Cecils' Hertfordshire house, Theobalds. Anne and Nicholas also acquired a Hertfordshire estate, Gorhambury near St Albans, about sixteen miles north of central London and twenty miles west of Theobalds. They needed to live close to London now that Nicholas had a government post, and in a house that reflected his status as Lord Keeper. Anne's stepchildren remained at Redgrave, which was maintained as a separate household headed by the oldest son of Nicholas's first marriage, the younger Nicholas Bacon.

Taking the opportunity of negotiations relating to the marriage of Anne's younger sister Margaret to Ralph Rowlett, Nicholas had bought Gorhambury from Rowlett. As he had done at Redgrave, Nicholas set about creating a new house and garden. Gorhambury was more modest than the vast prodigy houses by which other successful individuals competed to advertise their wealth and success with displays of magnificence. It was certainly dwarfed in size and splendour by the palace of Theobalds at Cheshunt, newly built by William Cecil and presided over by Anne's older sister Mildred. A popular portrait of the later part of Elizabeth's reign shows Cecil mounted on the white mule on which he pottered around his many acres of pleasure grounds.

Gorhambury was well designed, with innovative features, elegant and suitable to their position. Moderation, '*mediocria*', the middle way, was still the rule for the Bacons. 'The surest state and best degree/Is to possess mediocrity,' wrote Nicholas, in one of his poems of that period.[20] He nevertheless seems to have heeded the advice of Baldassare Castiglione in *Il Cortegiano* [*The Book of the Courtier*], that directs the courtier to 'erect great buildings both to win honour in his lifetime and to give a monument of himself to posterity', and of Aristotle, who directed that display – as opposed to vulgar opulence – was a virtue for men of wealth, standing and nobility of mind.[21]

Castiglione's courtier's manual was published in an English translation in 1561. The translator was Anne's brother-in-law Thomas Hoby. The end of Mary's reign and the early years of Elizabeth's saw the marriages of the remaining three Cooke sisters. Hoby married Anne's sister Elizabeth on the same day in June 1558 that Margaret married forty-five-year-old Sir Ralph Rowlett, a Hertfordshire gentleman and member of parliament, as his second wife. But only weeks later, by the beginning of August, the newly married Margaret was dead. The cause of her death is not recorded. By contrast Elizabeth had a long and eventful life. When Thomas Hoby was appointed ambassador to France in 1566, she accompanied him. In another of the random blows of fate that struck in an era of infectious diseases with little hope of cure, he died the same year, leaving her pregnant and with three small children. Elizabeth rallied, returned to England and eventually remarried. Like her sisters, she maintained her classical learning and put it to use, becoming known for her composition of lengthy epitaphs in Greek, Latin and English, and her fearless pursuit of legal causes, often seeking the support and intervention of her influential Cecil connections. The final unmarried sister, Katherine, married Sir Henry Killigrew in 1565, bore four daughters and died in 1583 after the birth of a stillborn baby. She too is recorded as writing Latin verse after her marriage.

When Elizabeth's reign began there must have been reason to hope that the queen would marry and bear children, securing England's future as a Protestant nation ruled by new generations of Tudors. The politics of regal marriage-broking were already in play at home and abroad.[22] After Mary's ordeal of false pregnancies and her early death, Elizabeth's youth and health were attractive assets. But nobody could know whether, like her brother and sister, she might not survive illness, or marry but produce no heir. The many physical perils of sixteenth-century life affected all classes of the population. And Elizabeth would be at constant risk of political reverses and threats, among them the potential for uprisings at home or invasion from abroad. William Cecil's unceasing vigilance over her safety and that of the realm began with her accession and would continue until his own death, still in harness as her chief minister, forty years later. In 1558 nobody could have predicted that Elizabeth would remain unmarried and would reign until 1603, refusing to name an heir until she was on her deathbed.

Anne was thirty years old as Elizabeth took the throne, with many personal losses behind her. Her two baby daughters, her mother, grandmother and younger sister had all died since her marriage five years earlier. She had lived through the horror of the arrests, trials, forced recantations and brutal deaths of men and women who supported her religious beliefs, and the exile of her father and close associates of her family. Surely Anne must often have felt fear and anger as pious and learned Protestants personally known to her were imprisoned, humiliated and sent to the stake. She could not betray any such thoughts to Mary, the queen she had served from the first days of her reign, or to the loyal Catholics who surrounded her at court. Whatever her feelings may have been at Mary's death, Anne must have possessed immense strength of character to tolerate, we must conjecture for her family's benefit and safety, such proximity to the Marian regime which, for five years, had offered no visible end in sight.

Chapter 11
The Apologia

The early years of Elizabeth's reign saw Anne as close to the new queen as she had been to Mary, yet now free to express her views and beliefs without constraint. She mixed with the leaders of the new religious and political establishment who were intent on progressing reform and in 1564 she undertook a task of translation of notable political significance.

Anne's education, experience and connections had, in effect, prepared her for public life. She was skilled in classical languages, philosophy and rhetoric. She could refer to classical examples and sources, and embroider her correspondence with Greek and Latin phrases. But non-royal women did not lead public lives and Anne and her sisters lacked the practical training in disputation and public debate given to their male contemporaries at the universities and the Inns of Court.[1] Like her sisters, Anne was turning her skills to less visible forms of influencing and persuading, outside the arenas of religion and politics occupied by men. By now she had served a double apprenticeship for this role: as the published translator of a prominent reformist work at the outset of Edward's reign, and as a member of the staff of the Privy Chamber, serving at court and surviving the political and religious threats of Mary's reign.

In 1564 she was called upon to undertake a major literary task: a translation from Latin to English of Bishop John Jewel's religious polemic, *Apologia Ecclesiae Anglicae* [*An Apology or Answer in Defence of the Church of England*] published in 1562.[2] As at the outset of Edward's reign, the printing presses were rolling to disseminate pious works, with political and religious argument enmeshed, in support of the reformed church. John Day and other reformist printers were openly back in business after being closed down and driven underground during Mary's reign. Cecil and his government colleagues urgently needed to promote the revived English church's message both at home and abroad.

The role of women of this period as translators has attracted scholarly attention. Although women in continental Europe are known to have written secular prose and poetry as well as religious meditations and translations, the output of female writers in England was more limited. Historians suggest that educated women's voices in Tudor England were conventionally silenced by the requirement to maintain female reticence and modesty: 'Except the gravity of some matter do require that she should speak, or else an answer is to be made to such things as are demanded of her, let her keep silence,' ordered Thomas Becon (1511–67), writing during the reign of Edward VI, warming to his theme to add, 'For there is nothing that doth so much commend, advance, set forth, adorn, deck, trim and garnish a maid, as silence.'[3]

This prohibition extended to writing, with two exceptions. Women were permitted to translate religious works by other writers – who were usually men – and to write their own religious meditations.[4] Yet even in this limited arena women were constrained. We have seen how the accomplished young Margaret More Roper was forbidden to seek a readership beyond her own father and husband. Even enlightened educators confined women's studies to a prescribed range of classical works and religious texts, hedging their encouragement with repeated emphasis on proper conduct. In his *Instruction of a Christian Woman* of 1523, Vives wrote that it does not become a woman to 'rule a school, nor to live among men, or speak abroad and shake off her demureness and honesty'. She should instead be at home, 'unknown to other folks, and in company to hold her tongue demurely, and let few see her, and none at all hear her'.[5] Chastity – this consistently modest, contained behaviour – should be a woman's most prized virtue, including after marriage, and nothing should tempt her into the world to compromise it by word or action.

Women's work of translation was seen as acceptable because it was considered to be a secondary activity. Safely placed at one or more removes from the expression of original ideas, translation kept women within the domestic sphere and posed no threat to the male *status quo*. The task of translation could be denigrated as a second-hand act. John Florio, whose translation of Montaigne's essays was published in 1603, describes the work of translation as 'defective', and belonging to females, and thus he feels degraded by his association with it.[6] Consequently, women's work in producing translations could be labelled insignificant and of low value. At best, it might be seen as a useful pastime to keep women occupied and less liable to allow their minds to wander into 'peevish fantasies'.[7]

Not all women were content to be so restricted. Anne Locke, a well-educated Protestant contemporary of Anne Bacon's, was one of the Marian exiles and translator of several reformist works. In the preface to a religious translation that she published in 1590 she expressed her frustration at being confined to this dutiful work: 'Because great things by reason of my sex I may not do, and that which I may, I ought to do, I have according to my duty, brought my poor basket of stones to the strengthening of the walls of that Jerusalem whereof … we are all both citizens and members.'[8] However, there is a paradox here: translation was an important process for the spread of humanist learning and even more so for the furtherance of reformed theology with its emphasis on the individual relationship with God, based on scripture and its interpretation, which called for access both to scripture and to the thinking of reformers abroad. As Bishop Jewel wrote in the *Apologia*, translated by Anne, '…we turn the scriptures into all tongues … We allure the people to read and to hear God's word'.[9]

The Cooke sisters were of course all proficient in translation and the four who survived continued their classical studies after they were married. The religious poems and epitaphs and translations of key religious texts that they wrote were probably circulated among their social networks, but only Anne had published her work, the Ochino sermons. Despite her sisters' advanced education and their marriages to equally well-educated men, who apparently encouraged them to continue studying, none produced a significant volume of writings from their learning.

Perceptions of what was appropriate behaviour circumscribed all women's lives, reinforced by the teachings of the church and warnings about the consequences of stepping out of line. Women were repeatedly exhorted to cultivate the virtues of discretion and humility. It was considered unthinkable for a woman to use her intellectual abilities as a man would, in the public exercise of opinions, influence and power, or to preach. Educated women trod a difficult path between the personal fulfilment of putting their learning and abilities to use, and the risk of attracting opprobrium and suspicion that they might deploy their knowledge in 'subtlety and conveyance to set forward and accomplish their froward [i.e. wilful and disobedient] intent and purpose'.[10]

How does what we know of Anne Bacon's experience align with this picture? In gaining a wider readership for the radical preacher Ochino she was working to advance the early Edwardian reformation. She grasped the opportunity to present an imaginative rendering of Ochino's sermons, deploying her training in rhetoric and her facility with language to bring his ideas vividly to life in English. Anne's version outlasted duller translations that initially appeared before and alongside hers and that ultimately faded from public view. Far from disappearing into obscurity as a dutiful production by a young woman complying with conventions of reticence and modesty, it was Anne's translations of Ochino's fiery sermons that endured and were widely read.

She expressed herself confidently in her dedication to her mother: while suitably deferential, she made it clear that she followed her own wishes in resisting her mother's disapproval of her studying a modern language. Anne – then eighteen or nineteen – sounds self-sufficient and mature in this address to her mother and her confidence mirrors the assurance of her translation. Yet the fault line between what educated women were encouraged to do and the warnings and limits placed on them because of their sex is present here too. This trope resurfaced when her English version of the *Apologia* was published. The context of a translation by a woman had to be framed in this way, it seems, to render it socially and morally acceptable. Together with other committed reformers around the country, Anne would have welcomed the renewal of the English church's agenda through the changes ratified by parliament in 1559. For the wider population, however, the Elizabethan religious settlement imposed from the centre meant more local dislocation, upset and expense. Hardly had they settled back into the Catholic practices swept away by Edward and restored by Mary, when all those changes went into reverse: as Eamon Duffy evokes it, 'the newly acquired Roods and patronal statues, the untarnished latten pyxes and paxes and holy water stoups, the missals and manuals still smelling of printer's ink, which Marian archdeacons had demanded, were to be once more pitched into wheelbarrows and trundled to the fire'.[11] The 'heretics' of Mary's reign were now revered as heroic martyrs and the new queen was, at the outset of her reign, in conflict with the senior clergy. Catholic continental Europe was reacting to Elizabeth's accession with dislike and apprehension, at the same time manoeuvring to tempt Elizabeth into a Catholic marriage. Elizabeth's new administration, led by William Cecil, had to settle uncertainty at home and send a clear message to the Continent.

Towards the end of 1559 Bishop John Jewel of Salisbury preached a sermon at St Paul's Cross, the outdoor pulpit of St Paul's around which thousands gathered to hear the important sermons of the day. In Edward's reign Jewel had been an associate of Peter Vermigli (Peter Martyr), the Italian reformer who arrived in England with Ochino and became Regius Professor of Divinity at Oxford. After briefly conforming to Catholic doctrine in Mary's reign Jewel joined the Marian exiles, following Vermigli from Frankfurt to Strasbourg. Returning to England on Elizabeth's accession he became a figure of authority and influence in the new religious establishment, appointed as an ecclesiastical commissioner and a bishop.[12]

In his Paul's sermon Jewel put forward a set of propositions challenging the Catholics' historical justifications for practices and beliefs including the nature of the Eucharist, the elevation of the Host during the mass – the practice over which Elizabeth clashed with the bishops in the first church services of her reign – and questioning the prohibition on reading scripture in English. The sermon was the prelude to a letter in Latin, written by Jewel under a pseudonym, that attacked Catholic theologians and alleged cruel and immoral behaviour in the Catholic church. Written at the instigation of William Cecil, this *Epistola* was sent to Sir Nicholas Throgmorton, the English ambassador to France, to be published and distributed there.

After consulting with Nicholas Bacon and others, Cecil followed up this first volley in his propaganda campaign with more weighty ammunition. The next commission to Jewel was for a full-scale statement setting out the beliefs and practices of the English church, the justification for England's secession from the Catholic church and a full-blown assault on the teachings and practice of the Catholic church. Written in Latin, the *lingua franca* of Europe, and published in January 1562, the *Apologia* was designed to be 'an affirming statement,' writes Patricia Demers, 'conveyed by a trusted, informed ecclesiastical figure'.[13]

Lacking preachers after the many executions carried out under Mary, the church's supporters were 'scarcely putting themselves together again, as after a shipwreck,' wrote Jewel. They urgently needed new means of disseminating the church's message. A translation into English of the Latin *Apologia* would make the case for the church closer to home. An anonymous, literal translation into English followed the first publication of the *Apologia*, but it did not satisfy Cecil and his associates who had commissioned the original work from Jewel. They wanted a new version, written in an accessible and simple style that would reach the widest possible readership. They needed a popular manifesto for the Church of England that could be read by anybody, and they turned to Anne Bacon to produce it.

Anne tackled this significant and demanding task with great erudition. This affirmation of the Church of England's creed was a vital task, given the shortage of preachers to give religious instruction to the congregations of the revived Protestant church. In contrast to the preachings of Ochino, there was limited reference in the *Apologia* to the doctrine of justification by faith, and almost none to predestination. Although those doctrines underpin the *Apologia,* the document concentrates on the history and authority of the Church of England, church practice and a rejection of the practices of the Roman church. A major theme is that the practices of the Church of England conform much more closely to the practices of the early church as derived from scripture and described in the writings of the early church fathers.

As she translated, Anne leavened the text with an idiomatic immediacy of phrase, creating a narrative that is persuasive and instructive, with notes of the charismatic preaching tone of Ochino. Anne's work rendered Jewel's text into straightforward language that would ensure the wider understanding of the new Church's message, and she used devices of style and phrasing that put an added emphasis on the importance of communal belief – 'we say', 'we judge', 'we have'. Like a preacher, Anne addressed the reader directly, changing Jewel's series of logical statements into popular rhetoric: a phrase literally translated as 'These be those heresies' becomes 'Behold, these are the horrible heresies'. She used vernacular words and colloquialisms in place of learned phrases that would put the reader at a distance. God will not be made a 'mocking stock', the beliefs of the Catholic church are 'tales', parasitic people are 'clawebacks', her readers are 'folk'. *Magnum silentium* becomes the everyday 'all mum, not a word', and *sacrificuli* (literally, 'sacrificing priests') becomes 'massing priests'. She used techniques from classical rhetoric to ornament and enliven the text and enhance its persuasive intent. Demers characterises it as a 'humanistic' rather than a 'technical' translation, that reflects an 'engaged, learned intelligence'.[14]

Anne's work in producing this translation was immensely valuable to the promoters of the Church of England. The Reformation in England was proceeding at different levels: within individual thought and conscience, in the meeting of

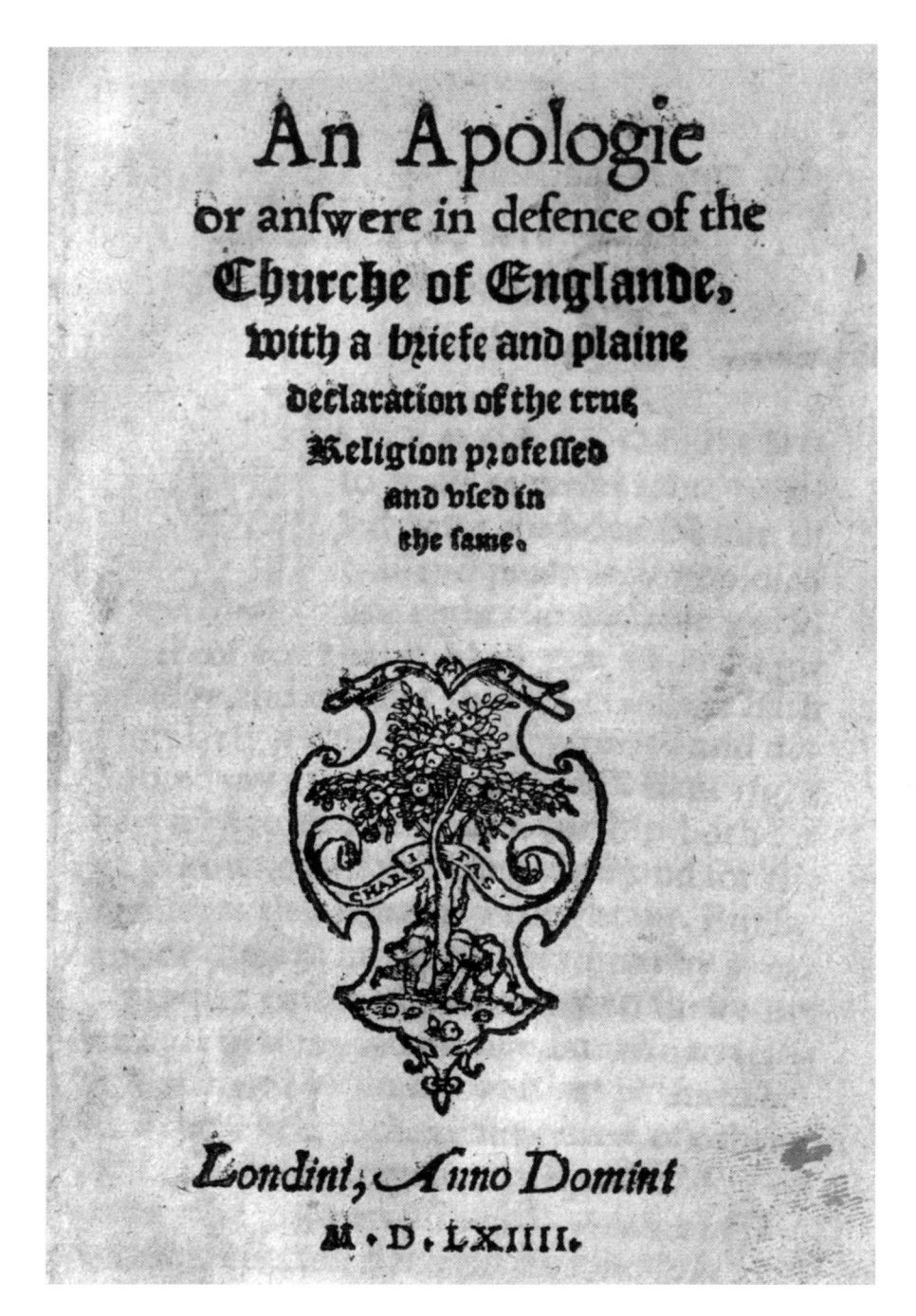

The title page of Anne Bacon's translation of John Jewel's *Apologia* (1564). Courtesy Williams Special Collections, Chapin Library, Williams College.

Church and politics, and in print. There were inevitably variations of response to the new ideas and assumptions. Considering the ways in which these ideas were communicated in print and images, Ian Green suggests the emergence of at least three different versions of English Protestantism.[15] In Anne Bacon's lifetime, it was constructed mainly by the clergy, with some input from educated lay people. Another version, which Green identifies as stemming from the educated elite and rooted in the 'constructive tension between Reformation ideas on the one hand and classical, humanist, or Renaissance ideas on the other, and by a tendency towards moralism, rationalism and anti-clericalism' is also an approach we can also associate with Anne and her educated circle of godly humanists.[16]

Contemporary writings variously instructed the reader in the doctrine of the new Church – reinforcing the key messages of justification by faith alone, rejection of elaborate ritual and the use of English not Latin in church services and the Bible – led to particular insights, and stimulated sentiment and imagination.[17] Through its direct appeal to a wide lay readership in the words and style of popular preaching, the *Apologia* became a core text for the Church. It was a work in the spirit of Tyndale, that defiant translator of the Bible into English, who was executed in 1536.[18] Tyndale used everyday, vivid words. Like Luther, he wanted Biblical translation to be straightforward, declaring every ploughboy should be able to read scripture.[19] In 1609, the collected works of Jewel, including Anne Bacon's translation of the *Apologia*, were published in one volume and distributed to every parish church.[20] Anne's work thus became one of the most widely read publications of the age. Eleven editions of the *Apologia* were published between Jewel's Latin original in 1562 and 1692.[21] It was Anne's translation that Jewel himself and a senior Catholic opponent, Thomas Harding, cited in an extended theological disputation.[22]

On its first publication in 1564, the translation was prefaced by a dedicatory letter written by Archbishop Matthew Parker, addressed to the 'right honourable, learned and virtuous lady A.B.' 'Madam,' it begins, 'I have perused your studious labour of translation.' The letter goes on to say that the author had sent him the translation, and he had returned it to her printed, 'to prevent such excuses as your modesty would have made in stay of publishing it'. It suggests it was a happy accident that the lady had employed her time this way and sent her work for the archbishop to judge, and that he anticipated a modest reluctance to publish. The work was thus distanced from those who commissioned it for a specific purpose, and the attribution to an amateur female author avoids any identification with a particular political faction. Anne's reputation as a chaste, dutiful woman is protected by the fiction that the work was undertaken as a harmless pastime and it was never her intention to seek publication.

Nevertheless, Archbishop Parker acknowledges the importance of Anne's rendering into plain English: 'you have ... honourably defended the good fame and estimation of your own native tongue, showing it so able to contend with a work originally written in most praised speech'.[23]

In his account of 'the True Causes of the Great Troubles' – by which he meant the rise of Protestantism in England – published in 1592, Richard Verstegan, a Catholic, declared 'The apology of this Church was written in Latin, and translated into English by A.B. with the commendation of M.C., which twain were sisters, and wives unto Cecil and Bacon, and gave their assistance and helping hands, in the plot and fortification of this new erected synagogue [church]'.[24] His suspicions led him to mistake the initials 'M.C.' on the preface to the *Apology,* which were Matthew Parker's (the 'C' standing for Canterbury), for Mildred Cecil – but this mistake reveals how ready both supporters and opponents of the new religion were to credit the influence of the educated, connected Cooke sisters.

Four centuries later, Parker's praise for Anne's clarity of writing was echoed by the critic C.S. Lewis:

> Latin prose has a flavour very hard to disguise in translation, but nearly every sentence in Lady Bacon's work sounds like an original. Again and again she finds the phrase which, once she has found it, we feel to be inevitable … If quality without bulk were enough, Lady Bacon might be put forward as the best of all sixteenth-century translators.[25]

In this translation Anne was directly promoting the established church view as it was formulated by Jewel. However, later in life she would question the mainstream view set out in the *Apologia,* promoting a markedly more radical line as she supported the Puritan preachers suppressed first by Parker and later by John Whitgift (Edmund Grindal, who served as archbishop after Parker and before Whitgift, was more supportive of the Puritans).

In February 1568 Anne received a long letter from Matthew Parker, whose tone was very different from the condescension of his preface to the *Apologia.* Addressed to her alone, and certainly not for her husband's eyes, it was personal and confiding. The archbishop needed her help because he and Sir Nicholas were at odds. He was distressed but did not want anyone to know there was trouble between them. He had not even told his wife of the problem. After long diversions laced with Latin tags, pouring on to the page his worries about corruption in Norfolk, where *omnia errant venalia* [everything was for sale] and benefices were being bought in batches and held by unauthorised people, he reaches the point. It is being said that a legal ruling made by Sir Nicholas seems to unfairly favour Bacon's nephew, one of his sister's sons who is a student at Cambridge. When Parker raised this with Sir Nicholas, concerned that such a ruling would affect his conscience and his honourable name, Sir Nicholas took offence. Unable to make any progress with his friend, the archbishop asks Anne to intervene, 'at this brittle time':

Because ye be *alter ipse* [another self] to him, *unus spiritus, uno caro* [one spirit, one flesh], I make you judge, and therefore I transmit the very copy of my letter sent to him... Whereby ye may take occasion to work as God shall move you. And thus I leave.[26]

Archbishop Parker was confident that Anne would understand the delicacy and complexity of the situation and had the power to persuade her husband that his friend was acting in his best interests. She was Nicholas Bacon's 'other self'. Although the outcome of this particular *contretemps* is unknown, Matthew Parker's appeal for help is one example of how Anne's influence came to be acknowledged and relied upon in a world far wider than that of home and children.

Her translation of the *Apologia* had given Anne a public purpose, a resolution of what Lynne Magnusson describes as the contradiction between her humanist education and the denial of the means for her to fulfil its aim of fitting individuals for public office and to do good in society.[27] As a woman she could not take up any such office, but in producing what Parker credited as a 'public work ... truly and well translated', she further fulfilled the sense of vocation that had impelled her early work translating Ochino and her dedication to reform. Her humanist training in classical rhetoric combined with a fresh and lively style resulted in clear, compelling prose that, again in Parker's words, avoided 'the perils of ambiguous and doubtful constructions'.[28] Through this translation, Anne had steadied and unified the voice of the English church.

Chapter 12
Family

Anne's translation of the *Apologia* was first published in 1564. She had worked on this substantial task while attending to her infant sons and running the large and busy household at York House in the Strand, where Francis had been born in January 1561. Her name does not appear in the lists of Privy Chamber staff after 1559. Mildred's position as Gentlewoman of Honour continued for a further year, then she too disappears from the Privy Chamber record. As the wives of the two most senior of the queen's ministers, the sisters frequently attended court, and it was no longer a matter of safety and expediency for women of the family to be formally attached to the intimate circle of the queen, as it had been in Mary's reign.

The Lord Keeper's household occupied the ancient building by the river at Charing Cross, first known as Norwich Inn, that had been the London residence of the bishops of Norwich. In 1536 Henry VIII moved the bishop out and granted the house to his friend Charles Brandon, duke of Suffolk, whose heirs subsequently surrendered it to Mary I. She granted it to the archbishop of York, who was the Keeper of the Great Seal, and it became known as York House. Nicholas Bacon was the first secular holder of the office of Lord Keeper. The house was leased to him and to his successors as Lord Keeper for the next seventy years by the archbishopric of York. Arriving at the same destination as his father by a very different route, Francis Bacon would ultimately become Lord Keeper himself at the age of fifty-six. He moved into his childhood home and celebrated his sixtieth birthday there at a feast (complete with a celebratory poem written and declaimed by Ben Jonson).[1]

York House was a substantial property, described at the time of the transfer to the archbishop as 'the appurtenances and 50 messuages, 10 cottages, 4 stables and 7 gardens in the parish of St. Martin in the Fields'.[2] The garden ran down to the Thames, the capital's main highway, where steps provided access to the boats that ferried Londoners up and down and across the river. Although well situated for river transport and the court at Whitehall, York House was an inconvenient building to live in and had been poorly maintained. Sir Thomas Egerton, Lord Keeper later in Elizabeth's reign, complained 'my indisposition of health increases, and the physicians promise me small comfort in this unsavoury house'.[3] It was given a makeover by the duke of Buckingham in the 1620s, including the construction of the classical Portland stone watergate which is all that remains of York House

Detail from 'Civitas Londinium', also known as the 'Agas' map of London, showing the Lord Keeper's residence, here named York Place, and the royal palace and court at Westminster in 1561 (edition published *c*.1633) © London Metropolitan Archives

today, standing marooned on the Embankment, more than 100 metres inland from the modern river bank.[4]

In the boys' infancy, when Anne was in her mid-thirties, the family began to use their newly built country house at Gorhambury, which was sited on a hill above the remains of the Roman city of Verulamium at St Albans in Hertfordshire. Formerly the property of the Abbott of St Albans, the manor was part of the lands surrendered to Henry VIII in 1539. Bacon acquired it in 1561 from Anne's brother-in-law Sir Ralph Rowlett of St Albans. Rowlett had married Anne's younger sister Margaret as his second wife in 1558. She died soon afterwards, and Rowlett had no children to inherit his land.[5] An old medieval hall house was demolished, the construction of a new house on the site began in 1563, and Bacon had spent just over £3,000 on the building project by the time it was completed in 1568.

While work on the new house progressed under his methodical supervision, life at court was not plain sailing for Nicholas Bacon. Falling badly out of favour with the queen over suspicions that he had advised on a tract supporting Lady Jane Grey's sister Lady Katherine Grey's claim to the succession, he was banished from court at the end of 1564. Bacon's biographer suggests that the earl of Leicester used the issue to strike out at Cecil and Bacon, seeing them as his opponents in the Privy Council.[6] Whatever the reasons behind his banishment, Bacon felt the disgrace keenly. Anne had to turn her attention to a husband who became physically unwell and severely depressed: he 'is not void of peril by heaviness of mind,' wrote Cecil.[7] After four or five months of misery, Sir Nicholas was reinstated in April 1565, but could not take up his duties fully as he was still too unwell to travel to sit in parliament and had temporarily to relinquish his role to another senior judge. The episode left Bacon permanently wary of taking any controversial line with the queen, while identifying more closely with Cecil's faction on the Privy Council.[8]

He was finally restored to the Privy Council, the queen's favour and his duties as Lord Keeper, with York House continuing as the family's London home. Fewer than twenty miles away, their country estate provided respite from the intrigues of court and the noise, dirt, and disease of the city. Anne would have been anxious to safeguard the health of her young sons, after losing two children in infancy and nursing two-year-old Anthony through a dangerous fever in 1560.

Hertfordshire was considered a salubrious place to live. Henry VIII had sent all his children to be brought up there, safe from the noxious city air. It was 'much repleat with parkes, woodes and rivers', reported the cartographer John Norden, 'the ayre for the most part is very salutary, and in regards thereof, many sweete and pleasant dwellings, healthful by nature and profitable by arte and industrie are planted there'.[9] The county's proximity to London attracted prosperous incomers who made their money from trade or lucrative office in the capital, rather than on rents and revenues from great landholdings. The Bacons and Cecils were among the new arrivals who built houses and gardens that were intended to enhance the status of their owners as well as signalling their awareness of the newest ideas and displaying their knowledge and culture. Writing towards the end of Elizabeth I's reign, in 1592, Francis Bacon looked back to what had been an affluent era of house building and garden making:

> There was never the like number of fair and stately houses, as there have been built and set up from the ground since her Majesty's reign, insomuch that there have been reckoned in one shire that is not great [most likely a reference to Hertfordshire] to the number of thirty-three, whereof the meanest was never built for two thousand pounds. There was never the like pleasures, of goodly gardens, and orchards, walks, pools and parks as do adorn almost every mansion house.[10]

The first known image of Anne dates to her early years at Gorhambury, when she was in her thirties (Plate 2). The three-dimensional, painted terracotta bust of Anne's head and shoulders introduces us to a slender, capable-looking young woman with plump cheeks, dressed in day clothes rather than the court dress of formal portraits. Anne's features are regular, set in an oval face with brows in an evenly curved arch. She has a straight nose and wide eyes, her mouth is full but compressed and she appears poised and a little tense. Her pointed chin neatly framed by a small starched ruff, her expression purposeful with lips slightly set, she appears ready to get on with whatever task presents itself next. This lifelike image captures the intellect, focus and determination of Anne Bacon at this stage of her life. She looks as if she is impatient to be away: perhaps there were long sessions sitting for the artist. He may have been Italian; if so, she could have whiled away some time in conversation. Such three-dimensional terracotta portraits had been made in England by Italian craftsmen since the arrival of Pietro Torrigiano from Florence in the early 1500s, followed by other Florentines who supplied Italianate sculpture to the Tudor court after Torrigiano left England.[11]

There are matching portrait busts of Nicholas (Plate 3) and of one of the sons – it is not clear which, but the child of the right age at the time the busts were made was probably Anthony. Her husband looks more relaxed than Anne and is clearly much older than his wife. The wary, veiled glance common in Tudor politicians' portraits is absent, and he is far from a sleek courtier. His countryman's ruddy complexion, heavy features and broad shoulders are offset by the slouchy black hat and sober clothes suitable to his profession of lawyer. His thick black brows, slightly raised, give his face a sardonic, questioning air, but his expression is mostly hidden behind a heavy beard. Nicholas Bacon looks immensely capable and steady, with an undercurrent of inscrutable steel.

How much do we know of the fine new house and their lives there? Today, the last remnants of Tudor Gorhambury stand in fenced pastureland at the top of the hill, surrounded by the open countryside and woods of the park (Plate 5). The ruin was left on the skyline, forming a fashionable eyecatcher from the gardens of the classical eighteenth-century mansion that succeeded the Bacons' house. From the front entrance the view opens out across the fields and woods of the estate. The approach today is a footpath, not a grand drive, and high above the ruins red kites wheel overhead, as they must have done four centuries ago. Beyond the site of the house, a group of spreading oaks survives from the oak wood that bordered the gardens in the Bacons' time. Broken walls lined with Tudor brick stand in quiet fields by the old oak trees, together with the remains of a graceful stone porch and the foundations that underlay the hall, parlours, chambers, gallery and kitchens. Now a silent ruin, Gorhambury was once a house of sixty rooms, filled with the purposeful bustle of a great household.

A survey of the manor of Gorhambury carried out between 1569 and 1573 describes the park extending to 581 acres, but the land remained subdivided, with 282 acres in use in a square block around the house.[12] Sited near to the remains of the Roman city of Verulamium, with a ruined Roman theatre within the estate boundaries, the house and garden were designed to echo the classical ideal of *otium,* cultivated leisure in a country villa, as opposed to *negotium,* business. The Bacon family lived among books and portraits, with quotations from the classics, *sententiae,* inscribed upon the walls and around the garden. They once again enjoyed a piped water supply, this time pumped for over a mile uphill from ponds by the river Ver and supplying every room.

Gorhambury was one of the first houses in England with classical features (Plates 4 and 5). The porch was an expensive item constructed from a mixture of brick, clunch and imported limestone, with Doric columns flanking it on the ground floor and Ionic columns and niches framing the upper windows. Over it was the familiar motto, *Mediocria firma*, and an inscription recording that the house was completed in the reign of Elizabeth. Apart from the porch, the house was constructed from flint – an economical option, plentifully available locally – and brick. Like Bacon's previous building project at Redgrave, the exterior walls were rendered and painted white. The main entrance, set in a long façade, led to an interior court with the main hall at the far end. East of the hall were kitchens and buttery and, to the west, a chapel. There were cloisters with a well-stocked library above, and living quarters for the family, guests and servants in a further twenty-five or thirty rooms on the first floor.[13]

The Gorhambury garden was one of the most extensive of its time in England. Nicholas and Anne Bacon were absorbing new continental cultural influences in many areas of life, including the revival of ideas about gardens and their settings in the landscape, derived from Italian villa gardens and the study of the classical sources that inspired them. The Bacons read Seneca to each other. They may have drawn on the philosopher's idea of a garden reconciling wealth and comfort with the belief that virtue could be achieved by living according to nature. The Gorhambury gardens were designed not for display, but to express such moral and philosophical attitudes, as well as for the enjoyment of solitude, contemplation and private discussion. They were stocked with a mixture of native plants and new treasures brought from overseas by plant hunters. Francis Bacon was seven years old when the house was finished. His famous essay written many years later, 'Of Gardens', which provides a detailed contemporary description of a great garden, may be an idealised version of the garden that he grew up with at Gorhambury.[14]

The estate map of 1634 (Plate 9) was made after the Bacons' time but the layout of house and grounds had not changed. It shows a garden with three enclosed areas, extending to approximately twenty-eight acres. To the south front of the house, a turfed rectangular court of some three acres is edged on three sides with a herber (a planted garden) or trees. Two ornamental gates in the north wall of the court give access to the house and a loggia below the gallery. Francis Bacon's essay proposes just this kind of grassy enclosure: 'a green in the entrance … I like well, that four acres of ground be assigned to the green'. Beyond the entrance court was the main garden, consisting of further courts to the west, north and south of the house with a 'handsome door' to the Oak Wood. To the east side were outbuildings, and trees that may have been an orchard. Francis Bacon describes a 'heath or desert', and something similar was a notable feature of the Gorhambury garden, forming a transition between the formal garden and the woods and parkland beyond. A walled area with summerhouses or belvederes at each corner, it mirrors the description of the heath in the essay, 'framed, as much as may be, to a natural wildness' and surrounded by alleys of shrubs and fruit trees, with, at each corner, 'a mount of some pretty height, leaving the wall of the enclosure breast high, to look abroad into the fields'. Oaks still grow in the Gorhambury parkland that was once the Oak Wood beyond the 'heath'.[15]

A substantial house, supplied with every comfort, Gorhambury was modest in comparison with the residence William Cecil was building at Theobalds, some twenty miles east. The two Hertfordshire houses and gardens were developed in parallel over the same period. The Bacons' house was not set up expressly to receive the queen and her court, as was Theobalds, where she stayed frequently, but she did visit Gorhambury on at least two occasions. The Bacons were anxious about hosting an unexpected royal visit in 1572. It seems the queen visited Gorhambury on a whim during her summer progress, and preparations to receive her had to be made in haste. Flattered and alarmed, knowing nothing about when she would arrive or where she was to stay, Nicholas dispatched a servant to his more worldly brother-in-law Cecil at Theobalds, with an anxious message. 'Understanding … that the Queen's Majesty means to come to my house', he asks for help, 'that I might understand your advice what you think to be the best way for me to deal in this matter, for in very deed, no man is more raw in such a matter as myself'.[16] When she arrived, Elizabeth was mockingly disparaging. According to Francis Bacon, who recorded the exchange in a later collection of witty aphorisms, she remarked, 'My lord, what a little house you have gotten!', to which her Lord Keeper diplomatically replied, 'Madam, my house is well, but it is you who have made me too great for my house.'[17] By now a corpulent man, Bacon no doubt amused the queen with this neat *double entendre*. No more details survive of the visit, but Elizabeth would return to Gorhambury, staying for several days in 1577. For that occasion, Bacon prudently added a long gallery to the house to make it more fit for the queen, above an open loggia in which a large statue of Henry VIII looked down from a prominent niche.

Sufficient details about the gallery survive to conjure a picture of this sober but elegant room, which was decorated with reference to the Bacons' humanist learning. Described by John Aubrey as 'stately', it was 120 feet long and 18 feet wide, with an anteroom at the east end and private apartments at the west end. Francis Bacon's will records that it was luxuriously furnished with rich hangings, table carpets, and long cushions.[18] A large fireplace on the long inside wall faced painted windows looking south over the garden. Two surviving stained-glass panels composed of small leaded panes with coloured images of plants, persons and creatures, many of them from the new world of the Americas, are the patched-together remnants of the windows made for the gallery (Plate 6). The Bacons were as entranced by the Elizabethan explorers' new discoveries as any of their contemporaries.

Long galleries in houses of the period were used for a variety of functions: for exercise during bad weather, as libraries and picture galleries, and for entertaining. At Gorhambury the gallery was also a place for quiet study. The walls were embellished with pithy quotations from Seneca and Cicero, inscribed in Latin, carefully framed and decorated. This was the outward expression of the humanist and Stoic values, including moderation and constancy, found in Cicero's *De Officiis* and Seneca's *Epistolae Morales,* that were guiding principles for the Bacons. Seneca wrote that 'the mind needs many precepts in order to see what it should do in life', and to refresh the memory.[19]

Despite the subsequent destruction of the house, an intact record exists of these *sententiae* in the form of a contemporary manuscript in which they are decoratively set out. It was a gift from Sir Nicholas to Jane, Lady Lumley that was probably made in 1575–6.[20] Jane Lumley (1537–78) was an aristocratic, learned woman who like Anne had received an advanced education at home. The translator of Euripides' *Iphigenia at Aulis*, she was the first translator of the classical Greek playwright into English.[21] It is not hard to imagine this educated woman visiting the Bacons at Gorhambury and requesting a copy of the carefully chosen sequence of aphorisms set out in the gallery. The decorated vellum manuscript in which they are preserved, which presents each aphorism, limited to two lines, within a rectangular frame, may mirror the layout of the inscriptions as she saw them on the walls.

The *sententiae* were, writes Elizabeth McCutcheon, 'an external mirror of and for [Bacon's] conscience and consciousness', with each line containing a perfect epigrammatic point.[22] Concise and pithy, they would serve as a daily reminder of how life should be lived.

Were the *sententiae* chosen by Nicholas alone, solely for his own edification? There is no evidence to provide clues about how the scheme was planned and executed. Yet we know from Nicholas's poem to Anne that they read Cicero and Seneca together, Cicero her favourite author and Seneca his. It is surely unlikely that the *sententiae* project excluded Anne. It went to the heart of their shared moral framework, was derived from the works of authors they read together and was the most significant decorative element in the gallery. Who better than Anne to join with Nicholas in seeking the most apposite texts and debating which to exclude, how many to use, and in what order to display them?

Gorhambury, the well-appointed country seat that showcased the Bacons' classical erudition and culture as well as their prosperity, and musty, medieval York House by the marshy banks of the Thames were the contrasting settings in which Anne brought up her sons. She supervised their early education and guided their studies through her choice of tutors when they were older. The boys were intelligent and quick to learn. One of their tutors, John Walsall, a scholar of Christ Church Oxford, was the Bacons' household chaplain from 1566 and first tutor to Anthony and Francis at Gorhambury. He said of the brothers that 'he never knew any to excel them'.[23]

Anne became a prominent patron of Puritan nonconformist ministers and preachers in Hertfordshire and chose her chaplains from among them. The nineteenth-century historian Urwick declared the Cooke sisters and their husbands to be 'a galaxy of Puritan patrons closely associated with our county of Hertford, and foremost among the illustrious Protestants of Elizabeth's reign'.[24] However it would be more accurate to identify the sisters with the Puritan cause, not their husbands, whose political responsibilities obliged them to conform to the conventions of the Anglican church. The queen was conservative in her religious tastes and disliked radical Puritanism.

The Puritan clergy declined to conform to the church's articles of observance, believing that prayer should not be mediated by ritual or prescribed texts. They variously refused to wear formal apparel such as surplices, make the sign of the cross at a child's baptism or use the prayer book, and they preached improvised sermons instead of set-piece homilies. Anne's allegiance to the preachers' cause opened up differences between her views and those of her old friend Matthew Parker. One of the Bacons' chaplains, Robert Johnson, was summoned to appear before Archbishop Parker at Lambeth in 1571 and suspended when he refused to conform.

In 1572, the Cooke sisters were united in trying to get another of the preachers, the influential Edward Dering, reinstated. It is likely this effort was initiated by the youngest sister, Katherine Killigrew, who was closely associated with Dering. In 1570 Dering had offended the queen, preaching a sermon in her presence in which he criticised her as head of the national church for allowing the appointment of unsuitable leaders and badly educated clergy.[25] With his licence to preach suspended after this challenge to the queen, Dering took a more radical position than he had previously, compounding his exclusion from royal favour. As his sympathisers attempted to soften the queen's view, a group of them presented her with a beautifully illustrated edition of an Italian treatise, the *Giardino cosmigrafico coltivato* by Dr Bartolo Sylva of Turin, adorned with dedicatory verses that referenced Dering's position and demonstrated that he had well-connected support. Dering, together with Anne's sisters Mildred and Elizabeth, contributed a page of verses in Greek. Katherine and Anne wrote verses in Latin. Anne's sisters' full names appear in Latin on the manuscript, but hers is redacted to A[nna]

B[aconia], with space for the full name but all except the initials erased.[26] The likely cause of this erasure is that after Anne's pursuit of Dering's reinstatement, it was her husband who as Lord Keeper prosecuted Dering in the Star Chamber the following year, when his licence to preach was permanently revoked. Bacon's professional duty must have sat uneasily with his wife's support for the preacher.

Anthony and Francis, through their mother steeped in the sterner reaches of Protestantism as well as the classical humanist curriculum, were clever and apt pupils. They outshone their more stolid stepbrothers in intellect and scholarly achievement. Following their early education at home, guided and managed by their mother, they entered Trinity College Cambridge together in 1573, when Anthony was fourteen and Francis only twelve. The boys were not physically robust. Anthony was often unwell, experiencing a temporary loss of sight when he was fourteen and subject to sudden episodes of illness that were a prelude to lifelong ill-health.

In 1572 Nathaniel Bacon, Nicholas's second son by his first marriage, wrote to his stepmother regarding a request for a particular servant to attend the boys when they went up to Cambridge. Bernard Paternoster, a servant of Nathaniel's in Norfolk, had attended the older Bacon brothers during their time at the university. But Bacon's second family were of a different generation, and Paternoster was not enthusiastic about reprising his old role after a decade or more. 'I will truly write your Ladyship word what answer he made me,' wrote Nathaniel to Anne, going on to detail Paternoster's many objections – he had broken his foot two years earlier (and it still hurt), had a bad back, was over fifty years old, loth to enter a new service and 'not able to take any pains'.[27] The plan was not pursued.

At Cambridge the brothers lived with the Master of Trinity, John Whitgift, a future Archbishop of Canterbury. His records show considerable expenditure on their behalf, on everything from special food and books to glazing for their windows, extra fuel to cosset Anthony during the summer (a costly habit that he kept up as an adult, to his mother's annoyance), and regular medical expenses.[28] They twice had to leave Cambridge when the university closed during episodes of plague. On at least one of these occasions, in August 1575, they went to Redgrave rather than home to Gorhambury, no doubt on their father's orders: 'My brothers of Cambridge the next week come to Redgrave and there remain; the plague is about Royston and Cambridge,' wrote their youngest half-brother Edward to Nathaniel.[29]

Edward, the youngest son of Bacon's first family, was based in Gray's Inn until he departed for continental travels in 1577. He wrote regularly to Nathaniel, lively letters relaying London gossip, international political developments and family news, and responding to requests for luxury goods to be sent from the capital.

Relations between the Lord Keeper's first and second families seem to have been amicable during the 1560s and 70s. Edward writes of occasions when his sister Elizabeth (married name D'Oyly) visited the Bacons both in London and at

Gorhambury. In November 1572 she stayed with them for four days: 'My sister D'Oyly is at this present in London … My Lady [i.e. Anne] gave her good entertainment.'[30]

In the same month Anne added a friendly, informal postscript to a letter from Sir Nicholas to his oldest son in Suffolk, regarding a local dispute between a widow and her son over the father's will that he tells the younger Nicholas to resolve. Anne writes, 'I pray you son … help the old mother to live in quiet and comfort with her own children in her old and few days by likelihood … She saith it grieveth her to have her children at variance,' adding that Sir Nicholas's gout has flared up.[31]

In 1574, Edward wrote 'My sister D'Oyly with her husband … will be at Gorhambury this Whitsuntide by my Lord's desire.'[32] He mentions his brother Nicholas being 'sent for' by their father to Gorhambury in August 1575, and in 1577 Nicholas is again recorded staying for some days at Gorhambury, in a letter from Robert Blackman to Nathaniel.[33]

Anne was thus involved in her grown stepchildren's lives from time to time, though not as closely and regularly as Nicholas. His adult sons and sons-in-law were under his permanent scrutiny and control, through his frequent correspondence with them about land transactions and other business matters in East Anglia. No detail, great or small, escaped his attention and he applied himself with equal rigour to the details of measurements for a ditch or roofing for a barn as he did to his legal and political work. There are many examples of his letters in his son Nathaniel's collected papers, which bring to life the complicated to-and-fro of the extended Bacon family's practical, financial and personal arrangements at this time.

Anne's two older stepsons, Nicholas and Nathaniel, were settled with marriages and estates. The Lord Keeper acquired land in Suffolk for his third son, Edward, who studied at Gray's Inn before setting out in 1577 to tour and study in Europe. He remained unmarried during his father's lifetime. Nicholas had arranged good marriages for his three daughters, choosing alliances that would consolidate the family's social and political networks.

Older brother Nicholas came in for his father's disapproval more than once for his dilatory approach to letter writing (in his few surviving letters to Nathaniel, he is keener to discuss falconry than business). Disorganised Henry Woodhouse, who was married to one of the daughters, Anne, exasperated his methodical father-in-law, earning a lengthy letter requiring him to set out his debts and assets and 'repair hither to me … you shall have the best advice that I can give you.'[34] He was better pleased with another son-in-law, Francis Wyndham, a lawyer who advanced to become a judge of the common pleas, whom he could rely on for legal drafting and transactions.

Before going to Cambridge Anthony and Francis had been joined for half a year in the Gorhambury schoolroom by Nathaniel's young wife. Anne Gresham, whom he married in 1569, was the illegitimate but acknowledged child of Sir Thomas Gresham, a wealthy and influential merchant and financier from an established

Norfolk family. Gresham's wife was the sister of Bacon's first wife Jane Ferneley, making him Nicholas's brother-in-law. Gresham's daughter, Anne, was born of his liaison with a woman in his household at Antwerp, where he travelled and stayed frequently on business. The expectant mother was made respectable by marriage to Gresham's Antwerp factor, becoming Mistress Dutton, and the child was eventually absorbed into the Gresham household in England.

Negotiating the match between Anne Gresham and Nathaniel, Nicholas Bacon built on his existing advantageous connection with Gresham, which both cemented their family ties and carried connections and business opportunities that for him outweighed the bride's illegitimacy. As her father's acknowledged daughter, Anne brought considerable wealth to the marriage, but after her mixed upbringing she lacked the polish and education required of a gentlewoman. Nathaniel began sounding out the Greshams about asking his stepmother Anne to help form his wife's mind and manners. When all was agreed she duly joined the family at Gorhambury. In about 1572, after his wife's period of attendance on Anne at Gorhambury, Nathaniel wrote to his stepmother:

> Your Ladyship knoweth how, being matched in marriage as I am, it stood me upon to have some care of the well bringing up of my wife, for these words of Erasmus are very true: *plus est bene instrui quam bene nasci* [it is more important to be well trained than well born]. Hereupon, being not able to remedy the one, I did as much as in me lay to provide for the other, and therefore I sought by all the means I could to have her placed with your ladyship.

He feels greatly beholden to Anne for troubling herself with his wife, 'to have such care over her and better to use her than I myself could have wished', while revealing his wife may not have been as tractable as he hoped (on her return from Gorhambury) and a firmer hand might have helped: 'Yea, I often said, and yet say, a more strait [strict] manner of usage would have wrought a greater good.'[35]

In a further letter around the same time he thanked Anne for settling his wife's tailor's bill, generosity he says he had not expected as he would have arranged for Edward to see to the bill.[36] His wife sent her own warm letter of thanks – perhaps after some family prompting, as it was rather late: 'I ... acknowledge myself greatly bounden to you for the great care that you always had of my well doing during me being with you,' she writes, concluding with an affectionate mention of her young brothers-in-law, 'my brother Anthony and my good brother Frank'.[37]

In the summer of 1573, Nathaniel invited his stepmother to be godmother to their first child, a daughter. Anne accepted, sending a piece of gold each for the midwife and nurse and promising the baby a gift, over which she took some trouble: 'my gift for the child I cannot (as I gladly would) send now by this bearer, because I cannot in so short time send to London for it, where it is, but as soon as

1 Nicholas Bacon's family tree. He sits between his two wives, Jane Ferneley and Anne Cooke, with their respective children in the branches above. Anne's two lost daughters, Mary and Susan, hold a doll and a feeding bottle. Private collection.

2 and 3 Anne and Nicholas Bacon in their early years at Gorhambury. Painted terracotta busts, *c.*1565. Private collection.

4 Watercolour of Gorhambury, eighteenth century, artist unknown. On the left is the gallery with its painted windows, over a long loggia which housed a statue of Henry VIII. Private collection.

5 The ruins of Gorhambury as they are today, viewed from what was once the main courtyard. The great hall and chapel lay to the left of the porch. The porch was constructed from costly French Caen stone, limestone, black marble and Carrara marble. On the top were figures of angels with trumpets, in the niches stood statues of Roman soldiers and there were classical heads in relief in the roundels. Elizabeth I's arms are in the top central panel. Beneath the window is a Latin inscription: 'When Nicholas Bacon brought these buildings to completion, two lustras [periods of five years] of Elizabeth's reign had passed. He had been knighted and made Keeper of the Great Seal. May all glory be ascribed to God alone'. Photograph: Erich Schlaikjer.

6 A detail from the stained-glass windows that originally decorated the long gallery at Gorhambury. Exotic flora and fauna, mythical characters and beasts reflect contemporary curiosity about the wider world. Private collection.

7 Anthony Bacon. Attributed to Nicholas Hilliard. Private collection.

8 Francis Bacon, after Paulus van Somer. By kind permission of the Honourable Society of Gray's Inn.

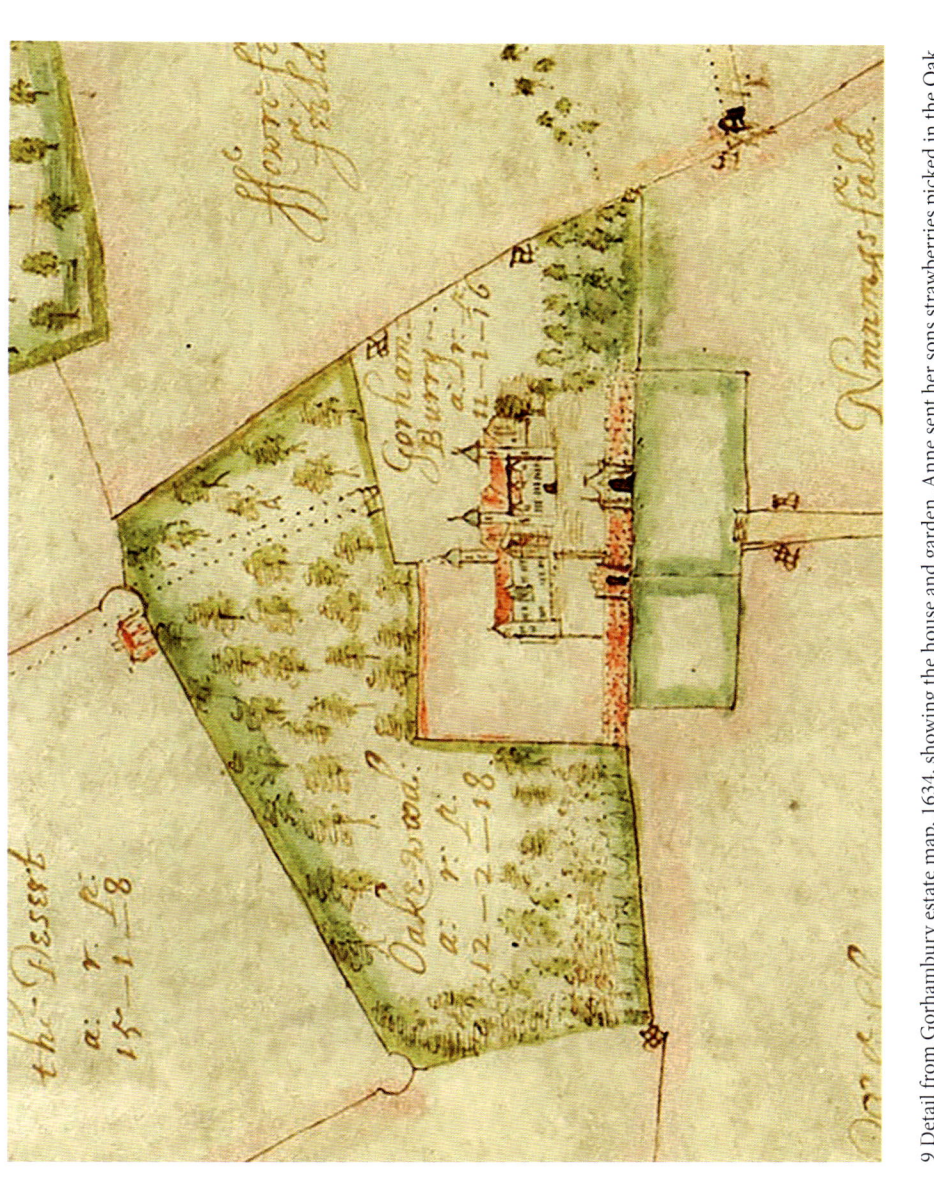

9 Detail from Gorhambury estate map, 1634, showing the house and garden. Anne sent her sons strawberries picked in the Oak Wood. Image courtesy HALS. DE/V/P1.

10 Lady Anne Bacon in 1580, aged 51. Attributed to George Gower, a court painter. The date indicates that Anne was newly widowed when the painting was completed and dated. Could it have been commissioned before her husband's death, or have been intended as one of a pair? She is dressed in black, a sign of wealth, as are her several gold chains, magnificent brooch and high ruff. Her wrist ruffs and bodice 'collar' are elaborate and probably include gold thread. There is gold braid on her headdress. She carries a book, indicating her learning and piety. These clothes would have been appropriate both for court wear and widowhood. She shows that she is a person of importance and standing, with or without her husband.

I shall go thither and have a fit messenger I will send it'. She adds in a postscript, with motherly concern, 'God be thanked for my daughter's safe deliverance', and includes an extra message to the younger Anne advising her to save her strength: 'Desire her from me not to be bold of herself in childbed for all she is so young and strong.'[38] The senior godparent of the same sex as the baby could expect the child to be given their name.[39] Anne waives this custom in her letter, writing 'The name for my part I put to the choice of the mother for any name she liketh.'

Although Anne Gresham Bacon's time at Gorhambury went well, it had been difficult to arrange. Nathaniel had to negotiate tricky family sensibilities. Lady Gresham had been persuaded to acknowledge and accept her husband's child by another woman. Then the young woman's position in the family was cemented by marriage to Lady Gresham's nephew Nathaniel. And now Nathaniel wanted his young wife to be shaped and influenced by his stepmother, the woman who had so quickly succeeded Lady Gresham's sister, Jane Ferneley, as Nicholas Bacon's wife. Nicholas's swift remarriage, which may have aroused suspicions of a pre-existing attraction between him and Anne Cooke, had left a coolness between the families.

Nathaniel was treading on eggshells when he proposed his plan, writing a painstaking justification to Lady Gresham.[40] The tension of the familial Ferneley/ Gresham/Bacon tangle is apparent in Nathaniel's letter. He reminds Lady Gresham that when they last met, he had little hope of gaining agreement to his plan – he does not say why – but had proposed it because he believed it would be to his wife's benefit. He reminds her that 'they that love their children best, being about these years that my wife is, seek to place them for a time in some good place from them' and that young people sent away from home learn to know themselves better than in their parents' houses. He knows that Lady Bacon will only take his young wife into her household if the Greshams agree and have a 'good liking' of her going there. He undertakes that they will not be put to extra expense, which seems to have been an objection raised by Lady Gresham.

Having put his best case, Nathaniel turns to his feelings for his stepmother, possibly referring to misgivings or suspicions raised in his last meeting with Lady Gresham. 'Perhaps, Madam, you marvel how it falleth out I have this great liking of my Lady [Anne Bacon]. In this respect I have ever liked of her, though in other things, as cause moveth me, it may be I have as great misliking of her.' We could understand from this that Nathaniel admired his stepmother's approach to raising and educating her children, but for other reasons, not spelled out, he was not in favour of her. Or we might guess he added the acknowledgement of feelings harboured by the first wife's family about Anne to soften his request.

In a letter written about the same time to his friend Anthony Stringer, whom he often took into his confidence, he says his father-in-law may believe Anne will be too sharp with her stepdaughter-in-law. In Nathaniel's view, 'the only sharpness that my Lady will use will be in restraining her of liberty, and what harm can thereby grow to one which is young who can not judge?' He feels the arrangement would help their marriage to a good beginning: 'good for me, better for my wife, and mete for us both to be so brought up as the one might have best liking of the other' and thinks that his wife being there 'will be so much better than where she is' (presumably in the Gresham household).[41] Lady Anne, he says, is well content with the plan and has promised to have a care of his wife when she comes to Gorhambury. There is certainly no trace of reserve or stiffness in his letter of thanks to his stepmother, where he refers to the difficulties he encountered as 'much ado … and those sticking most who had least cause to stick at it' (perhaps an allusion to the Greshams' objections), going on to thank her fulsomely for her care of his wife and attention to his wishes, 'for the care had of her, I account it had of me; the good done to her, I account it done to me, for I persuade myself it was done in respect of me'.[42]

Nevertheless, given the Greshams' reservations about the plan, we are left wondering whether Anne was in truth thought to be a little peremptory and harsh. Or was it rather that people sometimes felt daunted and uncomfortable under the scrutiny of her brisk intelligence? There is another hint of this in a letter from Edward Bacon to Nathaniel in 1573 when he writes of a visit by their cousin, Robert Blackman, who was often employed by the Lord Keeper to fulfil tasks relating to family business. Blackman, a Suffolk country cousin, had a difficult time with Anne that day, recounts Edward: 'Brother, my cousin Blackman had small [little] talk with my Lord touching anything concerning you, for want of a convenient time, being both chidden and oft interrupted by my Lady.'[43] Anne could clearly be affectionate and thoughtful, as we have seen from her husband's fond poem to her and her kindly interactions with Nathaniel and his wife – this does not rule out occasions when she could be brusque and impatient.

Nicholas Bacon was putting in place plans for a new house and lands in Stiffkey on the north Norfolk coast for Nathaniel. As well as reinforcing the Gresham connection through his marriage, Nathaniel was being positioned by his father as a future political leader in Norfolk, to extend and consolidate the Bacon influence in East Anglia. Nicholas's first son, also Nicholas, had been advantageously married in 1562 to an heiress, Anne Butts, after complex negotiations and was established at Redgrave, with a comfortable income and a future in the politics of Suffolk. The Lord Keeper also acquired land in Suffolk for his third son, Edward.

Anne Bacon's contribution to this aspect of family advancement had been to give Nathaniel's young wife the rudiments of education, show her how to present herself and behave, and how to manage a gentry household. Nevertheless, the younger Anne Bacon had to wait several years for her own house, in the meantime lodging with Nathaniel in his married sisters' households. 'My husband hitherto hath provided nothing towards our going to house,' she wrote sulkily to her Mother Dutton, wishing that when they do have a house, her mother might come and live with them. Young Anne seems to have missed her natural mother (who was still a member of the Gresham household), after being whisked away to Norfolk, a gentry marriage and the birth of her first baby.[44] In October 1573 she wrote to Nathaniel's stepmother Anne to thank her for the baby's christening cup and tell her that she and Nathaniel have a house at last: 'though the house be but mean [small] yet I am very well content withall'. She rather wistfully adds that her baby daughter is with a wet nurse in Stiffkey, not too far away: 'I dwell within a quarter of a mile of her, so that I may, as I will, look unto her.'[45]

At around the same time, Nathaniel undertook to help a young female relation to be trained in the household skills she would need as a wife. 'I give you hearty thanks for bringing up my daughter in your household,' wrote Jane Tuttoft, a widowed cousin. Then, perhaps quoting from a contemporary instruction book, '"Let her learn to write and to read, and to cast account, and to wash, and to brew, and to bake, and to dress meat and drink, and so I trust she shall prove a great good housewife".'[46] These skills were the foundations of every well-ordered household. While women of the status of Lady Anne Bacon at Gorhambury and her stepdaughter-in-law Anne would not carry out such practical housewifery themselves, they would of course acquire a working knowledge of all the tasks involved in provisioning and running a house and family, in order to instruct and supervise the staff who undertook them.

Anne's household skills, as well as her experience of service in the Privy Chamber and of court life, were put fully to the test when the queen showed her favour by announcing a second visit to her Lord Keeper and her erstwhile Gentlewoman of the Privy Chamber in 1577. For five days in May the court descended on Gorhambury. Royal visits were preceded by an inspection from the Harbingers, officials of the royal bedchamber, to check the accommodation. Once it was approved, there would have been frantic activity to put everything in order for the queen's arrival: house, gardens, stabling, food, drink and entertainments, a military-scale operation. The scale of the royal entourage was daunting: 'When the queen breaks up her court with the intention of visiting another place, there commonly follow more than three hundred carts laden with bag and baggage,' wrote an awestruck foreign visitor in 1592.[47] The great train of two-wheeled carts and pack horses would have been seen and heard from a mile or more away, making its slow way up the long hill to Gorhambury, where extra staff had been drafted in to cope.

Careful accounts were kept of 'The Charges expended at Gorhambury by reason of her Majesty coming thither on Saturday 17th of May, 1577, before supper, and continuing until Wednesday after dinner following.' The final bill was £577 6s 7¼d, the equivalent today of around £225,000. Cooks and 'them of the revells' – court entertainers – were brought from London at high prices. The food included 10 dozen geese, 13 dozen herons, 19 dozen pigeons, 8 oxen, 26 pigs, and 41 dozen rabbits. There were fine wines, beer and ale. The house and gardens were put into immaculate order. A costly silver cup was presented to the queen. As the courtly throng and their attendants swept through house and grounds they helped themselves to less precious souvenirs, making off with the Tudor equivalent of hotel towels and teaspoons: in the final accounts, a sum of £6 15s 6d was written off for missing pewter and 40s 6d for missing napery.[48]

The Bacons did not usually entertain on a grand scale, unlike the Cecils at Theobalds, who were veterans at receiving the queen and court and included royal apartments when building their house. Anne no doubt used her connections at court as well as her formidable energy, intellect and domestic management skills to make sure things ran smoothly. The queen's visit was a great occasion for them, confirming the family's status and place high in royal favour. Nicholas Bacon's professional life was again as secure as it could be given the unpredictable turns of Tudor political life.

Thomas Twyne, a physician and translator, had dedicated *The Garlande of Godly Flowers*, a collection of prayers and meditations, to Sir Nicholas and Lady Anne Bacon in 1574. In the dedication he lavishly praises Anne's attributes and connections:

> a loving lady, the offspring of an excellent race, niece to a rightworshipful grandsire, daughter to a worthy knight, scholar to a learned schoolmaster, sister to a right honourable lady, mother of much hoped imps, aunt to a peerless countess [Mildred's daughter Anne had married the earl of Oxford], wife to a noble counsellor, lady of a godly family, subject to a loving prince, a true worshipper of Almighty God.[49]

Another dedication to Anne, prefacing a sermon published in 1578 by her sons' former tutor John Walsall, speaks of her and her husband's advancement of 'true religion' as well as their care in governing and educating their family and 'countenancing of virtue and learning'. Addressing Anne, he says, 'this your care of God his glory is universally known to the whole realm, and so joyfully acknowledge[d] of the godly therein, that I need not produce myself for an experienced witness of the same'.[50]

Now approaching fifty, Anne was at the hub of a successful and thriving family network. Not only respected for her family and position, as would conventionally be expected of a Tudor courtier, she was also publicly recognised for her scholarship and godliness.

Chapter 13
Death and aftermath

Favoured by the queen, financially secure, with no recurrence of the royal disapproval of 1564–5, in 1577 the Bacons were making plans for the future of the family. Although the Lord Keeper did not possess the extensive lands and titles of longer established gentry and aristocratic families, his land acquisitions had been shrewd and he accumulated substantial cash reserves from the many sources of income attached to his role in public life. He had become very rich, with an income that had risen steadily from about £2,600 per annum in 1560 to more than £4,000 by the late 1570s.[1] While some of this wealth had gone into the building and maintenance of his new estate, he was also thorough and conscientious in his financial planning for the long-term future of the Bacon dynasty he had founded.

He was turning his attention to provision for his sons with Anne. A young heiress, Dowsabell Paget, had been proposed as a wife for Anthony in 1574, but though well advanced, the wedding plans came to nothing.[2] No alternative bride was found for him: Anthony was only sixteen in 1574 and his parents must have thought there was plenty of time ahead. Instead, both brothers were admitted to Gray's Inn in the summer of 1576, but fifteen-year-old Francis's introduction to legal studies was diverted into a broader path. In the autumn he set off for France in the retinue of Sir Amias Paulet, newly appointed ambassador to the French court, with the prospect of studying Roman law as it was practised in France as well as the opportunity to observe the mechanics of diplomacy and the role of the ambassador in gathering 'intelligences' to report back to the queen and her senior ministers. Taken to the court to bid a formal farewell to the queen and kiss her hand, a moment that impressed itself indelibly on his memory, Francis arrived in Paris with Sir Amias's train of family and staff on 3 October 1576. He was to spend three years away.[3]

The Bacons were not free of personal troubles. Sir Anthony Cooke died just before his grandsons entered Gray's Inn. Anne must have felt keenly the loss of the father whose steadfast piety and dedication to his children's education had enriched her life. Nicholas's health was often poor. Now in his mid-sixties, the Lord Keeper was overweight and suffering from painful attacks of gout. He also had kidney stones, causing intermittent disabling pain, and neither his memory nor his hearing were as sharp as they had been. Anne supplied advice and remedies, including drinks of almond milk and baths of water, milk and herbs. Attentive to every detail of diet that might support his health, she recommended what he should eat and drink, and when.[4] Yet there was no diminution in the Lord Keeper's appetite for work. In September 1577 we see him travelling to London on a Monday on official business, returning to Gorhambury on Tuesday to see his oldest son Nicholas, and then 'sent for to the court with all speed', Anne being there already.[5]

At the end of January, when the legal Hilary term finished, the Bacons customarily went to Gorhambury, a more congenial place to pass a winter week or two than damp and draughty York House. But in the early weeks of 1579, they were trapped in London by a great storm that struck overnight. The streets filled with snow, driven into banks a yard and a half deep by the bitter north-east wind, as a great freeze gripped the city. The snow fell without pause for five days, and when the thaw began, heavy rain brought fresh misery as the low ground by the river Thames filled and flooded. Water washed into the gardens of the riverside palaces of the Strand, flowed through the streets and seeped into buildings. Fish were left flapping on the floor of Westminster Hall when the floodwater finally drained away.[6] It was a dank end to one of the coldest winters anyone could remember.

Sir Nicholas was heavy, gouty and, at sixty-eight, feeling his age. Passing a quiet afternoon as the world outside froze, he summoned the barber to rub and comb his head. Soothed into a doze, he fell heavily asleep by an open window, later waking as Francis described it, 'all distempered and in a great sweat'.[7] Sir Nicolas asked the barber why he had been left in the cold draught.

'Why, my Lord, I durst not wake your Lordship.'
'Why then, you have killed me with kindness,' said the Lord Keeper.

Anne was skilled and experienced at treating her ageing husband's illnesses, but none of her trusted remedies lifted the fever that rapidly set in. His physician, Dr Smythe, could not save him, though he was paid handsomely for his efforts.[8] Within three days, Sir Nicholas was dead, of what was probably a severe bout of pneumonia. He died on 20 February, in the morning. Twenty-six years had passed since that other harsh February day in 1553 when Anne Cooke married Nicholas Bacon. Now Anne was experiencing the sudden transition into widowhood. She faced unaccustomed social and financial uncertainty, but also independence, free for the first time in her life from the obligations and constraints of the roles of daughter and wife.

The funeral took place seventeen days later on 9 March. It took time to gather everyone together and organise the procession, burial and funeral feast, all of which were on a grand scale. As well as the family and other high-ranking mourners, the household officers and servants, gentlemen and yeomen from Gorhambury, Redgrave and Stiffkey travelled through the winter weather to London to take their places in the funeral procession. A team of surgeons and physicians, led by senior surgeons Mr Baltroppe and Mr Fylde, with two of the queen's physicians and two of her surgeons in attendance, opened the body. They seared and embalmed the corpse with the assistance of Leonard Cox, a more lowly barber surgeon, wrapped it in canvas and put it in a lead coffin, itself placed inside a further coffin of wood.[9] The Lord Keeper's body lay in state in the chapel at York House.

Inside St Paul's, the tomb of John of Gaunt was boarded up to protect it from harm as workmen broke out the ground next to it for the burial of the Lord Keeper. The heralds of the College of Arms, who regulated the formalities of elite heraldic funerals, were organising the covering and decoration of the hearse and the pall. Two tailors made up plain mourning gowns for the sixty-eight poor men, one for each year of Nicholas's life, who would lead the procession and enjoy a one-shilling dinner afterwards. Stephen Treacle the cook was engaged to prepare the more important mourners' funeral feast, and the food and drink ordered included fish, jellies garnished with gold leaf, wafers and Hippocras, a spiced wine. The dinner cost £60 3s. As at the royal visit to Gorhambury, light-fingered guests made off with a substantial quantity of tableware: 'for 40 pounds of pewter vessel lost the day of the funeral' there was a bill of £1 3s 4d.[10] Anne herself claimed £16 10s 8d, the equivalent of between five and six thousand pounds today, from her husband's estate, which was paid to her on 9 March for 'provision spent at my Lord's funeral' – the itemised 'bill subscribed by my Lady' that explained what this comprised does not survive.[11]

Nicholas had declined so quickly, dying after only a few days of fever, that Anne had had no time to call Francis home from France to see his father. Only Anthony, now twenty years old and studying at Gray's Inn, was near at hand. Francis did manage to get a ship back in time to be at the funeral. He later wrote of a nightmare presaging his father's death, 'which I told to divers English gentlemen, that my father's house in the country was plastered all over with black mortar.'[12]

The rooms at York House and Anne's bed were hung with black valances. When it was time for her to dress for the funeral, her attendant gentlewomen, robed in stiff new mourning garments, came to assist with the heavy black clothes. Their steps stirred scented rushes on the floor. Nathaniel Bacon's schedule of accounts for his father's funeral tells us that William Sykes, the royal perfumier, supplied perfumes to scent the chambers on the day of the funeral and dozens of new rushes were strewn by women who were hired to clean and dress the house.[13]

Black cloth for the mourners' gowns was allocated by rank and importance, with the amount and quality of fabric allowed to each mourner regulated by the Heralds of the College of Arms. Anne had for herself nine yards of the best quality cloth at £1 10s a yard, her four gentlewomen had between them thirteen yards at 18s a yard, and her two chamber maids shared six yards at 12s a yard. Next in importance on the list of ladies and gentlewomen came her stepdaughters and her stepsons' wives. Their status as mourners was fixed slightly below Anne's: each had three-and-a-quarter yards of cloth priced at £1 6s 8d a yard, with cloth at 16s a yard allocated for one gentlewoman attendant each.

Sir Nicholas had drawn up a will about two months before his death. In it he specified the exact amount of expensive cloth for his chief mourners, according to the heralds' rules. William Cecil, by now Lord Burghley, was the principal mourner, reflecting the long friendship that had been forged into a formidable working partnership as together they rose to power. Twelve yards of best quality black cloth were allocated to him. Eight yards went to Sir Francis Walsingham the spymaster, another of the principal mourners. Each important mourner had a retinue of attendants who must also be clothed in black.

Sir Nicholas knew such funerals could cost as much as a lengthy visit from the queen, and the heralds who controlled them loved to spend other people's money. His estate paid for the purchase of a thousand yards of black cloth, at a total cost of £668 11s 10d (about £230,000 in today's values), a large proportion of the total estimated cost of the funeral, some £900.[14] He would be buried with all the display and ceremony due to his position as one of the highest officers in the land, though he had instructed his executors to curb extravagance, ordering that with a few exceptions those wealthy enough to pay for themselves should buy their own mourning garments. Nevertheless, for a man who advocated moderation, the Lord Keeper had anticipated a lavish send-off.

Anne and her four attendants were the only women at the funeral. The accounts detail lengths of lawn, an expensive fabric woven from fine linen, supplied to Anne and her gentlewomen. Lawn was used for the touches of white in bodices and tippets that edged the funeral clothes. Anne's three ells of lawn cost 10s a yard, a total of over £300 in modern money. Her women had slightly less costly fabric at 7s an ell. After this entry in the funeral accounts is a note that shows Anne was the only woman of the family in the procession: 'Memorandum, the rest of the ladies and gentlewomen had no lawns because they were not present at the funeral.'[15] It would not have been usual for any woman to attend the funeral of a man, following a royal ordinance that decreed 'a man being dead he to have only men mourners at his burial. And at a woman's burial to have only women.'[16] Anne's presence must have attracted attention and comment.

Like all the principal mourners, Anne wore a black, draped gown. Beneath it were a white lawn bodice and a ruff. Her head was covered by a black hood with floor-length, flowing tippets, edged in white. Based on the gowns worn by medieval monks and nuns, unvaried by fashion, these clothes signified the mourners' withdrawal from ordinary life. Chief mourners wore their hoods over their heads to mark the importance of their role in the funeral, while hoods were usually left over the shoulder by mourners of lower status. In William Camden's drawing of the procession at the funeral of Elizabeth I, we can see the gowns worn by women, and their variation by rank.[17]

As Anne was pinned into her mourning gown, the bells of the nearby church of St Martin in the Fields began to toll, echoing the more distant notes from St Paul's where the service would be held, its pulpit and arches hung with black cloth to honour the dead Lord Keeper. Lady Anne's attendants would have helped her put on the long black hood as she prepared to leave the house. She was fifty-one. This would be her last appearance as the wife of the Lord Keeper, the end of her place by his side at the heart of the Elizabethan political world.

In the courtyard, sombre lengths of black bay cloth, a type of baize, hung from temporary wooden railings put up for the day. Two men were set to guard the valuable cloth from thieves, but even so the accounts record that seven yards were 'stolen at my Lord's chamber door'.[18] Three black-draped horses waited to carry the Lord Keeper's sons Nicholas, Nathaniel and Anthony, as the procession began to form up. Others would follow on foot. All wore black, from the sumptuous heavy wool of Anne's cloak to the servants' thinner mourning livery. There is no provision in the funeral accounts for drapery for a horse for Anne, as there is for the sons. She may have ridden with the men, or she may have been carried in the family coach, as among the funeral accounts there is a bill for it to be repaired and refitted.

The sixty-eight poor men lined up in the chilly street, walking in pairs to form the front ranks of the procession that set off slowly up the Strand, to the sound of tolling bells. Sixteen beadles struck the paved road with their staves, clearing the way and pushing back onlookers who pressed in too close.[19] In the crowd would have been legal clerks and City errand boys, black-gowned lawyers and richly dressed merchants, pulling off hats to bow their heads as the coffin passed. Behind the poor men walked the members of the household, also in pairs, from the least important groom to the steward and treasurer, each dressed in mourning according to his rank, joined by staff from the family properties at Gorhambury, Redgrave, and Stiffkey. Then came the principal mourners, the Lord Keeper's family and friends, some riding, some walking. The long tail of the procession stretched back along the Strand as three hundred mourners accompanied Sir Nicholas on his last journey past Chancery Lane, Fetter Lane and the Temple, along Fleet Street towards Temple Bar, through the heart of the legal world he had known since he first came to Gray's Inn aged twenty-two, without rank or fortune.[20]

The painted and embellished hearse was flanked by four mounted heralds and preceded by the emblems of his rank – armour and coat of arms. Behind it the crowd saw the slight, upright figure of Lady Anne Bacon. Around her, mounted on their black-draped horses, were the men of the family, bulky in their black cloaks and hoods: the three sons from Sir Nicholas's first marriage, his sons-in-law, and Anne's own two sons, Anthony and Francis.[21] Anne's pale, composed face with its appraising eyes, long nose and narrow mouth, framed in a black hood, would have

The tomb of Sir Nicholas Bacon in St Paul's, London, as it was before the great fire, with effigies of his two wives Jane Ferneley and Anne Cooke. Early nineteenth-century etching by William Finden. National Portrait Gallery D40123 © National Portrait Gallery, London.

been the focus of all who gathered to watch, as the procession moved slowly past the jumble of shops and great houses on the Strand.

Funerals still retained features of pre-Reformation ritual, such as processions, singing and bell ringing, that had been long discontinued in other Protestant religious ceremonies. Yet while brightly coloured heraldic decorations on the hearse were still acceptable, the overall effect was sombre, with no display of banners and torches as there would have been in earlier times. The unstated purpose of the ritual and display of a high-status person's funeral was to signal continuity and stability and to reinforce the public perception of social hierarchy.[22] As the procession passed, the crowds of onlookers would experience a progression from the steady tramp of ordinary mourners on foot to a visual and emotional climax as the coffin appeared, borne on its decorated hearse. Then there would be a tailing-off behind the central section, with more ranks of followers on foot. The numbers in the procession reflected the importance of the deceased. Three hundred mourners made a good show for the Lord Keeper, but other funerals of the time eclipsed his. In 1572 the earl of Derby's funeral had featured 900 mourners in a procession that extended for two miles.[23]

The burial service in St Paul's would have been conducted from Cranmer's Book of Common Prayer of 1552, in which the minister was directed to turn away from the dead to address the living mourners as the body was committed to the grave. This referenced the Protestant belief that the soul had already been taken by God and there would be no prayers of intercession. The Lord Keeper would still be remembered in the world and his status marked forever, he would have hoped, by the tomb he had commissioned to be placed over his grave, next to the tomb of John of Gaunt. The stone monument was constructed in two tiers, supported on pillars. On the top tier lay Sir Nicholas in effigy, dressed in armour with hands lifted in prayer and his feet resting not on a dog, as was often seen on tombs, but on a curly-tailed piglet, the Bacon emblem being a boar. Beneath him on the lower tier lay the effigies of his two wives, side by side. Anne would have had the odd experience of seeing herself carved in stone, lying next to Jane Ferneley. The monument was destroyed in the Great Fire of London, when old St Paul's burned down. A battered and scorched remnant of the effigy of Nicholas, now in the crypt of St Paul's, is the only fragment left.

The making of wills was a relatively recent development. Previously inheritance had been a matter of custom, with any disputes determined by the church courts. Now wills were sometimes used to circumvent earlier rules, including primogeniture – men with no sons could use a will to divert the inheritance to other male kin instead of it going to the daughters of the family. An executor's duties included arranging and paying for the funeral, paying out legacies, ensuring that the heir inherited land and that conditions laid down in the will were fulfilled, discharging debts, collecting credits and following through on processes that could last many years when heirs did not immediately inherit.

Nicholas and Nathaniel were named as executors of their father's will. While widows were often appointed as sole or joint executrix of a husband's will by the mid-sixteenth century, Anne was not.[24] Rich men named their wives as executrix less often than those of lower social status.[25] There was much at stake in the inheritance of large estates such as Bacon's. Did he anticipate problems in the execution of his will, or have limited faith in his sons' abilities to manage it? He left nothing to chance, appointing the formidable Lord Burghley as overseer of the executors.[26]

The younger Nicholas Bacon, now the new Sir Nicholas, was thirty-six, living at Redgrave with his wife and children. His marriage to heiress Anne Butts had set him up with a substantial income. A dependable country squire, he was involved in local administration and government, but lacked his father's flair and ambition and never entirely fulfilled the potential that his local position and family connections offered.[27] Nathaniel, thirty-three at his father's death, was the more methodical of the older brothers. Under his father's direction he had become a reliable administrator active in local affairs in Norfolk.

Education, hard work, a shrewd eye for property and the political acumen to build networks of influence through family connections and alliances had brought Nicholas Bacon far from his origins as the son of a Suffolk yeoman. As he succeeded professionally, he had systematically invested in property in East Anglia for his older sons, and in Hertfordshire for himself and Anne with their two boys. However, one piece in the jigsaw of provision he made for his family was missing. Nicholas had not provided any income or land for Francis. Having accrued estates and arranged good marriages for his older children, and ensured an inheritance for Anthony in the Gorhambury estate, he died before he could arrange marriages for either of Anne's sons or acquire the land and capital that would have left Francis as secure as his brothers and sisters.

Sir Nicholas's substantial income from his appointments, estimated to have been at least £4,000 a year by the time he died, ended with his death.[28] Once the funeral was paid for, creditors satisfied and bequests handed out, there was not much ready cash to spare.[29] One of the bequests to Anne was £100 to keep the seventy household staff for one month after his death. After that, the household would be scaled down. She would still sometimes attend court, and her husband had left her his interest in the lease of York House, but otherwise she would live in Hertfordshire with a life interest in the house and estate at Gorhambury, together with leases on other lands in and near St Albans. This would all revert to Anthony after her death.

Anne entered widowhood with limited reserves of money, a country estate to manage, and facing rifts in the family. In between the fitting of mourning clothes and expressions of grief, bitter skirmishes over the details of lands and leases left in the will had broken out between the sons of the Lord Keeper's first and second marriages. 'When brethren do fall out,' wrote Nathaniel Bacon grimly, four months after his father's death, 'the dislikings between them are more hardly appeased than between strangers.'[30]

Chapter 14
Feme sole

Why mourn ye so, you that be widows… now you be free in liberties, and free propria iuris *at your own law.*[1]

The nature of the conflict simmering between Anne, with her older son, and her two older stepsons was not unusual after a father's death, especially if the man had children from more than one wife. Widows often had to make claims against their husband's heirs, particularly stepsons. It was usual for widows to receive the income from property rather than being given outright control over it: a woman had marginal family status both as daughter and wife, as it was the continuance of the male bloodline that mattered. This often led to tensions between mothers and sons, with heirs resentful of the burden on their inheritances where the widow retained a life interest. The death of a husband meant a power shift within the family – even if she was left financially independent by her husband's will, a widow would formally be her son's social dependant for her lifetime.[2]

If the inter-generational conflict had gone to law, what would Anne's position have been? The widows whose ranks she now joined exercised many of the private legal rights held by men. As a widow Anne gained legal and financial independence, having previously been subject to her husband's control. In legal terms, she was a 'feme sole', a category that included both unmarried women over the age of majority and widows.[3] Widows could inherit and own property and rights over property. A widow could make a will leaving property and gifts as she chose, enter binding legal contracts, sue and be sued, and plead in person: she was held to be fully capable and accountable.

While her husband was living Anne had no individual legal identity. Like all married women she was categorised as 'feme covert', literally a 'covered woman'. 'Coverture' was the legal doctrine that a married woman could not be a legal entity separately from her husband that remained in force for many centuries. Eighteenth-century legal commentator William Blackstone spells out the principle in his treatise 'Of husband and wife':

> By marriage, the husband and wife are one person in law: that is, the very being or legal existence of the woman is suspended during the marriage, or at least is incorporated

and consolidated into that of the husband: under whose wing, protection, and cover, she performs every thing; and is therefore called in our law-French a feme-covert; is said to be covert-baron, or under the protection and influence of her husband, her baron, or lord; and her condition during her marriage is called her coverture.[4]

For legal purposes, during her marriage Anne was classed with everyone categorised at that time as incapable of autonomy, a category that included wards, lunatics, criminals and idiots.[5] 'T.E.', the anonymous editor of an early treatise on women and the law, likened the impact of the married woman's loss of legal identity to a stream subsumed into a river:

> the poor Rivulet loseth her name, it is carried and recarried with the new associate, it beareth no sway, it possesseth nothing during coverture. A woman as soon as she is married, is called covert ... that is, veiled, as it were, clouded and over-shadowed ... she hath lost her stream ... her new self is her superior, her companion, her master.[6]

In the eyes of the law, 'T.E.' goes on, all women are 'either married or to be married' and their desires must be subject to their husbands'. During the sixteenth century the balance of power among the different English legal codes had been shifting in favour of common law, and conflicts between their principles were often resolved to women's disadvantage.

'T.E.' says that women are denied rights of their own because of the original sin of Eve's disobedience, adding pragmatically that 'some women can shift it well enough' nevertheless.[7] Perhaps 'T.E.' knew of determined women who would find a way through or around the legal restrictions that limited them. Certainly the Bacons had come across at least one such in their business dealings. In 1573 Nathaniel had written to his father of a possible land transaction with one John Calthorp. Calthorp's wife proposed to handle the sale of land to the Bacons herself, for, Nathaniel says, 'the man himself is of a simple wit'. At first sending her brother to discuss matters with Nathaniel, Mistress Calthorp rapidly took over, opening the negotiation with a robust valuation Nathaniel thought shockingly high.[8]

The law relating to women was a mixed collection of traditional provisions, including church law, local manorial law and custom, and common law. The jurist Edward Coke identified sixteen different jurisdictions, some of which gave women more legal opportunities and rights than common law.[9] Local customs still varied widely. Although conflicting principles between the different codes were often made to conform to common law, frequently disadvantaging women, the rise of equity law during this period introduced flexibility. Different legal remedies could be favourable to women 'waging law' in the Chancery court and the Court of Requests, and a feme covert could appoint a 'prochain amy' (next friend) to sue on her behalf.[10] A woman could apply to the Court of Chancery, which ruled on the most equitable course to take in each individual case, to assert or defend her rights, or have property she had acquired before marriage held on her behalf by trustees rather than it going into her husband's ownership.[11] Research continues to explore the extent to which women could and did act outside the restrictions of the common law.

As feme sole, a widow was able to conduct business and legal cases alone. However, a widow should not meddle in courts, but rather seek the counsel of a wise older man, rely on her male kin, and request help from the heir who should go to court on her behalf, wrote Vives.[12] It was not always so straightforward.

Although the transition from wife to widow could leave a woman vulnerable to being cheated or exploited by other claimants to her husband's estate, on the death of her husband she was in theory immediately protected by the doctrine of dower. The common law right of dower, first set down in Magna Carta, had been in use for three centuries, but its definition could vary. Dower was a woman's right to a proportion of her husband's property as a widow. It should not be confused with 'dowry' – a financial portion brought to a marriage by a woman. In principle, the right of dower gave a widow the use of a third of her deceased husband's freehold property for her lifetime. When she died, the property passed to the heir named in her husband's will. However, it could be difficult both to establish which land was included in the total and whether it was in a category excluded from the right to dower. Although dower rights were absolute and could not be limited or removed under the husband's will, a widow might still have to resort to legal proceedings against an uncooperative heir – possibly her own son – to establish and claim her dower. This could be a protracted process. Situations could be further complicated where customary law brought local variations regarding inheritance. Given wide variation in local customs and their impact on women's lives, where a woman lived could have significant outcomes for her if she was relying on dower.[13]

By the sixteenth century the right to dower was often superseded by jointure, a settlement that more reliably guaranteed a steady income for a widow, and which avoided the uncertainty and potential legal pitfalls of dower. Jointure was a pre-arranged settlement, usually in the form of an annuity drawn from the rents of specified land. It was thought to be safer than dower as it was tied to named land. Although a woman could lose her right to dower if she opted for jointure – the 1536 Statute of Uses excluded dower in cases where a jointure had been agreed before marriage – she could choose either option if the jointure was made after her marriage.[14]

A formal jointure agreement was usually made before, not after, the marriage. In the early days of jointure this had meant the purchase of lands held in the joint names of husband and wife. The wife's portion or dowry might be used to fund the purchase, with whoever survived the other having the benefit of profits from the land. By the time of Anne's and Nicholas's marriage the system had evolved, so that a surviving widow was guaranteed a fixed annuity from the rental income of the land. This became payable immediately she was widowed and stayed in place until she died or remarried. The equity courts could enforce jointure arrangements, if necessary, but as jointure lands were clearly defined, there was usually no need for a widow to resort to legal process as she might have to do under dower.[15]

Anne had a jointure on her marriage, and the arrangements it set up were confirmed and updated by her husband's will. We saw that at the end of January 1553, the recently widowed Nicholas Bacon drew up an agreement between himself and Sir Anthony Cooke in preparation for his marriage to Anne Cooke, a transcription of which survives in the Suffolk Archives.[16] It indicates that the marriage date had been fixed, as the provisions were to be brought into effect by 12 February, about two weeks later. Nicholas made over to Anne 'a good sure and parfit estate' of land in the Manor of Ingham, Suffolk, and some other neighbouring properties, to be her jointure for the term of her life. To the property he added the profit from a stock of 400 sheep that were 'going and feeding' upon it. Anne was bound by covenant to maintain the flock at the same level to pass on after her own death. Nicholas did not need to use the substantial marriage portion of 400 marks given by Sir Anthony for his daughter's marriage to purchase land for the jointure.[17] By the time of his second marriage Nicholas was securely on the Tudor property ladder thanks to his shrewd business sense and useful position in the Court of Bequests. He already owned the Ingham land allocated for the jointure and the other associated property. Beginning immediately after his death, regular payments to Anne of £100 at each Lady Day (March) and Michaelmas (September) are recorded by her stepson, the younger Nicholas, as the fixed annuity paid to her from the income of Ingham.[18]

His 'dear and well beloved wife' is the first person named in Nicholas's will. He gives her one thousand five hundred ounces of plate, to be chosen by her, with all his linen, napery, hangings, coaches, litters and the household stuff remaining in London at York House, apart from the contents of his study and a small number of specific items he leaves to others. He sets aside the £100 in ready money for her to keep on the household staff for a month and says she can keep 'such jewels and goldsmiths work as remain with her' and all his horses and geldings. In keeping with his origins as the sheep reeve's son and lifelong investments in livestock, Nicholas makes provision for her rights in the flock of sheep at Ingham, near Bury St Edmunds in Suffolk. Anne will have the property of Gorhambury for her lifetime, together with lands and leases nearby comprising the lease of Aldenham and copyhold lands or tenements in the parishes of St Michael and St Stephen in St Albans, and others associated with his estate lands at Westwick, Gorhambury and Pre. After her death this property will go to Anthony and, in the meantime, he may have half of the house contents when he reaches the age of twenty-four. She has all the remaining household stores, goods and chattels at Redbourn and Windridge not otherwise allocated in the will, and Nicholas's remaining interest in York House. In consideration of these lands and legacies, he writes, and 'for all loves that have been between us', he charges her 'to see to the well bringing up of my two sons Anthony and Francis that are now left poor orphans without a father'.[19]

In his will Anne's husband updated the provisions of the jointure, bequeathing her the life interest in the proceeds of his flock of sheep at Ingham on condition she provided a bond of £200 and maintained the flock to be passed on to his son Nicholas at her death in accordance with agreements made at the younger Nicholas's marriage.

He also ensured that she did not invoke her right to dower, overriding it by directing her formally to give up her right to dower in regard of all the property of his that was dowable, 'within one year next after my decease and before she be married again'.[20] If she did not, she would forfeit all his legacies, gifts and bequests. The possibility of Anne's remarriage is woven into the will's provisions. If she remarried within the year, and before meeting the requirement of the will to release the dower, all her husband's legacies and bequests to her would be voided and would pass to the younger Sir Nicholas.

'A release from my Lady Bacon of her dower to Sir Nicholas Bacon' and 'My Lady Bacon's bond for the stock of Ingham' are among the 'writings' delivered by Nathaniel Bacon to his brother, the new Sir Nicholas Bacon, on 18 February 1580 almost a year to the day after their father's death.[21] Anne had fulfilled the conditions of her husband's will and was secure in both her jointure and all the bequests made to her under the will.

Although his will made adequate provision for Anne's maintenance, the sudden drop in household income from the loss of the Lord Keeper's official revenues must have caused a decline in the ease and comfort of her life. Nevertheless there was no sign that she contemplated improving her finances and social status through remarriage: 'truly she is as far off that, as when you departed from her nor none ever came to her for that as far as I can hear of,' reported a Gorhambury servant, Thomas Cotheram, writing to Anthony the year after Nicholas's death, adding he would send word if he ever heard to the contrary, 'But I hope to God there shall be no such occasion.'[22]

As the executors' overseer, Lord Burghley had the authority and responsibility to arbitrate in any dispute over the will. Three months after the funeral it is clear that matters were still not settled. In May 1579 Nicholas wrote to Burghley, complaining about Anthony. He has received Burghley's letters, he says, and understands that '... great speeches have passed between my brother [Nathaniel] and your Lordship concerning the matters in question between my brother Anthony and myself touching my father's will', going on, 'whereby as I think I may find myself justly grieved to see my brother Anthony to have greater care to get what he can than to be anything thankful for such benefits as we [Nicholas and Nathaniel] have promised him'.[23]

Having set the tone for his letter – that he has been generous and Anthony is grasping – Nicholas details some of the points of contention between them, which have previously been drawn up into a schedule (this is not included with the letter to Burghley). Anthony has been left land at Pinner Park, near Harrow, but there is a dispute about who will have the livestock that is on it. Nicholas says he agrees to give up the stock to Anthony, together with other unspecified goods. On the second point, the resigning of his interest in the lease of the manor of Redbourn, which was left to Anthony, he is more stubborn – he writes that he will not 'depart with the profits nor yet the lease unless I may have perfect assurance for my money'. He is suspicious that Anthony is concealing 'more leases than we know of which he is loth to have known in respect of the stocks', as well as other details of leases and covenants that are still at issue. He wants to resolve matters in order to fulfil his father's will, he also says he wants 'a continuance of a perfect friendship' with Anthony, but this is in jeopardy as a result of '[Anthony] my brother dealing so hardly with me and I so friendly with him'. Nicholas says that he and Nathaniel made a 'frank offering at the first' in token of their goodwill to Anthony, and such brotherly friendship should have outweighed wrangles over worldly goods. But underlying his protestations is the revelation that the older brothers' expectations have been disappointed: 'we thought my father's [e]state to be much better than we find it is'.[24] As executors they had to balance the books, and as Nathaniel revealed in a letter to Burghley later in the year, there were assets not allocated in his father's will, such as livestock associated with some of the land, that they wanted access to if necessary to settle any outstanding debts of the Lord Keeper's estate.[25]

Burghley worked hard to resolve matters with the older sons, in correspondence stretching into the summer following Sir Nicholas's death, but their answers were slow in coming. 'Where a good time past I wrote a letter to you and your brother Nathaniel … I have of long time looked for answer … I found myself deceived in my expectation therein,' he wrote to Nicholas at the beginning of July 1579. In a broadside that shows his impatience with the whole business, he ordered Nicholas to send a 'full perfect answer to my satisfaction to the articles which I sent … that by the imperfections of your answers I be not left as evil unsatisfied as I had now'.[26]

The patriarchal tone of Burghley's letter must have reminded the older Bacon brothers of their own father's style. All their lives they had received his stern reminders and admonitions, their lapses of duty or effort greeted by an epistolary raised eyebrow: 'I marvel…'. Indeed, letters from Sir Nicholas to his oldest son complained of the same faults that were annoying Burghley ten years later: 'Write at large and not scantly,' he had admonished, in response to Nicholas's scrappy answers, and as he impatiently waited for letters, 'Son, the sooner I hear answer of those things I committed unto ye, the better.'[27]

Sir William Cecil in the early years of Elizabeth I's reign. Unknown Anglo-Netherlandish artist, 1560s. National Portrait Gallery 2184 © National Portrait Gallery, London.

Burghley reminded them that Anne had been a good wife to their father. He says she has already conceded a great deal in the negotiations over the will (we do not know precisely what), and he does not want them to drift into legal proceedings.

The dispute between the stepbrothers festered on into the year following the Lord Keeper's death, and in line with the advice to widows, Anne deferred to her brother-in-law to resolve matters. A letter from Anne to her stepson Nicholas in the summer of 1579 indicates that Burghley was still mediating between members of the family over the will and had resolved to formally hear the matter the following day. However, Nathaniel failed to be in London for the hearing, for unknown reasons that Anne alludes to in the letter as 'a great pain'. Relations were still strained. Anne appealed to her stepson Nicholas to reconcile their differences: 'I pray God work in your heart as ready a disposition to end well, as I at the first by his grace gave a very rare example to begin well immediately upon your father's death, of a most faithful heart ever to him, and the like desire to confirm your good will still,' she wrote, going on to hope that he has not been influenced against her and her sons by 'any ill counsel, as the world is full of subtlety' to alter his nature, which 'hitherto I have taken to be well inclined,' concluding 'I pray you, good Sir Nicholas Bacon, let it do no hurt between us where there has been so long a continuance of more than common amity. You being the son, and I the wife, and now the widow of the same good father and husband.' She ends with the hope that they might 'meet together friendly', signing herself with a conciliatory 'your well willer [wisher] always'.[28]

The matter did not end up in court, but rumbled on in correspondence, with Burghley showing further exasperation at Nicholas's and Nathaniel's slow response to his questions and deadlines and chiding them for their behaviour to Anne. In July he wrote to Nicholas that he had received only one inadequate letter from him, with no input from Nathaniel as he had requested:

> I have received a single letter from yourself, irresolute for me to understand, altogether dilatory, without motion of [any contribution from] your brother Nathaniel, whom I joined with you in my letter. And though this your letter contain good words towards me, yet finding lack of good words or sense towards my Lady Bacon your late good father's good wife, and also towards your natural younger brother Anthony Bacon, I was moved to think somewhat hardly of all these hard circumstances…

He says they should him answer speedily, and show:

> a reasonable, kind and courteous regard … to the lady that hath so long time deserved well of you and yours, and hath been so good a wife to my Lord your father, and lastly who in the time of your father's death in my sight and hearing yielded so much unto you for your benefit as surely no natural mother could have yielded more to her own children, whereof my conscience moveth me to … exact of you both some more courteous and natural dealing than hitherto I see or can perceive. And in this sort I had rather deal with you than for lack of my intercession to permit you to take a course to go to the law, as by your letter you seem to mean to drive my Lady unto, a matter surely unmeet to be attempted by her or provoked by you or any of yours, to whom so many benefits have come from your father and her since their intermarriage and by reason of the same marriage.[29]

He has not passed on to Anne and Anthony some of the contents of Nicholas's letter that 'might miscontent them,' he writes to Nicholas, another indication that Anne's attempt to smooth over the situation with her stepson had not succeeded.

Nathaniel responded within a fortnight. The family wrangle now included ill-feeling between himself and Nicholas, who had disagreed with a proposal to resolve the dispute that Nathaniel had been on the way to agreeing with Burghley. But his real complaint was against Anne for, he says, interfering in what should have been the last stage of the negotiations: 'When the matters were thus near the end, and yet not at an end, and your Lordship had somewhat accepted of my promise to treat with my brother to consent to that point, by my Lady['s] meanes your Lordship was stirred greatly against me.' He thinks she is causing trouble between himself and Burghley and refers to Burghley's 'sharp speech' to him. He is defensive about failing to meet Nicholas to draft a joint reply: he was ill with an ague, he says, then Nicholas had a sick child and could not travel.[30]

Nicholas also responded, after receiving a further letter in which Burghley pushed for a resolution, reminding him to remember his obligations to the memory of 'your late good father in what reputation he lived and died' and to Burghley in his role as overseer of the executors: 'the solemn promise you made with oath when you agreed to stand by my order should any controversy arise between Lady Bacon and you for herself or her children your brethren'. Nicholas also thought that Burghley was favouring Anne in the dispute, and in his letter even accuses her of 'embezzling' goods due to them, contrary to assurances made at the outset:

I may very well in honesty now refuse to stand unto the same [keep to the agreement], for there were promises at that time [after the Lord Keeper's death] made unto my brother and me whereof there is no word spoken, which with your Lordship's favour have been in many ways broken. For my Lady promised that no goods should be embezzled from us, which she hath not only broken, but also hath been in offence with every man which hath informed us of them … Also your Lordship promised to deal indifferently between us, which hitherto (if without offence I might speak it) I have not tasted of, as it may very well appear in the form of an order set down by your Lordship.[31]

We do not know whether the goods Nicholas believed to be rightfully his and Nathaniel's consisted of more than the livestock at issue, or whether the scope of the dispute had widened to include other possessions of the late Lord Keeper. Either way, both her stepsons saw Anne as responsible for breaching earlier verbal agreements, as well as instrumental in trying to turn Burghley to support her and Anthony in his decision, which they would all be required to obey. It is perhaps indicative of the failing powers of the Lord Keeper in his final months that these loose ends were left to be contended over after his death, when his lifelong habit had been to keep tight control over every administrative detail.

The records of outgoing correspondence preserved in Nathaniel Bacon's papers and used here to trace the progress of the dispute are in the form of drafts or copies, often with additions or deletions included. In relying on them, we cannot of course know whether a document always records the final form of the letter that was sent, but their overall content is corroborated by the incoming letters from Lord Burghley preserved by Nathaniel.

Burghley's authoritative intervention finally effected a resolution. Matters seem to have been settled by February 1580, when Nathaniel delivered to Nicholas a note of the 'writings concerning my Lady and Mr Anthony Bacon' that lists the legal agreements over lands and leases then in place.[32]

The dispute over the will had left a breach between the Lord Keeper's first and second families that was never repaired. After July 1579, once the details of lands and legacies were agreed between them and recorded, the pattern of Anne's future as a widow took shape. The focus of her daily life was greatly changed. With the flow of the Lord Keeper's legal and political business terminated, the constant comings and goings to and from court over, her sons absent, and friendly visits from stepchildren at an end, the important press and bustle of activity that had surrounded Anne at both York House and Gorhambury for almost two decades fell suddenly silent.

Sons often left their mothers to deal with important property and estate business, and this was the pattern that emerged during Anne's long widowhood, as she took on all the responsibility of managing Gorhambury and the associated properties that had been left to her for her lifetime, without the benefit of ownership. Anne's duty was to maintain the estate in good order for Anthony. Running Gorhambury was to absorb much of her energy as she took on responsibility for the practical decision-making and financial outgoings that Nicholas had always controlled down to the last detail. Although it was no longer either the focus of family life or the reflection of his high office and material success, Anne had to maintain Gorhambury, depending on the income from rents and leases to keep up the house and estate for Anthony to inherit. However competent and dutiful she was in taking this on, Anne found it an unwelcome burden and perpetual source of worry. Her sons were no help. It soon became clear that, in contrast to their father and the older sons he had trained in the methodical management of money and property, neither Anthony nor Francis showed any interest in or aptitude for business dealings and financial management. The result was to be a steep decline in the family's material fortunes, despite Anne's efforts to manage and preserve the assets left in her control.

Her energy over the coming two decades would be divided between supporting her sons through the vicissitudes of financial and career troubles; her personal faith and the furtherance of the religious causes she promoted and defended; and the management of the estate, a task whose demands she found an onerous distraction from her preferred life of pious observance. In 1593 she would write to Anthony lamenting the death of John Finch, a trusted tenant farmer whose careful management of her 'rural business,' she says, 'procured me … much quiet of mind and leisure to spend my time in godly exercises, both public and private.'[33]

We know of such details because, most unusually for the period, a cache of Anne's personal letters has survived along with a collection of Anthony's correspondence, in the archives at Lambeth Palace. Anne would recognise the castellated, turreted buildings that still stand on the south bank of the Thames across from today's Millbank. Lambeth Palace has stood for 800 years and would have been part of her view across the Thames, upstream from York House. For one decade of her widowhood, the 1590s, the letters that are preserved there are a window into Anne's life. Placed into folios between heavy marbled covers, Anne's surviving letters are dispersed among her son's official correspondence. Thin cream-coloured leaves are inscribed with her uneven handwriting in faded ink, filling the pages from top to bottom.

These letters, written in her energetic, often barely decipherable hand, bring to life the world of a sixteenth-century woman indefatigably defending her family's interests and doing her best to stay in control. They illustrate a period of her life during the middle of her widowhood. Scattered with classical references and quotations from the scriptures, Anne's letters speak of many things: morality, money, faith; strawberries and beer; leases, pictures, carpets; feckless servants, ungodly fashions and pious sermons. We will see that they preserve Anne's vehement declarations, her warnings about treacherous companions, cautionary advice and occasional rages. She wrote to her sons of life on the Gorhambury estate – brewing, poachers in the woods, trouble with tenants – and advised them on politics, religion and health.

The letters' appearance and the organisation of their content help round out what we know of Anne's personality, as well as her preoccupations and state of mind in her sixties. Unlike the carefully structured translations and formal letters from earlier in her life, there are no paragraphs in these family letters, no gaps before the signature, and sometimes a postscript expands to become another letter. Phrases in Greek and Latin often punctuate her sentences. Extra notes and instructions embellish the texts, in corners and margins or on the outside of the letters. Subjects are juxtaposed as if Anne wrote each thought as it occurred, pouring words onto the page. The freshness of expression so notable in her translations is present here in unfettered form.

For her first decade as a widow, before the period covered by the letters, evidence about Anne's life is sparser. We have seen that Nicholas left Anne £100 to maintain the household for a month after his death. What happened after that was spent? As executor of his father's will, her second stepson Nathaniel kept methodical records of the financial transactions made as he and his older brother Nicholas wound up their father's estate during the spring and summer of 1579.[34] These accounts include the costs of the funeral and other payments, valuations of land and other property, money due from creditors, and the legacies paid to some sixty household servants together with their wages for the first quarter of the year, to Lady Day (25 March) 1579. Recording and settling all the credits and debits, a mass of detailed entries ranging from £2 owed by Edmond Stoneham of St Albans 'for an old gelding called Windham' to bequests to prisoners in Newgate and a legacy of £100 to the chapel of Benet College, Cambridge, Nathaniel was assisted by Bartholomew Kemp, his cousin's husband, who had been employed in the management of the Lord Keeper's accounts. 'Cousin Kemp, I pray you pay…' is Nathaniel's customary introduction to the lists of sums due. Wrapping up what proved to be a long and complex ledger, 'The sum total of legacies and wages paid to "my Lord's men as appeareth by this book", concluded Nathaniel, was £160 10s 6d.[35]

It is safe to assume that many of these employees were being paid off and their services dispensed with, as the Lord Keeper's household was heavily scaled down. Lacking detailed household accounts for the years that followed, we cannot know how many of the staff were retained. However, there was no longer the need for a large retinue to provide the professional support and display of personal magnificence required for a leading statesman. Neither was there the substantial cushion of cash from the Lord Keeper's official revenues that had previously underpinned household expenses and investments.

From the details that emerge from her later letters we can construct a tentative outline of Anne's daily life and occupations. Who were her daily companions in the reduced household at Gorhambury? First, there were the remaining servants and tenants she depended on to keep the house and estate running and to manage the newer responsibilities associated with her life interest in Gorhambury and other properties. Second, and no doubt more congenial to her inclination to spend her hours in scholarly reading and pious reflection, she had the company of the nonconformist clergymen who frequented Gorhambury.

Unusually for a gentry household headed by a woman of Anne's social status, no female members of the extended family on either side seem to have been there to keep her company or to act as upper servants. At the funeral she had been attended by four gentlewomen, according to the expenses for their mourning clothes. Who they were is not recorded, and although in her letters she often refers by name to household servants, estate tenants, godly men and local politicians known to her sons, there is an absence of references to any female visitors, companions or personal attendants in her accounts of local people and events. While most of her time was spent at Gorhambury, she occasionally went to London, where she did sometimes seek out female company. We can infer the pattern of her visits from her letters of the 1590s, some of which are written from lodgings in Fleet Street. She occasionally went to London to seek medical advice, at other times she recorded going to her sister Elizabeth's house at Blackfriars after hearing a sermon, and to Lord Burghley's house in the Strand to seek an opportunity to speak to him. She infrequently attended court to see the queen and her old friends there, otherwise keeping up with the news from London through correspondence.

Her pious occupations – personal prayer and study, and her support for the nonconformist preachers of Hertfordshire – would have occupied a great deal of her time and attention every day. Everyone in the household who could do so, excluding only the ill or infirm and those with pressing practical duties, would have met daily for prayers in the morning and the evening. For the very pious, rising early in the morning was the best way to ensure lengthy uninterrupted private prayer – perhaps Anne followed such a regime. As the widowed head of the household Anne may have led the household prayers herself. This was accepted practice, though Anthony may have been expected to take the role if he was present.

If a chaplain was part of the household, or one of her favoured godly preachers was visiting, it is likely they would have led the prayers as well as joining Anne privately to read and discuss scriptural texts and works of religious meditation. We know from her later letters that Anne took domestic religious observance seriously. Members of her household were tested by godly preacher Mr Wildblood on their catechism. In letters to Anthony she more than once told him to ensure that his whole household said prayers and read psalms morning and evening.

Under Anne's patronage the area around St Albans would become an enclave of radical Puritanism, with Gorhambury a haven for radical preachers in trouble with the church authorities, after nonconformist preachers were put at risk of suspension following Archbishop John Whitgift's imposition of rules for religious conformity in 1583. The Hertfordshire preachers she supported were often mentioned in her letters, notably Humphrey Wildblood and Percival Wyburn, who made themselves comfortable at Gorhambury to the extent that Anthony wondered if there was a risk that she would marry one of them.

Anne adopted the role and status of godly widow that she maintained for the rest of her life. She was vigilant over her sons' welfare, and continued to direct her energies into religious reform, while her identity remined entwined with the memory of her husband: 'certainly among my blessings,' she wrote to the Genevan theologian Théodore de Bèze in 1581, 'I especially count the fact that God wished me to be the wife of such a man', signing herself 'Yours in Christ A. Bacon, widow of the Lord Keeper'.[36]

Anthony and Francis may have been attentive to their widowed mother during the tussle over the will, but neither of them was interested in leading the life of a country gentleman at Gorhambury or engaging in the local politics of Hertfordshire. They were seeking footholds in the worlds of law, politics and diplomacy. Francis moved into the accommodation built by his father in Gray's Inn in order to resume his legal studies, his only other option being to remain with his mother at Gorhambury. Anthony stayed with him while preparing to leave England for a continental tour. His mother expected Anthony back after a conventional year or two as student and traveller, but it proved to be a prolonged absence that would transform him into a player in the world of Elizabethan overseas intelligence. After his departure at the end of 1579, she was not to see her older son again for twelve years.

Francis Bacon's life and career have been well documented by later generations, his letters and writings preserved and published. Historians have drawn on Anthony's letters, and his career is now recognised to have been more closely linked to Francis's than previously known.[37] He has never had the prominence of his famous younger brother. Yet in 1579 there was no secure trajectory ahead for either brother, the 'poor orphans without a father' the Lord Keeper had left to their mother's care. She felt the weight of responsibility for them, and acute anxiety about their uncertain futures.

Chapter 15
Golden lads

Since her old friend and brother-in-law Lord Burghley had been willing to sort out the will and settle the dispute with her stepsons, Anne may have expected him to help her secure careers and incomes for her sons. Of his own sons, Thomas, from his first marriage, was comfortably established, while Robert was the only surviving son of his marriage to Mildred. Then only sixteen, Francis and Anthony's cousin was pitied for his physical disability – he had spinal scoliosis, a condition that affected his posture and mobility – but was as precociously intelligent as the younger Bacons and had benefited from a similarly rigorous education under Mildred's guidance. Anne did not yet realise the impact the rise of the young Robert Cecil would have on her own sons' prospects.

The rift with her husband's first family over the will had ruled out turning to the older Bacon half-brothers for help and guidance. Anne hoped Lord Burghley would fill the void and direct Anthony and Francis towards settled paths in life. He did offer some limited help, initially. However, Anthony and Francis carried no dynastic significance in the family. That lay with the sons of Bacon's first marriage, in particular Nicholas, who had inherited his father's title and much of the property. Anthony and Francis, though brought up with all the trappings of high status and wealth, had no easy path laid for them to maintain that life. They had to make and maintain connections that would sustain and advance their position. The estrangement from their father's first family lost them valuable networks of kin, compounding the precarity of their position. Lord Burghley was their most powerful kinsman, whose support would have been pivotal, but he had no family obligation to further the interests of the sons of his brother-in-law's second marriage, who were at one remove both as nephews by marriage and as less important in dynastic terms than the sons of the first marriage, and over the coming years his interventions on their behalf would be only partial and intermittent. He never offered wholehearted and consistent support.

After their father's death the brothers tried to recruit their uncle into a paternal role in their lives, talking in letters to him of his friendship and fatherly dealing with them. Burghley's response to these overtures was equivocal from the beginning. When Anthony set off for Paris at the end of 1579, the letter of introduction he carried reveals Burghley's caution about how much responsibility to take for his nephews' futures. In the course of writing that Sir Nicholas had charged him with the 'care of the bringing up of him [Anthony] and his brother', Burghley had second thoughts, amending the phrase to read simply 'the care of him and his brother'. The term 'bringing up' then would have included an obligation to assist the brothers towards social and financial stability, and Burghley was not prepared to commit himself so far. Anne possibly anticipated a level of long-term support that he had no intention of providing.[1]

Francis wrote to his uncle in 1580 to ask for help in obtaining a legal post from the queen, as he established himself in a legal career. He made it clear that practising law was a choice he was forced into to make an income, being left so poorly provided for. In response Burghley put in a word on his behalf to the queen and from time to time he promoted opportunities for Francis to build a career in royal service. He briefly employed Francis as an interpreter in 1581, during a visit by French dignitaries and helped to establish him as a member of parliament, also in 1581, alongside his fledgling practice as a lawyer.[2] However, when Francis later spoke in parliament in opposition to a proposed timetable for the payment of royal subsidies, he fell out of the queen's favour. Although she called on him for legal advice over the years, he failed time after time to get a foothold on the lucrative ladder of official appointments until the accession of James I in 1603.

Accompanied by one of Burghley's reliable retainers, a Mr Windebank, Anthony had left England for France in December 1579 with a standard three-year licence to travel and, according to Burghley, with the intention of seeing the country and learning the language.[3] No one in Anthony's family would have predicted that the three years would stretch into twelve, during which Anthony developed into something between political correspondent and spy, the role known as 'intelligencer'. After a stay in Paris on first arriving in France, Anthony left Mr Windebank behind and travelled to Germany and Geneva – the centre of religious reform, where his grandfather had waited out the years of Mary I's reign with other Marian exiles – in the company of a friend from his Cambridge student days, Honoré Blanchard, before returning to France.

While in Paris he had had a first taste of intelligence work, mixing with a duplicitous Catholic sympathiser, William Parry and covertly reporting back on his activities, on Burghley's orders.[4] News of this association, in the course of which he had lent money to Parry, reached hostile ears in London and Burghley was forced to reassure the queen that Anthony was acting in her interests. Anthony also began to report to the queen's spymaster Francis Walsingham who in 1580 encouraged him to continue the correspondence: 'your letters are very welcome unto me'.[5] He met another of Walsingham's intelligence-gatherers Nicholas Faunt, a continental traveller of around his own age. Faunt became a close friend and correspondent and would prove a valuable source of information to Anne, who trusted him to relay news to her in person of and about Anthony. In a letter to

Anthony, Faunt recorded how he had met with her in 1582. Walking with Anne in Lord Burghley's gardens, he had answered her probing questions about Anthony's health, how much he was spending, how he occupied himself and what plans he had for further travel.[6]

Anne's anxiety about Anthony and the heavy responsibility she bore for her sons' welfare and advancement is evident in two letters to Théodore de Bèze that she wrote – in Latin – in May and July 1581. As both his half-brother Edward and his new friend Faunt had done, Anthony was lodging and studying in Geneva. He stayed in the household of de Bèze, who had succeeded John Calvin as leader and principal teacher of the reformed faith.

'My lord husband has left me, his second wife ... just two sons, the whole hope of my offspring in these years moreover,' wrote Anne to de Bèze, adding that her sons 'particularly miss and need the guidance of a father's authority and the solicitous concern of a loving parent'. While she had been 'greatly desirous that he should set out from here and see your Geneva – or rather, God's Geneva, as well as your face', she feared Anthony was too young to wander abroad unsupervised when he left England, rather than supported by the 'help and frequent counsel of a godly and truly prudent father', as Edward had been.[7]

Her fears were fuelled by uncertainty about Anthony's whereabouts, and it was not until receiving a letter from de Bèze, to which she replied in July, that Anne knew that her son had reached Geneva. 'While Anthony remains with you,' she wrote back ' – and the longer he stays the happier I am – act as a parent to him, I beseech you, giving him your counsel and assistance, both for the sake of piety and so as to carry out the rest of his journey more advisedly and safely by means of your wisdom, if now he decides to remain abroad still longer.'[8]

As she suspected, Anthony was indeed on course for a longer absence from home. Whilst uneasy that he was away for so long, for now Anne was glad to know that Anthony was using his time responsibly and in irreproachable company. De Bèze dedicated a volume of meditations on the Psalms to her in November that year, 'in testimony of the honour and reverence I bear to the virtue of you and yours', telling her it was Anthony who had encouraged him to revisit the manuscript and publish it. He praises her husband's and her father's fine qualities, as well as Anne's own, and hopes she will find consolation for her losses in spiritual meditation.[9]

One of de Bèze's associates, Walter Travers, had recently returned to England after a decade in Geneva and Antwerp, having been driven out of his Cambridge post by John Whitgift, the Master of Trinity College, who disliked his Puritanism. Aided by Burghley, whose household he joined as chaplain for a time on his return, in 1581 Travers obtained an appointment at the Temple church in London. Anne accompanied Francis to hear Travers's sermons. This was a public display by them both of support for the Genevan style of Protestantism and for Puritan practices, such as communal public fasting undertaken as a sign of repentance, that were out of favour with the religious establishment.[10] Thus in the early 1580s, mother and sons were in accord over religion as Anthony enjoyed the atmosphere in Geneva and Francis accompanied Anne to hear Travers.

There was no such harmony between Anne and Anthony in respect of his financial affairs, around which dark clouds were gathering. He was spending and lending money freely, drawing on income from Gorhambury. His business affairs at home were partly administered by Hugh Mantell the steward, who managed property transactions including rent collection, transferred money from the proceeds to Anthony twice a year, and sent him reports on estate business. Anthony had further updates on how his interests at home were being managed from two Gorhambury servants, John Stalling and Thomas Cotheram. Anne was saving woodland to be felled when Anthony came home, so the timber could be sold to cover his likely debts, Cotheram reported in March 1580, adding that she was displeased with Stalling, who 'doth not do his duty at Gorhambury' and she regretted giving him a lease.[11] Anne was already feeling the strain of running the estate alone and keeping Anthony's precarious finances afloat.

Although Anthony charged his servants to be courteous and helpful on his behalf and stay on the right side of his mother as they managed estate business, he paid scant attention to the details of financial management at a distance. He was neglecting to answer Mantell's letters or provide the seals and signatures Mantell needed for transactions. He was spending freely on his servants and horses and lending cash to friends, until his outgoings were consistently outstripping his estate income. Anthony had never managed anything practical in his life or had money of his own, aside from the allowance from his father that a young gentleman at the Inns of Court might expect. If he thought about the estate at all while he was away, it may have seemed to him a distant cornucopia of resources that were his by right, which others were looking after for him. But Mantell was borrowing money from Anne, and even dipping into his own resources to cover expenditure that was due.[12] He was at his wits' end over Anthony's cavalier attitude to money. 'There is not one penny in my hands,' he declared, in a despairing response to an instruction from Anthony to pay bills in 1581.[13] Anne's patience ran short as her limited resources were depleted to support her son's spending. Hugh Mantell tried to prompt his conscience:

> I am verily persuaded that if you did enter into a reckoning and consideration of the great charge you have been at since your going over and the troublings of her Ladyship and other of your worship's friends, you would certainly have greater desire to return to England than you hitherto seem to have.[14]

The drain on Anne's income was such that she was threatening to keep all Anthony's revenues and convert them to her own use to cover the sums she had paid out, as 'she is utterly unable to pay these great sums out of her Ladyship's so small a revenue,' wrote Mantell who was by now old and weary, and did not have long to live.[15]

Anne wanted Anthony to come home. So did the beleaguered steward, who hoped he would return to repair his disordered financial affairs. Francis, too, looked forward to his brother's return. However, after Anthony had attracted the queen's attention and approval when he transacted some business on her behalf in Bordeaux, she authorised his continued stay in France with a further three-year licence issued in 1582. By 1584 he had become an unofficial contact between the English court and the Huguenot prince, King Henri of Navarre, at Henri's court in the city of Montauban.[16]

There Anthony had a second narrow escape from marriage, following the failed match with Dowsabell years earlier, when he rebuffed the daughter of a lady of the court who had him in her sights. He doubly offended the mother, when he did not support her campaign to wear wigs in church: the 'scandalous excess in her head attire', a female frivolity banned by the Huguenots.[17]

Michel Berault, a French Protestant minister of the city, wrote to Anne to reassure her about her son's wellbeing. He knows she must be anxious, as it is a turbulent time in France. He was referring to the long conflict between Catholics and Huguenots. He tells her that Anthony is a most generous and distinguished young man, shining with virtue, who has increased in piety. Perhaps he too had noted Anthony's careless attitude to spending, as he added that Anthony had made more gain spiritually than he had lost financially. The minister mentions Anthony's ill health, giving this as a reason why Anthony could not risk a journey back to England, even though he seemed keen to return home.[18]

The truth about Anthony's prolonged stay in Montauban was darker than the minister's account suggests, though he does caution Anne not to believe everything she might hear about her son. In 1586 Anthony was accused in Montauban of sodomy with Isaac Bougades, one of the pages of his household. This was a terrifying charge: sodomy was a capital offence, punishable by burning at the stake. Anthony was saved from public disgrace at the least and a hideous death at the worst, by the personal intervention of Henri of Navarre.

Of course, the existence of such an accusation did not mean that the allegations were true. The accusation could have come from a disaffected servant, been based on malice and rumour, a deliberate slander on Anthony's reputation or the result of an attempt at blackmail. In an age when households were crowded, beds routinely shared with others of the same sex, and servants and masters lived in close proximity, that was always a risk and such accusations could be used as a political weapon. In Anthony's case, the main evidence seems to have come from two servants, father and son, who could have had any number of motives. Anthony had numerous servants in his household, doubtless vying for favour and preferment, and in historian Will Tosh's view 'the depositions tell a story of domestic mismanagement, jealousy and favouritism'.[19]

Although the scandal of the accusation seems never to have become public in England, Burghley and Walsingham, with their extensive information networks, must have known of it. It appears that, in time, Anne also knew. Some ten years later she would write to Anthony, who remained unmarried and childless, that she would have been happy to have grandchildren, 'childer's childer', but 'France spoiled me and mine', surely a reference to Anthony's deeply compromised position as a marriage prospect.[20] Whatever the truth of the episode, which is not discernible from the available evidence, and whether or not Anne knew the whole story, Anthony avoided returning home for another six years.

In the years after he had left the safe haven of de Bèze's household in Geneva his mother suspected Anthony of drifting into dangerous friendships with Catholics. Three friends in particular were the focus of her mistrust: Thomas Lawson, Anthony Standen and Antonio Perez, who had been a secretary to Phillip II, the king of Spain. Thomas Lawson was a young Catholic servant of Anthony's who joined the household in Montauban. Anthony sent him to England with messages in 1588, including both personal letters and cloak-and-dagger reports – 'certain advertisements of great importance to her majesty's service, and dangerous for himself' – writes eighteenth-century historian Thomas Birch, whose memoir of Elizabeth's reign draws heavily on Anthony's letters.[21] But Lawson earned no reward for his mission. Instead Lord Burghley put him in prison, where he stayed for ten months. Lawson's incarceration was instigated by Anne. Convinced that he was a dangerous influence who was corrupting her son, Anne had called on her brother-in-law to have Lawson locked up.

Anthony later dismissed his mother's suspicions as unfounded, stirred up by M. de Plessis and his wife – the lady of scandalous wigs and a spurned daughter, who had turned against Anthony in Montauban. Anne's animosity towards Lawson never abated. 'Let not Lawson, that fox, be acquainted with my letters,' she wrote when Anthony eventually returned to England, asserting that Lawson had commonly opened letters sent to Anthony while he was away, and would 'pry and prattle'.[22]

In the tenth year of Anthony's absence he was still in Montauban, mired in debt and tangled in lawsuits. He had received a royal summons home from Walsingham on behalf of the queen, another intervention instigated by his mother. But even though he now said he wanted to leave, he did not have the means to do so. His situation had worsened after the usually reliable Nicholas Faunt failed to persuade Anne to pay what she considered to be exorbitant charges by money-changers when she sent funds to France. Anthony was becalmed in Montauban with both his mother and Lord Burghley demanding to know why he did not return.

Anthony recruited another friend he had met in France, Captain Francis Allen, to travel home to reassure his mother and others in England about him, see if he could raise some funds, and retrieve his servant Thomas Lawson. Allen went to Gorhambury, where Anne received him courteously. All went well until he produced letters from Lord Burghley and Francis in support of Lawson, intended to soften her view of him. Anne refused to look at the letters and, Captain Allen reported to Anthony, she became hostile and distressed.

> She expressed the utmost resentment at her son's so long continuance abroad, calling him traitor to God and his country, and alleging that he had undone her, and sought her death … That she was resolved to procure the queen's letter to force him to return home … She declared that she could not bear to hear of him, and that he was hated of all the chiefest in France, and cursed of God in all his actions since Mr Lawson's being with him, whom she was determined not to suffer to return to his master Mr Bacon … She used several other expressions of her concern for his delaying to come back, urging that she had spent [sold] her jewels to supply him, and had borrowed the last money which she had sent him of [from] several persons.[23]

She further told Allen that her daily misery because of Anthony would 'be her end', leading Allen to advise Anthony to come back as soon as possible for fear of 'shortening her years'. Anthony's prolonged absence, his demands for money and her suspicious fury about his companions were having such an impact on Anne that her temper was barely in check. She went so far as to say she would rather Anthony were dead.

Captain Allen wrote that she had repented these words and taken them back immediately, yet she was adamant she would not send back Lawson, declaring: 'if there were no more men in England, and although you should never come home, he shall be hindered from coming to you'. Allen metaphorically threw his hands in the air: 'It is as unpossible to persuade my Lady to send him, as myself to send you [St] Paul's steeple.'[24] She was infuriated at any mention by Francis of Anthony's situation. Although Francis was eager to help his brother, said Captain Allen: 'the apprehension of his mother's displeasure prevented him from interposing much in his affairs'. He warned Anthony that Anne was prepared to resist any attempt he might make to sell Gorhambury and would appeal to the queen to stop it.[25]

Piecing together what information she could glean about Anthony's activities and reaching her own negative conclusions, despite attempts to reassure her, was Anne dwelling upon the duty laid upon her in her husband's will to watch over and support their sons? Nothing was as he would have wished and expected. Her fears and regrets about her sons weighed heavily as she struggled to maintain the property Nicholas had so shrewdly acquired and steadily managed for his family's future, while its revenues were ransacked and depleted by Anthony's demands. Yet while Captain Allen found Anne angry and distraught at Gorhambury, she was not helpless. She had demonstrated that she could muster the influence of the most powerful allies – Burghley, Walsingham and the queen herself – in her determination to gain control and get her son home.

Anthony was still away in 1591 when, through rumours that reached her from the English factors in Bordeaux, Anne heard that he had befriended Anthony Standen, a Catholic double-agent who was in prison in the town. Anthony was working to assist Standen into better prison conditions and to procure his release. Anne again suspected her son of Catholic sympathies. She was convinced that he had 'some design of retiring with that gentleman to Rome'.[26] There was no truth in this, but Anne nevertheless did her best to thwart such a move by forbidding the merchants to do business with Anthony. Once again, she expressed extreme anger with him, as she (temporarily) renounced her son, declaring him to be 'illegitimate not to be born of her body'.[27]

Although Standen was released and returned to England a free man, Anne's suspicion of his influence over Anthony was undiminished. In June 1593, she wrote to Anthony 'Be not too frank with that papist. Such have seducing spirits to snare the ungodly.'[28] She signed this letter 'your carefull mother', which for her at this time must surely mean she felt beset by, 'full of', cares rather than our modern use of the word. Given her attitude to these companions of her son's, it is unsurprising that later in the summer of 1593 both Standen and Lawson made themselves scarce 'to avoid the resentment of Lady Bacon', after spending time at the brothers' country retreat in Twickenham.[29]

Anthony had finally responded to the clamour for his return and arrived back in England in early February 1592. He was thirty-four years old, in poor health and badly in need of money. His mother was sixty-four. Anne sent Nicholas Faunt to Dover to meet him and escort him to London. Faunt carried a letter from her to Anthony. It was a qualified welcome home. 'That you are returned at length, I am right glad', she began, but expressed her dismay not only that Thomas Lawson was back on the scene, 'how welcome that could be to your long-grieved mother, judge you', but also that there was bad news about Anthony's health. Like his father, Anthony was periodically crippled by gout: 'I can hardly say whether your gout or his company was the worse tidings'. She would prefer Anthony to rely on the bearer of her letter, Nicholas Faunt, who was a more suitable companion and wise adviser than, she said, those around him who 'pretend and dissemble'. She also quizzed Anthony on his religious observance, reminded him that he had no father to counsel him and sharply remarked he had too little regarded her advice.[30]

Notwithstanding his long absence, after reading this letter Anthony did not hurry to cover the extra miles from London to Gorhambury to visit his mother. Neither did she go to London to see him. As would always be the case for Anthony, fragile health was his excuse, and the February weather did not encourage travel either to or from Gorhambury. A month later, Anne was still unsure when he would come. John Finch the farmer and others wanted to see him, she wrote, 'When your health and leisure serveth to be here'.[31] Although they continued to correspond, for now Anthony did not have to account for himself face-to-face with his mother.

He settled back with Francis in the chambers in Gray's Inn that they had occupied together twelve years earlier and set about trying to repair his disastrous finances. He immediately determined to sell some of his property in Hertfordshire. At the end of February, as she looked out the documents concerning the lease on Redbourn rectory, part of his inheritance from his father, Anne told him the neighbours were against the sale and would prefer him to let the rectory or sell a smaller property. Anthony had the use of the manor house at Redbourn, about five miles from Gorhambury, which he occupied as his occasional Hertfordshire base after his return. Perhaps the neighbours felt positively about the rectory continuing in the ownership of the Bacon family for reasons of local loyalty, or were apprehensive about the estate being broken up and sold piecemeal to unknown incomers.

Anne warned Anthony to be on his guard against those who would take advantage of his inexperience in business. He should be wise and circumspect as the world would be ready to judge him, and he could be vulnerable to taking advice from the wrong people. She wanted him to further his political career using his Hertfordshire connections, but the St Albans townspeople elected two local men as members of parliament, ignoring Anthony. Anne encouraged him not to give up but he did not at first pursue a parliamentary seat (he did later sit in parliament but took little active part); neither was he keen to serve as a Justice of the Peace.[32]

Anthony sought acknowledgement of his work as an intelligencer, and hoped his experience abroad would result in offers of work at home. However, expecting some material recognition from Lord Burghley of his long, unpaid service in France, Anthony received nothing but words, 'yet even in these no offer or hopeful assurance of real kindness which I thought I might justly expect at the lord treasurer's hands, who had inned my ten years' harvest into his own barn without any halfpenny charge', he wrote bitterly to the earl of Essex.[33] Over the years Anne's brother-in-law had continued to distance himself from her sons. In terms of family advancement his own younger son's career was his priority. They were operating as a political team, and in 1596 Robert became principal secretary to the queen. 'The father and son are affectionate, joined in power and policy', wrote Anne to Anthony. She mistrusted Robert Cecil and thought his kind manner of speech to her was intended to deceive.[34]

A powerful man would customarily extend his patronage to a wide network of members of the family, those dependent on him or in his service, recommending them for posts and seeking favours from those in high places. That was how business was done, the fabric of political and court life, and that is what Anthony and Francis expected of their uncle. But Burghley's reply to a letter Anne wrote to him in 1593, requesting help in securing a post for Anthony the year after his return, was silkily courteous and evasive. He regretted he really had less influence than people imagined:

> I thank you for your kind letter, and for your sons, I think your care for them is no less than they both deserve, being so qualified in learning and virtue … For my good will to them, though I am of less power to do my friends good than the world thinketh, yet they shall not want the intention to do them good; and so God continue you in his favour, by your meditations and that I as your old friend, may be the partaker of your good wishes and prayers.[35]

Anne's vital role in helping her brother-in-law into Mary I's favour, her willingness to work on the heavy task of translating the *Apologia*, their close political and family alliances over the years – all past and forgotten, it seemed. Her old friend had nothing to offer her sons. Burghley was training Robert for high office and was not inclined to encourage competition from the difficult and clever Bacon brothers. He did not need them as allies in his own circle. There were also the matters of Anthony's narrow escape from prosecution in France, the brothers' spendthrift habits and their questionable companions. Burghley may have decided to remain aloof from his nephews as they fell into debt and kept what their mother considered to be unhealthy hours and unsavoury company.

Anne's fears about Anthony's Catholic companions resurfaced in 1595 when she learned of his growing friendship with Antonio Perez, a Spaniard in his fifties with a past that included charges of murder, heresy and sodomy: 'I would you were well rid of that old, booted, polling papist,' she wrote. 'He will use discourse out of season to hinder your health.'[36]

She did not know that Anthony had been accumulating contacts and cultivating Catholic intelligence for years. Keeping company with Catholics was one of his tactics, informing his understanding of the international political landscape. His 1580s commonplace book contains lists of Catholics resident in Paris, and he collected and transcribed Catholic treatises. Anthony's web of contacts and informants was sustained through a heavy volume of correspondence. The letters in the archive are testament both to his capacity for hard work and his talent for establishing and maintaining friendships and connections. Although shunning public office – and falling sick any time there was a question of appearing at Elizabeth's court – rarely stirring from home and frequently confined to his room by ill-health (the gout would leave him almost crippled and he was troubled by kidney stones), he kept his finger on the political pulse of Europe and was recognised at the highest levels as a talented intelligence gatherer. Henry Wotton, later one of his political associates in the household of the earl of Essex, summed him up: 'A gentleman of impotent feet, but a nimble head … being of a provident nature … and well knowing the advantage of a dangerous secret.'[37]

With Anthony back in the country, Anne's worries about unsuitable companions found their focus in his household servants. Anthony's retinue aroused her suspicious disapproval. She thought his men were lazy and over indulged. 'Keep not superfluous servants to mar them with idleness and undo you,' she urged. Nevertheless the households of Gorhambury and Redbourn were intertwined and Anne took responsibility for some outgoings connected with Redbourn. One of Anthony's servants, Pierre, 'weeps for new clothes,' she reports, and she will pay for them. But she thinks the fashion for tight and skimpy hose is shocking. The Redbourn tailor makes everything 'so abominably scant, both men's and boys' hose before, that their filthiness is ready to be seen upon every step, going or stooping'.[38] Such flaunting of men's anatomy she thinks beastly and sinful – 'So ungodly becomes England under the holy and pure gospel'.[39]

Anne's letters are seasoned with many such caustic remarks about her sons' serving men, their careless habits and the cost of keeping them. 'If you keep all your Redbourn household at London, you will undo yourself. Money is very hard to come by and sure friends more hard … your debts will pinch you,' she warned Anthony. Francis she thought was 'robbed and spoiled wittingly by his base exalted men, which with Welsh wiles prey upon him'. They were too intimate and too indulged: she names 'that bloody Peerce' (probably Henry Percy, one of his servants), whom she says Francis keeps as 'coach companion and bed companion, a proud, profane, costly fellow, whose being about him I verily fear the Lord God doth mislike'.[40] While we might assume that it is a suspected sexual relationship that has caused her outrage, it seems equally fuelled by the servant Percy's position of general intimacy and access to the expensive luxuries enjoyed by her gentleman son. We do not know if Anne ever directly addressed the question of her sons' sexualities with them.

Applied to by Anthony to clear some of Francis's debts in April 1593, Anne wrote angrily about Francis's tangled finances and the hangers-on she colourfully describes as 'cormorant seducers and instruments of Satan'.[41] Anne had not lost her knack for a striking phrase. She names 'Edney, a filthy wasteful knave, and his Welsh men one after another' as among the worst of them, before conceding she might help. The chamber servant Francis Edney survived Anne's wrath, remaining in service until Bacon's death when he was left the substantial sum of £200.[42]

Anne still feared her adult sons were drifting in the wrong direction in the absence of a father to guide them. 'God help both my poor sons,' she wrote to her nephew Robert Cecil in 1594, 'They feel the smarting want of a father now in their ripe age'.[43] She did what she could for her sons but verged on despair: '…the state of you both doth much disquiet me,' she wrote to Anthony in the spring of 1593. 'I have been too ready for you both till nothing is left.' In the same letter she spoke of her grief that her sons were 'so besotted' with those that had 'greatly abused and spent you': she was convinced that the servants were dissolute chancers who took advantage of her sons, extracting money and favours while doing little. She doubts she can trust her sons to be her executors, saying she will instead give away what few goods she has left to her servants.[44] She found no echo of her standards of thrift, propriety, piety and order in her sons' lives.

Anne closely followed Francis's bids to land a government post, with regular exchanges on the progress of his attempts to enlist support from influential patrons. She advised where she could, spoke to her nephew Robert about Francis's prospects of preferment, and at least once approached Lord Burghley in person at his London house. Though her family connection kept open this privileged access, Anne did not succeed in her attempts to further her sons' careers. How much Burghley knew of Anne's state of mind regarding her sons can only be conjectured. While some contact was maintained between Francis and Anthony and their uncle, they had to use the connection carefully. In a letter to his mother Francis mentioned a wardship in Burghley's gift, but said he would not open the matter himself, as he needed at that time to 'reserve my Lord to be my friend with the Queen'.[45]

In 1596, Anne's younger sister Elizabeth Russell, then aged sixty, attempted to reconcile Anthony with Burghley. Having established with Burghley that he distrusted Anthony for reasons that included his continued association with Catholics and his intelligence work for the earl of Essex, she relayed a list of these 'charges' in person to her nephew. He refuted them, citing among other things his original commission from Walsingham to gather intelligence, maintaining that the imprisonment of his messenger Lawson had been in part due to his mother's 'passionate importunity, grounded upon false suggestions and surmises', and adding that his mother had told him his cousin Robert viewed Anthony as his mortal enemy. Elizabeth went back to Burghley with persuasive arguments on Anthony's behalf but she failed to heal the family rift.[46]

The gap between their fortunes and those of Robert Cecil grew wider. Robert, trained and promoted by his father, moved into high office and accumulated a great fortune of his own through shrewd investment of his official revenues in land purchases. His cousins became ever more indigent, drawing on the family resources and selling land to cover their debts, to the despair of their mother. The brothers extracted the best goods from Gorhambury, requesting carpets and cups, pictures and beds, globes and astrolabes, which Anne duly packed up and sent to their lodgings in London. Sir Nicholas had made provision in his will for Anthony to take possession of up to half the contents of Gorhambury. It is surely likely that he visualised his son married with a settled household, not leading a rackety life in bachelor quarters at Gray's Inn and Redbourn.

The house was being emptied around Anne as Anthony claimed the choicest contents. Packing up a valuable carpet and portraits of ancient philosophers to send to him in London, Anne wrote that she had diligently looked after the household furnishings her husband had left, but 'you have now bared this house of all the best.

A wife would have well regarded such things, but now they shall serve for use of gaming or tippling upon the table of every common person ... and so be spoiled as at Redbourn'. We can imagine dusty unkempt rooms at Redbourn manor, with servants lounging and squabbling. One of them, a servant called Streetly, had set the house out of order, Anne heard, and had hit another servant in the eye. 'I pray God you hear not of some mischief by him,' she wrote to Anthony, adding 'But my sons have no judgement. They will have such about them and in their house ... I cannot cease to warn as long as I am a mother that loveth you in the lord most dearly.'[47]

The two adult young men economised on their outgoings by dipping into estate resources for goods and services as well as money. Anne paid out-of-season coal bills for Anthony at astronomical prices and picked up their debts for groceries and physic. She supplied domestic goods to them both, and maintained a steady supply of food and drink carted from Gorhambury to London (at more expense) for them. In one letter in June 1593 Anthony asked for four hogsheads of beer to entertain company for Francis and 'a gentleman from beyond sea', a gilt cup of his father's, and two horses for his coach, despite Anne's warnings that he could not afford to keep a coach in London with all its attendant expenses of stabling, fodder and grooms.[48] These were not just occasional gifts and treats from the estate to supplement their London supplies. Anne was heavily subsidising their households. She tried to keep a grip over this expenditure and queried exorbitant bills from some of the tradesmen, requiring her sons to provide detailed records and accounts, but the demands piled up.

Anthony continued to drain the estate, attempting to cover his debts by selling off the assets his father had left. On 10 November 1593 Anne gave him her life interest in the manor of Napsbury. In 1597 he asked her to sign a deed of mortgage on land in Cheddar with an annual rent of £30, bought by his father in 1553, and at the same time told her of his intention to sell Napsbury. His mother was distressed about the land sale and that he had already disposed of lands in Barley and Pinner: 'I hope you mean it not. The chiefest manor hereabouts. Have you no hope of posterity?'

She was saddened that her sons had no wives and children, as we have seen writing that she would have been happy to have grandchildren, but she seems to have kept hope alive, advising Anthony five years later to look after his health so that God might bless him with a good marriage. Her outbursts about Francis's serving men indicate she understood that he too preferred relationships with men. Rumours circulated about his sexual tastes. The gossip became more open and detailed, naming names, after his fall from royal favour in 1621. Francis Bacon, reported John Aubrey in his *Brief Lives*, had 'his Ganymedes and favourites', and there were stories about how he indulged them with favours and money.[49]

We should not lose sight of the fact that modern assumptions about male-male relationships may not reflect their nature or significance in the early modern era. Men's relationships with each other existed across a spectrum of friendship, affection and intimacy, with or without the erotic contact today defined as 'homosexual'. Although it is likely that both Anthony and Francis were sexually active with men, they also cultivated intimate friendships that 'were varied, public, highly valued and sometimes contentious – especially when they clashed with more formalised alliance systems such as marriage,' writes Will Tosh in his study of male friendship in Anthony Bacon's circle. While we might assume that, as a pious woman, Anne would consider her sons' behaviour to be sinful, homosexual activity itself may not have been the most significant concern for men and women in the sixteenth century: rather it was the disruptive impact such relations could have upon the established social order of both private and public life at any level.[50] Whatever her feelings about this aspect of their lives, with her sons unmarried – perhaps, she may have feared, unmarriageable – and without stable careers, Anne was left in a limbo where social expectations of her family were not being met, and her relations with her sons could not progress beyond that of mother and unmarried child.

In his will Nicholas had charged Anne with the 'well bringing up' of their sons, thus handing her the responsibility of establishing them with financially stable households and rewarding professional lives. Her attempts to fulfil this, through invoking her brother-in-law's help, and warning and counselling her sons, were frustrated. For three decades, Anne had seen at first hand how careers were built in Elizabethan England. She knew that with no father or powerful patron to promote their advancement, her sons were unlikely to succeed. On a more immediate level, she was irked by Anthony's lack of energy and strategic retreat into illness, and Francis's carelessness. She rebuked Anthony for his lack of action, his indoor, invalid's life and his work that relied on words, not active experience of life in his own country:

> You are said to be wise, and to my comfort I willingly think so, but surely son, on the other side for want of home experience by action and your tedious unacquaintance for your own country by continual chamber and bedkeeping you must needs miss of considerate judgement in your verbal only travailing.[51]

Francis, she wrote, during angry exchanges about debts, was 'his father's first chis' – his chosen, dearest child – and had gifts of natural wit and understanding, if only he would use them rightly. She grieved the loss of Nicholas's influence over her sons and did her best to advise and assist them, but her admonitions were largely ignored. Anne expressed distress and anger, sometimes despair, at their tangled lives. Her letters include direct attacks about their behaviour, though she hopes that by heeding her guidance and counsel, her motherly and godly advice, they may improve.

When she found they had no learned man to advise them she thought of sending her minister, the elderly Mr Wyborn. It is unlikely that either Anthony or Francis, who kept both irregular hours and ill-regulated servants and whose early piety seems to have dwindled, accepted. While the correspondence records that Wyborn did appear briefly at one point in Anthony's company and is mentioned as a possible companion on a visit to Bath, at other times the brothers politely rebuffed their mother's offer of godly men to give them moral and religious guidance.

Perhaps Anne's insistence on the good influence of her 'learned men', and her occasional suggestion that she should send them to London to edify her wayward sons, contributed to Anthony's and Francis's reluctance to visit her. Meanwhile the godly preachers were working their way through the best wine in the Gorhambury cellars. They knew what remained in the household stores from the Lord Keeper's time and were not reluctant to ask for it: 'If you be content so, I would pierce a vessel of your old claret wine. I offer the white wine, but learned men and some others ask for claret,' she wrote in the spring of 1594, also mentioning that Wyborn had a touch of gout.

Though there was, over the years, a steady exchange of letters between her and Anthony over matters ranging from the supply of beer to property transactions, Anne felt there was too little regular engagement with both sons: 'I may think much lack of kindness and duty in you and your brother that never write to me,' she reproved Anthony. His response was sharp and defensive: he would rather hear nothing at all from her than be bothered with issues that, he wrote, 'springing many times more out of jealousy and motherly apprehension, than out of truth, trouble your Ladyship more than they can profit me'.[52] The tone of her letters sometimes irked him, and he found her demands and reproaches intrusive, but Anthony was enmeshed in the web of obligation that required him to be a dutiful son to his mother and attend – even minimally – to the estate his father had left to him, however unwillingly he conformed to this role. Francis too sometimes jibbed at his mother's demands and advice, once complaining that she was treating him like a ward, whilst he remained dependent on her for help in managing his debts.

In turn Anne had no option but to settle into an uneasy accommodation with their lives. Her financial predicament continued, almost entirely due to her sons draining the resources their father had left to maintain the family, and her inability to stop them. It cannot have taken long for her to realise they were never going to follow their father's practice of careful accounting and husbanding of assets, yet she continued to prop them up financially, no doubt hoping that if she supported them for long enough their standing in the world would be protected and their fortunes would improve. She was not the only casualty of their insatiable need for cash. Nicholas Trott, an old friend of the brothers from Gray's Inn, was mercilessly tapped for loans. They borrowed everywhere, leaving a trail of debt and keeping the vaguest of financial records.[53]

Although clashes over money occurred repeatedly, not all Anne's exchanges with her sons were confrontational. Very many of the letters between Anne and Anthony are busy with practical details and with news, both local and political. She remained attentive and affectionate towards both sons, despite her exasperation with their way of life. She supplied them with beer brewed at Gorhambury and sent Peter the kitchen boy to trudge the twenty-five miles to London with seasonal game, pigeons, fresh trout – a 'faint-hearted fish,' she wrote, that must be boiled as soon as possible – and baskets of strawberries. Her gifts and messages could be thoughtful and loving. She sent young pigeons in springtime, an extra delicacy for their London tables and reminder of childhood: 'I send between your brother and you the first flight of my dovehouse,' she wrote in April 1595, 'twelve to you and sixteen to your brother, because he was wont to love them better than you from a boy.'[54]

From long experience of treating her husband's gout, she advised Anthony on managing the condition. She would often tag on such advice at the end of her letters, a domestic and intimate reminder to take physic at the right time, or 'keep the affected part warm'. Anthony also suffered from kidney stones and kept her updated when the condition flared up. Again drawing on her experience of treating his father, who had had the same condition, she recommended a detailed regime: an almond milk and herb drink, baths of milk and boiled herbs (which he should sit in, up to his loins, for two hours), anointing the genitals with oils of almonds and linseed and, *in extremis*, gently inserting a crow quill to turn and dislodge the stone in the urethra. She offered to go over to Redbourn and prepare the bath for him herself, as she had done for his father.[55] Anne sometimes wrote at more length about their general health, exhorting both sons to have regular meals and sleep – she warns them sitting up late will make 'your limbs stark and your body bothered' – avoid late and heavy suppers, get up early and take exercise.[56] They should not stay awake at night thinking too hard then lie around in bed late into the morning, and she told Francis not to have musicians playing to lull him to sleep, which was a decadent practice, in her view.

Living alone at Gorhambury, Anne no longer had regular, immediate access to the most powerful and influential at court, but she still sometimes attended. She considered herself experienced enough in that world to advise and counsel her sons continually. 'I think for my long attending at court,' she wrote to Anthony, 'and a chief counsellor's wife, few *preclarae feminae mea sortis* [distinguished women of my sort] are able to speak and judge of such ... worldly doings of men.'[57] And she warned him to take her words seriously: 'Read not my letters either scoffingly or carelessly, which hath been used too much. For I humbly thank God I know what I write and counsel.'[58]

In 1594 Anthony moved from what Anne considered to be the 'good air and Christian company' of Gray's Inn to lodgings in Bishopsgate Street. She was alarmed: she had heard the area was unhealthy and full of lewd company. Francis was living in Twickenham. She was concerned that neither area had a competent minister, and there would be no godly instruction for her sons in either place. In

1595 she advised Anthony against a proposed move of lodgings into the earl of Essex's house on the Strand, which would confirm his position as adviser to the earl and member of the inner circle of the Essex coterie. She feared the move would unsettle him, remove his independence and leave him open to political manoeuvrings, suspicion and disagreement with those around him there. She again invoked her long experience and knowledge of princely courts, which led her to fear he would be seen as the earl's follower, not his friend, trading his freedom for bondage and observed by treacherous servants who would gossip about him. She quoted a line from Horace to reinforce her warning, *dulcis inexperto cultura potentis amici,* translated by Allen as 'those who have never tried it think it pleasant to court a friend in power'.[59]

Having devoted most of her letter to this serious cautionary advice, Anne moved on to a miscellany of other matters: a gift of venison she had received from her neighbour Mr Sadler – 'very good flesh and fair killed' – a mention of the earl of Essex's wife and his mother-in-law, and advice to Anthony about his health. The topics she addressed in a short postscript vary from a reminder in the first sentence that she is sending Anthony and Francis ten pigeons each, to a swipe in the next at her *bêtes noires* Standen and Lawson whose presence, she says, will cause Anthony to be 'more misliked and suspected' (i.e. of Catholic sympathies). Her letter ends, 'God keep you safe from Spanish subtleties and popery.' Anne could cover a dizzying mix of subjects in a few sentences in her letters to her sons. Like her translations, her letters are full of small word pictures – a man called Large is 'a whining and crafty fellow,' she wrote in her next letter to Anthony, while 'The Bishop [Richard Fletcher, bishop of London] is a grave and comely man.'[60]

The result of the distancing of the Bacons from the Cecils was that both Francis and Anthony sought secure patronage elsewhere once Anthony was back in England. They crossed over to the opposing faction at court, becoming allied with the earl of Essex and building influence in the inner circle around the earl. Francis provided political advice and Anthony built on his web of contacts to expand and run the earl's European intelligence network. Housing a full secretariat of well-informed staff, Essex House was in effect a political headquarters as well as the earl's London home. Anthony's and Francis's fortunes had become firmly entwined with those of the earl. Whether or not his mother's warnings gave him pause, Anthony once again ignored her counsel and in 1595 he moved into Essex House, the earl's London mansion on the Strand.

Chapter 16
Mistress of Gorhambury

'My two chief service horses are sick. God help me,' Anne wrote to Anthony in May 1593. Shortly after this, one horse was dead, another unwell. Just a month later, in the midst of June haymaking – when Anne writes that it is so hot and dry that the grass is burning away – there was more trouble: 'My fine black hobby [a medium-sized work horse] for service is complaining, not well. God save the beast; I know not how to do for service if it continue.'[1] Her worry about the horse was urgent. She needed good quality horses for the work of the estate and one of the best she had been left was ill – how would she manage? This forceful woman with a keen intellect, who had served at court and mixed with senior political and religious figures, was tied to a country estate where money was short and her sons stayed away.

Life at court can hardly have prepared Anne for the nuts and bolts of farming life, but now she was faced with daily practical problems and decisions. The estate's working horses were expensive pieces of living farm machinery that she could ill-afford to replace; there were other horses to worry about as well. Anthony wanted a saddle horse in London. She reluctantly sent him one (with the gloomy name of 'Loss'), but wrote this left her with no spare horse 'for friend or preacher'. She had too few saddles to give him one: 'If I had been able I would have bought more.'[2] Three of her 'great horses' and a 'special gelding' were lost or dead by 1596, while a 'furious fellow' brandishing a sword had tried to carry off a light riding horse of hers while it was waiting to be shod at Redbourn. 'The loss of such horses and my son's sickly state will even go very near my heart,' wrote Anne, reporting her local troubles to her nephew Robert Cecil, whom she must now respectfully address as 'good Mr Secretary'.[3]

Anne's letter to Anthony mentioning the black hobby begins with a proposal for a visit: 'About beginning of the next week, son, I mean, if it please God, to step to London to see and know how it is with you for your health and business and not long after to send some beer. July will come on a pace for your brother's debt to Cornellis.' That letter answered a deferential, careful one from Anthony, into which was woven a request for supplies of beer. Beer, a daily staple at that time, was one of the commodities the brothers found it convenient to source from their mother, at no cost to themselves. Anne's answer – I am coming to see you, then you will get the beer – was an unwelcome surprise. Replying the same day, Anthony fended off the visit. He warned his mother about dangerous infections in the parish she intended to lodge in and said that he and Francis could tell her anything she wanted to know by letter.[4] It seems clear Anthony did not want his mother coming to see about his health and business, or to ask difficult questions about Francis's debts. He did not want to have to think about working horses. Anne kept Anthony informed as far as she could but it was difficult for her to fix his attention on the issues relating to management of the estate, money and property that she felt were important. She was weary: 'Myself, my horses and my money is as good as spent all,' she wrote to him in 1594.[5]

Getting barrels of beer to her sons in London was not a straightforward matter. It involved arranging haulage, either by hiring someone, which was expensive, or sparing her own horses and carts, which she needed for estate work, and she sometimes refused to do this. She had to make sure that the brewing was done by a competent brewer and had been training estate worker Osborne's wife to learn the craft, despite the costs going up and her suspicion that this servant had been pilfering from the house (among other things, one of Anthony's best shirts was missing).[6] There must always be beer for the household, of various strengths, as it was everyone's daily drink in an age when supplies of clean water could not be relied on. It did not last for long, so had to be transported, stored and drunk before it was unfit. Anne often wrote to Anthony with detailed instructions about how the barrels she was sending him should be handled and when the latest brew should be drunk.

As well as farming and housekeeping Anne had general estate business to manage. She counselled Anthony not to turn out good long-term tenants in his quest for better returns on his leases: Goodman Rolfe and his 'ancient wife' were grieved to hear they might not have their farm lease renewed, she told him. Conversely the widow Finch unwisely had her eye on 'such a foul, blotted' man as a second husband, a loose-living, indebted man with numerous children, that Anne had advised her that if she married him she should not continue as a tenant, but 'go away and dwell with him to avoid obloquy'.[7]

Despite the many cares of estate life Anne's horizons remained wider than Hertfordshire and she received news from different sources. Through Anthony she kept up with the London political world, and conversations with her old friends at court yielded first-hand news of the queen. One of her informants was Lady Dorothy Stafford, a senior member of the Privy Chamber and an old friend. Anne mentioned that Lady Stafford had alerted her to the queen's 'marvelling' that Anthony had not been to see her. Anthony's letters sometimes referred to European politics and Francis Goad, another associate of the earl of Essex, reported directly to Anne on conditions in France, 'this ruinous kingdom', just before Henri of Navarre renounced his Protestant faith to take the crown of France as a Catholic. After her years at court, Anne had not lost the desire to be well informed.

A letter from Anne sent in early May, 1595, addressed 'To my son Mr Bacon at Bishopsgate. This was meant to be sent with the beere'. Anne goes into detail about the brewing and transport of the beer, in varying strengths, which if well kept will last until Michaelmas. She complains about Lawson's handing of the horses and ends with a prayer for Anthony's health to improve. The added note in the margin is about a mastiff Anthony has sent, that she suspects 'will hunt after sheep and is too old'. Lambeth Palace Library PL 651, f. 156. Image courtesy of Lambeth Palace Library. Photograph: Deborah Spring.

Domestic life at Gorhambury could be fraught when Anne thought servants were being careless or difficult. On occasion she terrified them with angry words and summary dismissal: 'A man master would go nigh to break thy head for this speech, but I bid thee get out of my sight like a lying proud varlet,' she exploded at Edward Spencer, a tippling horse keeper in Anthony's service, whereupon, she says, he ran to the stable and 'jetted away like a jack [rabbit]'.[8]

This episode happened in May 1593, when Anne complained that Spencer had not looked after the horses properly and had lied and 'wrangled disdainfully' with her. They got on badly. On another occasion she berated him for his behaviour when he came back late after hawking. It was the prelude to more trouble as there seems to have been a general breakdown of order and discipline between Anne and her servants, including Spencer and Osborne and the latter's wife the brewer, the next summer. She referred to this time in a letter to Anthony the following year – 'my servants of that sort [the Osbornes] with Edward [Spencer] and such brake out of order with me last summer'.[9]

She was indeed 'unquiet' with all her household, reported Spencer to Anthony, following a disturbing incident while Spencer was staying at Gorhambury. He was told to look after a bitch – it is not clear by whom – but according to Spencer when Anne saw the animal she demanded he kill it, sending a servant to tell him 'if I did not make her away she would not sleep in her bed'. Spencer, obeying what he took to be an order, hanged the bitch. Yet he says this only stoked Anne's fury: she told him he was mad and to go home to his master. She was still not speaking to him. 'I will give none [no] offence to make her angry; but nobody can please her long together,' Spencer told Anthony.[10]

What are we to make of this story? There is no corroboration by anyone else who was there, yet the detail is so particular and vivid that it seems credible. It is not the first time we have seen Anne apparently overwhelmed and out of temper. Our knowledge of her is too fragmented, and the passage of time too long to speculate closely on the state of her mind or health that lay behind such outbursts. We know enough of her circumstances, though, to guess that anxiety, loneliness, her sons' behaviour and her own ageing and fatigue probably all played their part. The comfort and prosperity of her married years, life at court as a respected figure, her hours of leisured study and the companionship of a loved and like-minded husband had been replaced by decades of a scrimping life in the country with little security or support.

A picture of Anne as an angry, even mentally unstable, elderly woman has built up over the centuries, not least because of a comment by the seventeenth-century bishop of Gloucester, Godfrey Goodman, who described her as 'little better than frantic in her age'.[11] We can only speculate on how reliable a piece of evidence that is: Godfrey would only have been in his twenties when she died, and his account was written some forty years later. Both Standen and Spencer complained to Anthony of encounters with Anne, framing her as irrational and impossible to please. This line has been followed by some historians of the Bacon family, including James Spedding in the nineteenth century and Jardine and Stewart in the twentieth, dismissing Anne as beset with anxiety and jealousies, her judgement in question. However more recently, Gemma Allen offers a more nuanced approach to the question of Anne's 'unquietness'. She suggests that Spencer's attitude to Anne, together with Lawson and other servants of Anthony's, arose from their unwillingness to acknowledge her power and authority as mistress of Gorhambury for her lifetime. They stirred up trouble and turned to Anthony for decisions. Allen contrasts their characterisation of Anne as perpetually difficult with the accounts of her written by Captain Allen, who was not entangled within the Bacon households. Despite her anger when he broached the subject of Lawson, he sympathised with her feeling for her absent son.[12]

Maintaining her authority over the servants and estate workers was an endless problem for Anne. While some of the men at Gorhambury were good workers, others took to drink and thieving and it became harder to keep control. Intruders hunted unchecked in the woods. Anne bemoaned her inability to tackle them: 'Idle Redbourn men hunt here almost daily; if I were not sickly and weak I would out myself with all kinds of dogs against them and kill theirs.' Anne had plenty to say about villainous locals and servants, at various times describing them as naughty and subtle, vile vagabonds and tipsy varlets. She struggled with the responsibility of asserting her authority over these local troublemakers – everyone knew that the real master was Anthony, yet he was rarely there. Nevertheless, when Anthony offered to ask Richard Lockey, the mayor of St Albans, to come out to resolve a dispute with a tenant for her she refused. She had no time for Lockey, 'an open mouthed man without all discretion, full of foolish babbling' who would only make things worse.[13]

In December 1596 Anne wrote to her now powerful nephew Sir Robert Cecil to complain about the people of St Albans. The town was always in disorder, she said. The poor were allowed to stray everywhere, breaking fences, begging, laying open enclosures and hacking and stealing wood, 'besides the hurt they do tippling, taverning and drunken idleness and gaming, which is almost this town's profession'. They had broken up the Gorhambury water conduit to steal the lead and attacked her servants.[14]

The master of a large estate with plenty of work to offer would have overseen the manorial court, which dealt with some petty offences and regulated local economic life, and probably become a Justice of the Peace for the county, taking an active part in local government through these institutions. By contrast, Anne had no formal legal authority over the community, and Anthony, though he had reluctantly accepted the appointment, avoided sitting as a county Justice of the Peace. The Gorhambury manorial court functioned under the direction of a steward, in this case a legally qualified official appointed by Anne with Anthony's agreement, to a certain extent policing social order. While Anne took a close interest in the business of the court and reported it to Anthony, a steward did not have the authority of a leading local figure.

Not all Anne's female contemporaries felt powerless in the face of local trouble. Her own sister Elizabeth engaged in high-profile law cases, pitching in at the highest levels of Privy Council and Star Chamber. Elizabeth went into these battles with ferocious energy, recruiting the support of Lord Burghley and Robert Cecil for her legal campaigns, and once insisting on addressing the court for half an hour despite being told she should remain silent.[15] By contrast Anne was cautious about taking to law, and there is no trace of her approaching any legal issue with the gusto that Elizabeth brought to the process. In her letters she told Anthony of the manorial court's business and discussed transactions connected with the estate such as the renewal and transfer of leases. Her known encounters with the legal system are formal transfers of land to and by her sons, and two recorded cases in which she is named.

Between 1587 and 1591 she was the plaintiff in a case involving property in Old Bailey, London.[16] In 1600, together with one George Orlibye, she was named in a suit brought by John Digby and Thomas Preston concerning the Gorhambury estate's watermills on the river Ver in St Albans. The estate included Prae Mill, which powered Sir Nicholas's waterworks pumping water uphill to the house; Kingsbury Mill in the parish of St Michaels (formerly a malt mill, it had been part of the St Albans Abbey estate before the Dissolution); and a mill 'lately erected by the Lady Ann Bacon' called the Abbey Mill.[17]

Over a distance of ten miles in and near St Albans the waters of the Ver, one of Hertfordshire's rare chalk streams, powered up to a dozen mills. They were used for grinding grain, cleaning cloth and sawing wood. The flow of water was variable, especially in the summer, so that the volume of water used by the Gorhambury mills and abstracted from the river to supply the house may have reduced the water available to drive an older mill further downstream. The complainants alleged that Lady Bacon's mills infringed the ancient custom of 'suit and grist' whereby a tenant was legally obliged to grind their corn at the landowner's mill. In other words, the older mill was losing revenue from tenants, whether because the water flow was insufficient or because the tenants were using the Gorhambury mills – or both. This case was brought when Anne was in her last decade. The other person named with her, George Orlibye, was probably her agent or tenant. She must have approved the construction of the new mill although, unless it was funded by the tenant or Francis, it is unlikely that she financed a capital project, given her lack of income.

Even adding to her variable estate revenues the generous personal annuity of £200 from her jointure, the total was insufficient to maintain the house and estate to the standard she had been used to during her marriage. Her husband had apparently left her adequately provided for, with land and leases to generate sufficient revenue during her lifetime, in addition to his house. Her position as a widow managing family property and money was not unusual. Other widows in similar circumstances were busy administering estates, hiring officials to help them, supervising tenants and employees and generating sufficient revenues to cover their expenditure.[18] Anne's own widowed step-grandmother Margaret Cooke had been astute in business, ably managing her stepson's property and financial interests until he came of age and leaving substantial assets in her will. Anne was not so fortunate.

As her husband had lacked funds to complete before his death the provision he had planned for his second family, the revenues from Gorhambury, with its associated manors and leases, had to cover the cost of maintaining Anne and her two sons as well as all the outgoings of the estate. We have seen how Anthony depleted his mother's revenues, spending freely as he travelled in France, then after his return in 1592 negotiating to sell property left to him directly. The following year he asked Anne to pass to him her life interest in three manors, Napsbury, Burston and Windridge, and other local land left with Gorhambury to generate revenue. She was reluctant but agreed, presumably seeing no other solution to his difficulties. True to form, Anthony began to sell those off too. Some years after Nicholas's death Anne had granted Francis, with conditions, the property of Marks in Essex. This was another of her manors, which Anne and Francis jointly leased to a tenant. She intended the revenue to help support Francis, as his father had only been able to leave him some low-value marshland in Woolwich. By 1592 however, Francis was ignoring her conditions and raising money against Marks by mortgaging it. By April 1593 he was £1,300 in debt and trying to sell the manor, which he finally did in 1596.

The cumulative effect of the selling-off of lands that had brought in revenue in multiple ways (from leases, rents, mills, produce), the inability of Anthony and Francis to secure reliable forms of income or look after the remaining family properties, and their plundering of their mother's ready cash and property assets created a long-running financial nightmare for Anne in her widowhood. Even her reliable twice-yearly jointure income was depreciating as inflation reduced the value of the fixed sum she received.[19] It is no wonder that the tone of her letters to her sons can sound beleaguered and angry. She herself, she wrote, had kept house and stayed out of debt, not buying anything of value.[20]

Apart from her unhelpful sons, who else could Anne turn to in the family? Three close members of her own family had died while Anthony was in France. Her sister Katherine, who was married to Henry Killigrew, a diplomat, died aged forty-one in 1583 after the birth of a stillborn baby, leaving four daughters.[21] She had lived just north of London at Hendon, some fifteen miles from Anne at Gorhambury, but no evidence has surfaced so far to tell us how much contact there was between them. Mildred's daughter Anne, who had a deeply unhappy marriage with the earl of Oxford, died in 1588 and Mildred herself died in early 1589, leaving Anne and Elizabeth as the surviving sisters.

There is scant mention of her sisters in Anne's letters, and nothing to shed light on how far Anne's relationship with Mildred survived the divergence in their fortunes. Anne no longer enjoyed being at court, only going there occasionally to see the queen and her own Privy Chamber friends, according to Nicholas Faunt.[22] By the time of her death Mildred had everything that Anne now lacked: wealth, status, influence, an important husband who was devoted to her, a successful son, and grandchildren. The Burghleys regularly entertained the queen at Theobalds. Mildred had money of her own to leave bequests to charities and colleges, and her wardrobe included luxurious gowns that had been owned by Anne of Cleves. Mildred's London funeral procession was almost as grand an occasion as the Lord Keeper's had been ten years earlier. A surviving document among the Cecil papers lists the great personages who attended. Anne's younger sister Elizabeth, Lady Russell, was the chief mourner and Anne joined the other women of the family and friends from court in the procession.[23] Burghley was deeply bereft, inconsolable. His lengthy Latin epitaph to his wife was inscribed on the large and elaborate tomb he built for her and their daughter in Westminster Abbey.

In the autumn of 1593 Anne was unwell at home with a fever. She told Anthony that she did not want to see him, or her sister Elizabeth, who had suggested a visit. She wanted to keep her house quiet and not be encumbered with lodging her sister, she wrote. Perhaps she preferred solitude, or perhaps the extra domestic effort and expense of entertaining her wealthy sister was out of the question. Elizabeth had survived two husbands, Sir Thomas Hoby, diplomat and translator, who died in his thirties leaving her pregnant with their third child (a son, inevitably named Thomas Posthumous), and Lord John Russell who died in 1584, with whom she had two daughters. Unlike her struggling sister, Elizabeth had no money problems, entertaining the queen and court at Bisham Abbey, her house in Berkshire in 1592.[24] Anne occasionally saw Elizabeth in London when they attended sermons together, and once recorded travelling home to Gorhambury in her sister's comfortable coach, carefully driven by 'a comely man'.[25]

Anne's relations with her stepchildren remained broken following the dispute over the will. Her connection with them never recovered. Even important family news arrived second-hand. Anne was taken by surprise at the news of the marriage of her stepdaughter Elizabeth to Sir William Peryam, a judge, in 1595. It was Elizabeth's second marriage and Peryam's third. 'I never had any inkling of [it] before Crosby told [me]', she wrote to Anthony, asking for more details. Anthony's reply does not survive, but it must have been uncomplimentary as Anne later wrote to him that though his half-sister's nature was unkind, he should keep his views to himself and not openly deride her.

Bartholomew Kemp, the cousin who had for many years assisted with managing the estate finances, occupied a London house that contained some of the residual household goods from York House, after Nicholas's death. But by 1594 Kemp was in financial trouble himself, owing money to Anne. Thinking she might have to go to law to recover it, Anne asked Anthony to advise how she should proceed. Francis joined in the correspondence, reporting to her that Kemp had left town, giving the keys of his house to Francis in case his mother might seek to recover property from it. Francis took the opportunity to ask for the house contents, having discovered to his surprise that domestic implements were very costly to buy for himself.[26]

Anne's closest connections outside the family were the radical clergymen she befriended and supported. She actively campaigned on their behalf, using her influential connections and her own patronage – she had the disposal of two clerical livings in Hertfordshire – to further the Puritan cause. Her support for the nonconformists during her widowhood may have led to a cooling of her relationship with Mildred, who had conformed to the established church and was friendly with John Whitgift, appointed Archbishop of Canterbury in 1583, and other senior church leaders.

Determined to bring the nonconformists into line, Whitgift imposed conditions on all clergy. They included rules about qualifications to preach, wearing the correct vestments, and an interdict on preaching and catechising in private places and families. This was a direct challenge to the Puritans who believed that prayer should not be mediated by any kind of ritual and who variously refused to wear formal clothing such as surplices, make the sign of the cross at a child's baptism, or use the Church of England prayer book. Anyone who did not agree with and obey Whitgift's rules was forbidden to preach. Whitgift established a Court of High Commission that operated through a swift and secret inquisitorial process, to adjudicate on dissident preachers' cases. Lord Burghley likened the court to the infamous Catholic Inquisition, but Whitgift was supported by the queen, who shared his dislike of Puritanism. Although Whitgift had been close to the Bacon family when he taught Anthony and Francis at Cambridge, his drive to oust nonconformists moved Francis to write to the queen complaining of his old tutor's persecution of 'careful and diligent preachers' – one particular target of Whitgift's campaign was Walter Travers, the Temple church preacher whose sermons Francis attended with Anne.

Anne was fiercely opposed to Whitgift's imposition of conformity. She sought justice for the dissident preachers and supported the opposition to Whitgift's Articles, the detailed list of rules that had been drawn up. Anthony's friend Nicholas Faunt admired her dedication to the cause, noting in a letter to Anthony that he had witnessed her attending at the royal court to solicit help for the 'poor afflicted church'. Of Whitgift's election as archbishop, Faunt wrote, 'The choice of that man at this time to be archbishop maketh me to think that the Lord is even determined to scourge his Church for their unthankfulness.'[27]

After objections to the Articles from members of the Privy Council, including Lord Burghley, Whitgift was sent a petition from the House of Commons opposing them. His response was read to the Commons on 25 February 1585. Highly unusually, for women were not usually admitted, Anne was present in the Commons chamber to hear this. She had been 'extraordinarily admitted' there by Lord Burghley. Whitgift gave no ground to his critics in the response. This grieved Anne, but not wanting to outstay her welcome she left the chamber before having a chance to speak to Burghley. Instead, she wrote to him the next day, again attempting to secure a fair hearing for the preachers. She suggested that 'those that labour for right reformation' should have the opportunity of a quiet audience before the queen or the Privy Council to put their case. They should not be left to the bishops who, she said, were parties in their own defence and sought worldly ambition. The preachers should be permitted to confer together and to be fully heard. She said she had profited more by hearing 'ordinary preaching' over the past seven or eight years than her twenty years of hearing preachers at St Paul's, and that hearing such sermons was a duty given by God to widows.[28] However, Whitgift did not deviate from the course he had set in his inaugural sermon of 1583, in which he denounced the disobedience of 'our wayward and conceited persons', meaning those that loved reformation. His Articles remained unaltered, and Anne continued to assist those who disobeyed them.

Anne had the disposal of the local livings of Redbourn and St Michael's parishes and used these appointments to support her favoured nonconformists. She appointed one of her Gorhambury circle, William Dyke, to the curacy of St Michael's, from which he was ejected by the church authorities, though with the help of the earl of Essex he obtained the living of Hemel Hempstead in 1594. He was succeeded at St Michael's by a minister in the same mould, Erasmus Cooke (who does not appear to have been a relation of Anne's). Cooke was radical, controversial, and preached fervent sermons. On Whitsunday in 1596 he organised a public fast at St Michael's, openly defying a ban on unauthorised fasts. A large crowd of enthusiasts from both within and outside the parish, including other ministers, attended the service. It was an epic occasion that went on for six and a half hours, with Cooke preaching three separate sermons in between prayers and psalm-singing.

Anne and her vicar Mr Cooke seem to have got on well: when Gorhambury was short of staff in the kitchen, she thought of going to stay at his house.[29] He was still the vicar in 1604 and benefiting from Anne's patronage: in that year he took over occupancy of the mansion house of Colney Chapel, one of the minor Bacon properties around St Albans, and he continued at St Michael's until resigning in 1607.[30]

Erasmus Cooke's defiant day of fasting and preaching had followed direct clashes between the local clergy and the ecclesiastical authorities. Matters came to a head under John Aylmer, Bishop of London, who was responsible for St Albans. In the early 1590s he summoned Cooke and other Hertfordshire radicals to be censured for hosting a meeting of Puritan ministers from other dioceses. The then mayor of St Albans, John Clark, was drawn into the ferment. A fervent Puritan, Clark was charged with allowing unlicensed ministers to preach in his house, including 'some such as have been especially disliked and disallowed by authority'.[31]

Anne was outspoken in her view of those who acted against the preachers. In a letter to Anthony she denounced Aylmer as 'a godless bishop' and those serving the archdeaconry of St Albans as 'biting vipers the whole pack of them'. She was aware of the risks she ran in opposing the establishment, warning Anthony to destroy her letter (evidently, he did not): 'Burn this though I write true. Beware of liberal speeches these captious days.'[32]

'I humbly thank God for the comfortable company of Mr Wyborn and Wildblood,' she wrote on 17 May 1592, adding there were those who might fear God's displeasure – 'work the woeful disappointing of God['s] work in his vineyard' – by silencing such men, 'in these bold sinning days. *Haud impune ferent* [they shall be punished] come when it shall'.[33]

These two Puritan preachers were Anne's regular companions at Gorhambury, the ageing Percival Wyburn and a younger man, Humphrey Wildblood. Neither any longer had church livings, after refusing to conform to accepted doctrine.[34] Percival Wyburn had been known to the Bacon household for many years. First employed as a chaplain in 1560, he was later one of the Marian exiles. When the religious climate became inhospitable to nonconformists in his later years, he found refuge at Gorhambury with the widowed Anne. She presented the parish of Redbourn, the second clerical living under her patronage, to Humphrey Wildblood in 1589. Three years later he was deprived of the benefice by the church authorities. He was partially reinstated in 1594, when he was permitted to teach in the archdeaconry, but not to connect with the wider community – he was forbidden to preach or act as a schoolmaster.[35]

In 1597 Anne took up arms on behalf of another of her Redbourn preachers, Rudolph Bradley, who had been excommunicated. She wrote to the man responsible, Dr Edward Stanhope, the Bishop of London's chancellor and a member of Whitgift's Court of High Commission. He happened to be a relation of hers. She opened her letter with a stern admonition: 'I cannot marvel what ails you, Mr Doctor, still to vex the godly ministers of Christ and by your undeserved excommunication to hinder the glory of God so pitifully.' Anne wrote she felt bound to assist Bradley who had been lawfully placed in his post by her. He was a good man whose parishioners needed him. She asked Stanhope to remedy this 'great undoing of her Majesty's people', reminding him of their family connection and her personal status as she signed herself 'In the Lord, A Bacon, your sickly and ancient cousin, late Lord Keeper's widow'.[36]

Anne believed that her status as a godly widow carried spiritual responsibilities for others. Such obligations were derived from the biblical authority of St Paul, whose first letter to Timothy speaks of godly widows engaged in continual supplication and prayer in return for support from the Church. When she appended the word 'widow' to her signature, either in English or in Greek, Anne was usually writing with a particular moral and advisory purpose, structuring her intervention around prayer for the person to whom her advice was being offered.[37] Two such letters were addressed to the earl of Essex, when she felt it her duty to chastise this lofty personage about his behaviour.

In 1595 she was in London attending a sermon. As she chatted afterwards to a court friend (whom she does not name) the subject of swearing came up. The friend told her the earl of Essex was 'a terrible swearer'. These words, says Anne, struck such terror into her heart that she cannot rest until she has sent the earl some useful texts for his remembrance in case he has forgotten them. She goes on to quote a paragraph's worth of biblical warnings against swearing. She adds a prayer for the earl and his 'posterity' – reminding him that he has an example to set for the next generation. Saying this might be the last time he hears from her as she is so old and ill, she signs off with a flourish that referred again to her connections, 'From the confines of ruinated Verulam'.[38]

Essex had not heard the last from Anne about his morals. She wrote to him again in December of the following year. He had just returned to England after a triumphant military campaign against Spain and she congratulated him on this success. However, she had again heard reports about him from a court source – 'upon some speeches of some and with some person at the court, where lately I was' – that worried her. This time, it is a rumour that the earl is having an adulterous affair with Anne's great-niece, the countess of Derby. Anne warns him of the damage to his and the lady's reputations and the risk of violent revenge by the husband, before quoting the Bible and exhorting him to consider the danger he is in, body and soul. Not to mention the sorrow he will cause his pregnant wife: 'O honourable and valiant noble … make not her heart sorrowful to the hindrance of her young fruit within her.' As in her previous letter to the earl Anne added the word 'widow' to her signature, a reminder to the recipient of her role as a godly moral guardian. This time, the earl replied immediately, thanking God for sending 'so good an angel to admonish me', but protesting that the charge was unjust and untrue. He was, he told her, 'hourly conspired against and practised upon' by those who want to put him out of favour with the queen.

The letter has been preserved, though Essex's last line is a request for her to burn it. Anne replied, hoping he would be free from crafty treacheries and subtle snares. Hastily written and dispatched late at night, she notes in a postscript to Anthony, to whom she sent the correspondence, that her reply to the earl carries no special weight. It does not assume either the moralising tone or the 'widow' in the signature that characterised her letters of reproof.[39]

There is evidence that Anne still found time and energy for the publication of reformist works during her widowhood. Her views shifted, as we have seen, from support for the newly established Elizabethan Church of England, evident in her translation of Jewel, to the more radical position of her later years, as she advocated for the Puritans persecuted by Whitgift. In a letter to Anthony in 1593, she mentioned 'two kallendars' that she wished to have very safely returned to her. These 'kallendars' are likely to have been what was then a significant work in progress. Starting with William Urwick in the nineteenth century, historians have suggested that Anne Bacon sanctioned and possibly financed the collation and publication of a work published that year, entitled *A Part of a Register: Containing Sundry Memorable Matters, Written by Divers Godly and Learned in Our Time, which Stand For, and Desire the Reformation of Our Church, in Discipline and Ceremonies, According to the Pure Worde of God, and the Law of Our Land.*

This collection of over 250 documents – Puritan papers, letters, petitions, complaints, arguments and proceedings of the ecclesiastical authorities – was written between 1570 and 1590. Collected and collated by a Puritan minister and preacher named John Field, it brought together evidence documenting the Puritan movement and the steps that had been taken to repress it. It was part of what has been termed the 'literary warfare' between nonconformists and their opponents, who included the conformist bishops.[40] It included a survey of ministers in England with assessments of their moral worth and how able they were to carry out their duties – from learned preachers to some described as simply 'dumb'. It has been suggested that some of the documents are stylistically typical of Anne's writing and that she was a direct contributor as well as patron of the enterprise. Unsurprisingly the authorities saw to it that, when it appeared, most copies of this controversial publication, overtly critical of the Church of England, were suppressed or destroyed.

In the first half of 1598, Anne told Anthony she was so short of money she had borrowed £50 from Lady Paulet. She had asked for £100 but would have to make do with the £50. Then seventy years old, she was relieved when her friend confirmed the loan: 'I was glad I knew this so soon. I will cease to trouble any more, growing sickly as I do and being behind-hand.'[41] 'Send me plain word,' she added in a postscript, referring to Anthony's proposed sale of yet another property, Redbourn. He sold the manor that year for £1,800 and Windridge the following year, as soon as she passed it on to him. This is where the surviving correspondence between Anne and Anthony ends. Their long dialogue falls silent in the records, but it is not the final letter in Anne's hand.

In early March 1600 Anne was in London, staying in lodgings in Fleet Street. She could not have avoided hearing of the growing furore over the behaviour of the earl of Essex. After leading a disastrous military campaign in Ireland he was being held under house arrest by the current Lord Keeper in Anne's old home,

York House, only a short distance from the lodging where she sat dwelling on her health and financial woes. From her lodgings, she wrote to her stepson Nicholas. This, her last known letter, is a weary plea. She hopes that Sir Nicholas and his lady are in good health. Her own health, she says, is poor, but she bears it with patience. It is nearly Lady Day, the March quarter day when her annuity is due and, she says, she always has need of the money before it is paid. One Mr Cooke has been charged with making the payment to her, but she is anxious: 'if he doth fail me and you then, at the day, I hope you will have care of me, to see me paid'. The letter is signed 'your Lordship's mother in the Lord, very friend', with her name and the Greek 'widow' – doubtless used here as an extra reminder to Nicholas of his family obligations to her.[42]

Now seventy-two, Anne had for years referred on and off to her poor health. She had back pain, episodes of 'quartan fever', a recurrent infection that may have been a form of malaria, and she sometimes wrote of her 'fits', which may mean other flare-ups of illness. She was sometimes too unwell and gloomy to receive visitors. While we have no record of whether Anne saw her sons that March, it is likely that she did at least see Francis. In a letter of 12 March 1600 to the queen, just over a week later than her letter to Nicholas, he described his mother's health as 'very worn'. Francis cited her health, and his love for her, as part of a bid for money, requesting a grant of land from the queen to give him a modest income in order that he may not only do her better service, but also free his mother from worry as he fears Anthony may otherwise sell Gorhambury. Perhaps he thought the reference to her old servant would soften the queen's heart (it did not).[43]

Anne's sons were in trouble. All the earl's friends had been turned out of Essex House by order of the queen, Anthony among them. Francis was steering a perilous course between his loyalty to his patron the earl and his service to the queen, who was demanding his legal advice on Essex's prosecution. When the earl was allowed back to his house on 19 March, he was kept under guard, with no visitors permitted. It was yet another negative twist of fate for the Bacons, now dangerously identified with the rebellious earl.

Francis tried to mollify the queen and to advise Essex how best to negotiate and survive her disfavour. But the headstrong earl's fall gained unstoppable momentum as he ignored the advice and played a disastrous hand. At his trial it was Francis Bacon who delivered the *coup de grace* of a fatally sharp cross-examination and rational summary of the arguments on behalf of the prosecution. Essex was condemned to death and beheaded at the Tower on 25 February 1601. Did Francis pursue the case so hard in return for immunity from prosecution for his brother? It seems that Anthony was never arrested or questioned, despite his close association with the earl. Francis intimated that a number of the earl's followers were saved because of his intervention – no names were named, perhaps they included Anthony.

In the event Anthony died within months of Essex. His health had completely broken down and his finances were as catastrophic as ever: he died 'so far in debt, that I think his brother is little the better by him,' wrote the diarist John Chamberlain.[44] Francis was now the heir to Gorhambury but what he had mostly inherited from his brother was debt. Anthony was buried in St Olave's church in London on 17 May 1601. None of his correspondence survives after 1597, closing that window into the Bacons' affairs more than a decade before Anne's death.[45] It is possible that his papers from that date until his death were destroyed to remove evidence of his dealings with Essex during the earl's rebellion. We do not know when Anne last saw him, how the news of his final illness and death reached her, or her feelings at the loss of her son.

Anne had kept her life interest in some of the manors out of Anthony's hands. She surrendered these to Francis in November 1602. Four years later, Francis finally married, at the age of forty-five. There is no record of Anne's response to the match and an eyewitness account of his marriage to wealthy, fourteen-year-old Alice Barnham on 10 May 1606 does not mention Anne among the guests. It was a fashionable London wedding at Marylebone Chapel, followed by a dinner given by Alice's stepfather Sir John Packington.[46] Francis spent a generous amount of his bride's money on celebrations and extravagant clothes: top-to-toe purple for his wedding outfit, and garments of cloth of gold and silver for them both.

In 1606, the year of his marriage and five years after Anthony's death, Anne made over her interest in Gorhambury to Francis. He may have wanted the option to sell the property, if he had to, but in the event his late marriage to a wealthy wife and wish to live showily at his family home saved the estate Anne had so long preserved for her sons. Perhaps the match revived her hopes for grandchildren, but there were none. The marriage was not a success. The couple lived apart for the last three years of Francis's life and he added a codicil to his will revoking all bequests to his wife. It is unclear how much time the couple spent with Anne at Gorhambury. A note Francis made in 1608 mentioned work to be done in the garden there. However, Francis was busy in London, at last acquiring the high offices and material success he had coveted for so long. The queen's death in 1603 and the accession of James I revived his hopes for the legal appointments he had been refused by the queen. Before his marriage he had acquired a knighthood, having petitioned his cousin Robert Cecil for one. His mother lived to see him appointed to the well-remunerated post of Solicitor General in June 1607, for which he had been tipped but passed over years before. He became Clerk to the Star Chamber in 1608, an even more valuable appointment for which he had been holding the reversion – the right to take over the office when it was vacated by the present holder – for nineteen years.

Anne may have been infirm and declining by the time of her son's late marriage and his professional success. Although it would be worth hearing her views on her teenage daughter-in-law and the continued absence of grandchildren, we have no

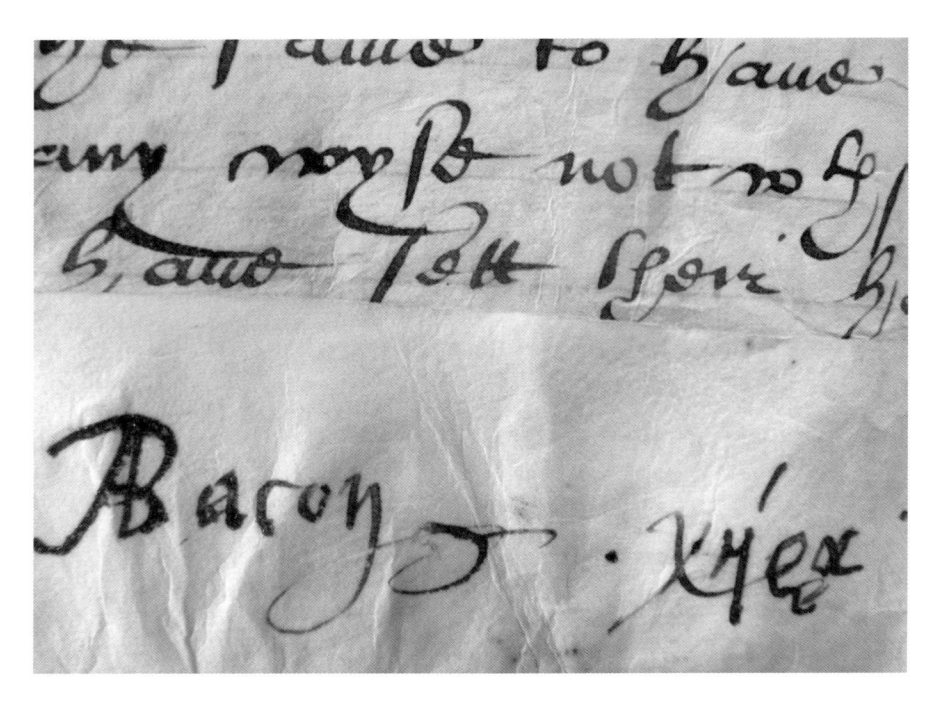

Anne Bacon's signature on a deed transferring her life interest in four manors to her son Francis. She adds the word 'widow' in Greek. Image courtesy HALS. IX.D.3.

sight or sound of her in those years. We equally cannot know whether she found Francis's eventual success and relative solvency a consolation after the rackety years she had endured and financed. With the injection of cash from his marriage and his appointments, and with his mother's life interest in Gorhambury surrendered to him after Anthony's death, Francis began to restore the estate from its depleted condition. In due course he added a tree-lined carriage drive from the house to a lavish new summer residence and water gardens, whose faint outlines in an area still called the Pondyards can be seen in meadows by the river Ver.[47] Francis was finally spending money that he did have. 'When his lordship was at his country house at Gorhambury, St Albans seemed as if the court were there, so nobly did he live,' wrote John Aubrey.[48] It was too late to remedy his mother's long years of scrimping, but it is to be hoped that her burdens of anxiety and financial hardship were eased in her final, silent decade. The last of her sisters, Elizabeth, died just before her in 1609, having commissioned an elaborate tomb for herself at Bisham and made arrangements for a suitably lavish funeral.

Francis did not mention his mother in his correspondence during those years, no other known correspondence or reports of her exist for that time. Then in late August 1610, Francis wrote to his friend Sir Michael Hickes:

It is but a wish and not in any ways to desire it to your trouble. But I heartily wish I had your company here at my mother's funeral, which I purpose on Thursday next in the forenoon. I dare promise you a good sermon to be made by Mr Fenton, the preacher of Gray's Inn; for he never maketh other. Feast I make none. But if I mought have your company for two or three days at my house I should pass over this mournful occasion with more comfort.[49]

Francis had been at Gray's Inn when his mother died at Gorhambury. Anne was buried in St Michael's, the modest parish church in St Albans where the godly preachers she supported and encouraged had stirred up dissent, defied Whitgift's rules and attracted like-minded Puritans to Hertfordshire. A preacher, just one friend, no feast. Her funeral was a quiet affair, as Francis records it, dignified with a sermon by the learned preacher of Gray's Inn. In his will, Francis asked to be buried near his mother. While there is a conspicuous monument to him in the church, Anne Bacon's grave is unmarked, its location unknown. There was, it seems, no funeral gathering to honour her, no black-clad procession to follow her coffin, no stone memorial, and no epitaph to record her death and mark the achievements of her life.

Conclusion

After all the vigour and passion of her long life, the last traces of Anne are her unsteady signatures on the documents transferring land to her remaining son. She outlived her husband, three of her four children, her sisters, and her royal mistress and contemporary Elizabeth I.

Anne Bacon experienced the religious and political reverses of four Tudor reigns at first hand and was publicly active in advancing the cause of reform. As a woman of the Privy Chamber, she had privileged access to the first reigning queens of England, Mary I and Elizabeth I. She intervened on behalf of her husband and brother-in-law at a critical point in the succession crisis of 1553 while her family remained under explicit threat, in the case of her father, or at risk of investigation and persecution as the ranks of her fellow reformists were thinned by detention, death and exile.

Formally excluded from the public arenas occupied by men, she nevertheless achieved national recognition for her published works of translation. She acquired the confidence to deal on equal terms with the scholars and lawyers who took on leading roles of church and state under Elizabeth I, and she knew her own worth in that world. An accomplished linguist with a knack for the telling phrase, she turned her skills and education to effective forms of influencing and persuading. She never wavered either in her commitment to the public cause of religious reform in England, or her pursuit of her family's welfare and advancement.

The conventions of the time saw women's education as a Pandora's box of hazards, threatening both the male *status quo* and women's reputations, which must be contained to keep women out of the public arena and in their proper place at home. Silence and chastity were the golden rules. Silencing Anne Bacon would have been a hard task. She found and used her voice, while fulfilling the conventional roles of dutiful daughter, wife and mother. As a young woman she confidently followed her own path, studying Italian under her mother's disapproving eye and taking the opportunity of her familial connection with William Cecil to have her translations published when most women were limited to the private circulation of their work in manuscript. She achieved the early public recognition and visibility that gave her confidence to advocate for the reformist cause, when she was free to do so, for the rest of her life.

She was brave and resolute in the summer of 1553: it is arguable that without her determined intervention on his behalf, William Cecil may not have survived to become the chief minister who shaped and dominated the government of Elizabeth I for forty years. Though constrained to silence during Mary's reign, Anne watched and waited, once again demonstrating strength of character and courage as she sustained her family's presence close to the monarch through the dark years that saw Protestants consigned to prison and burned at the stake for their beliefs. Released from dissembling after the accession of Elizabeth, Anne took on the significant responsibility of translating a major religious work. Her version of Jewel's *Apologia* was a vital building block in the revival of the Church of England under Elizabeth I, a translation both learned and perfectly pitched to be accessible to congregations throughout the country. Her brother-in-law Cecil who commissioned the work clearly recognised her value. It was Cecil whom she addressed in her later years to engage his support for Puritan preachers and who gave her exceptional access to parliament to hear the Whitgift debate in person, crossing another line of expectation and convention.

Her marriage to Nicholas Bacon was a loving, companionate partnership that carried them through a quarter of a century of danger and uncertainty, success and sadness: 'certainly among my blessings I especially count the fact that God wished me to be the wife of such a man,' she wrote. Aged only twenty-five, she had stepped into the breach to take over the household and mother Nicholas's bereaved children. Their years together during the reign of Elizabeth I were secure and successful. She felt his loss deeply and seems never to have considered another marriage.

There were other personal sorrows. Anne's grandmother, mother and younger sister all died in the early years of her marriage, her father was absent for the five bleak years of Mary's reign and the two daughters who might have been a delight and consolation to her did not survive infancy. She was sustained through these reverses by her evangelical faith. Anne never retreated into piety as an escape from the world but remained active and engaged with religious debate and in her later support for Puritan nonconformism.

By lucky accident we have unusually detailed insights into Anne's state of mind and her circumstances in later life through her surviving letters. Beset during her widowed years by financial worries, the burdensome details of running the family estate and her anxiety over her sons, in her letters Anne can sound overwhelmed by troubles. Yet throughout she maintained her sense of maternal duty and asserted her moral authority as a godly widow.

Anne's distinctive, assertive voice was sadly silent in her final decade, and her death unremarked. Her name disappeared from editions of the *Apologia*, from the seventeenth until the mid-nineteenth century.[1] Anne Bacon was for centuries almost hidden from history, yet the surviving evidence reveals the story of a woman of incisive intelligence, courage and tenacity who had a considerable impact on the

Tudor era. We can go some way to understanding how she was affected by both personal transitions and national events, and how patterns of thought grounded in religious faith, so unfamiliar to many in our secular age, shaped her intellect and governed her life.

Notes

Introduction

1. H. Mantel, First Reith Lecture (2017) <http://downloads.bbc.co.uk/radio4/reith2017/reith_2017_hilary_mantel_lecture1.pdf>.
2. G. Allen (ed.), *The Letters of Lady Anne Bacon*, Camden Fifth Series, vol. xliv (Cambridge, 2014); P. Demers (ed.), *An Apology or Answer in Defence of The Church of England: Lady Anne Bacon's Translation of Bishop John Jewel's Apologia Ecclesiae Anglicanae*, Tudor and Stuart Translations, 22 (Cambridge, 2016); P. Demers (ed.), *Anne Cooke's Englishing of Bernardino Ochino* (Cambridge, 2023).
3. Interest in Anne Bacon was first revived in early to mid-twentieth-century studies (M.B. Whiting, 'The Learned and Virtuous Lady Bacon', *The Hibbert Journal*, 29 (1931), pp. 270–83; M. St Clare Byrne, 'The Mother of Francis Bacon', *Blackwood's Magazine*, 234 (1934), pp. 758–71; R. Kelso, *Doctrine for the Lady of the Renaissance* (Urbana, 1956)), that principally framed her within a family and domestic context. Radical feminists of the 1980s moved on to consider how educated women of the period conformed to roles and identities within a patriarchal society (see for example M.E. Lamb, 'The Cooke Sisters: Attitudes toward Learned Women in the Renaissance', in M. Hannay (ed.), *Silent but for the Word: Tudor Women as Patrons, Translators and Writers of Religious Works* (Kent, Ohio, 1985), pp. 107–25). Subsequent feminist writers have addressed Anne's life and work in further examinations of aspects of female identity in the early modern period and the historical religious context in which Anne lived and undertook her work of translation: see A. Stewart, 'The Voices of Anne Cooke, Lady Anne and Lady Bacon', in D. Clarke and E. Clarke (eds), *This Double Voice: Gendered Writing in Early Modern England* (Basingstoke, 2000), pp. 88–102; G. Allen, *The Cooke Sisters: Education, Piety and Politics in Early Modern England* (Manchester, 2013); J. Goodrich, 'Reconsidering the Woman Writer', in P. Phillippy (ed.), *A History of Early Modern Women's Writing* (London, 2018), pp. 46–65, and others.

Chapter 1

1. See M.K. McIntosh, 'Sir Anthony Cooke: Tudor Humanist, Educator, and Religious Reformer', *Proceedings of the American Philosophical Society*, 119/3 (1975), p. 239, n. 34.
2. The family name was variously spelled 'Cooke', 'Cook' or 'Coke'.
3. M.K. McIntosh, 'Some New Gentry in Early Tudor Essex: The Cookes of Gidea Hall 1480–1550', *Essex Archaeology and History*, 9 (1977), pp. 134–5.
4. P.W. Hasler (ed.), 'Cooke, Sir Anthony (c.1505–76), of Gidea Hall, Essex and Abergenny Place, Warwick Lane, London', in *The History of Parliament: The House of Commons 1558–1603* (Woodbridge, 1981).
5. McIntosh gives an account of the incident, drawn from two contemporary sources, in 'Some New Gentry in Early Tudor Essex', pp. 132–3. See p. 137, n. 21 which cites the sources as PRO STAC 2/15/ff 95-6 and PRO SP2/Q/No.12.

6. PRO SP 1/85/207 cited in McIntosh, 'Some New Gentry in Early Tudor Essex', p. 133.

7. *Ibid.*

8. D. Calkins, 'Cooke, Sir Anthony (1505/6–1576), educator and humanist', *ODNB* (Oxford, 2004; online edn 2019).

9. Such 'licences to crenellate' permitted the addition of embellishments that referenced defensive castles, bringing grandeur to the ordinary manor houses whose owners added these details. 'Machicolations' were originally the apertures in castle walls through which defenders could rain down missiles or boiling oil on attackers.

10. P. Morant, *The History and Antiquities of the County of Essex*, 2 vols (1763–68; Chelmsford, 1978), vol. i, p. 66.

11. A. Sutton, 'Cook, Sir Thomas (c.1410–1478), draper and mayor of London', *ODNB* (Oxford, 2004; online edn 2004).

12. J. Summerson (ed.), *The Book of Architecture of John Thorpe in Sir John Soane's Museum* (Walpole Society, 1966), vol. xl, pp. 26 and 90; plate 78.

13. Morant, *County of Essex*, vol i, p. 66, n. G.

14. *Ibid.*, p. 67.

15. 'Romford: Introduction' and 'Romford: Manors and other Estates', in W.R. Powell (ed.), *VCH Essex*, vol. 7 (London, 1978), pp. 56–64 and pp. 64–72.

16. J. Norden, *Speculi Britanniae Pars: An Historical and Chorographical Description of the County of Essex, 1594*, ed. H. Ellis (London, 1840), p. 24.

17. J. Strype, *Annals of the Reformation* (1725; Oxford, 1824), vol. ii, pp. 604–6.

18. 'St Edward the Confessor, the Parish Church of Romford' <https://www.stedwardsromford.com/history>, accessed 15 February 2022.

19. D. Starkey, 'Intimacy and Innovation: The Rise of the Privy Chamber, 1485–1547', in D. Starkey *et al.*, *The English Court: From the Wars of the Roses to the Civil War* (London, 1987), pp. 89–90.

20. D. MacCulloch, *All Things Made New: Writings on the Reformation* (London, 2016), p. 160.

21. Henry VIII, King of England, *Assertio Septem Sacramentorum adversus Martinum Lutherum* (London, 1521).

22. See D. Coast, 'William Tyndale, Henry VIII, and The Obedience of a Christian Man', *The Historical Journal* 64/4 (2021), pp. 823–43.

23. 'An Act Abolishing Diversity in Opinions', commonly known as 'The Act of Six Articles' (1539), reflected the king's concerns about the issues dividing religious opinion in England, and his wish to establish 'concord and unity'. G.W. Bernard, 'The Making of Religious Policy, 1533–1546: Henry VIII and the Search for the Middle Way', *The Historical Journal*, 41/2 (1998), p. 339.

24. D. Thomas, 'Reconstructing Broadsheet Production in Reformation Wittenberg', in A. Pettegree (ed.), *Broadsheets: Single-sheet Publishing in the First Age of Print* (Leiden, 2017), p. 117.

25. D. Lloyd, *Stateworthies: or the Statesmen and Favourites of England since the reformation their prudence and policies, successes and miscarriages, advancements and falls during the reigns of King Henry VIII. King Edward VI. Queen Mary. Queen Elizabeth King James. King Charles*, ed. C. Whitworth (1670; London, 1766), vol. i, p. 250.

26. *Ibid.*, p. 254.

27. *Ibid.*, p. 250.

28. *Ibid.*

29. *Ibid.*, p. 252.

30. Allen, *Letters of Lady Anne Bacon*, p. 53.

31. *Ibid.*

Chapter 2

1. Machiavelli was writing to a friend, Francesco Vettori, describing his life in exile and the consolation of his books, 10 December 1513.

2. J. Goodrich, 'Class, Humanism, and Neo-Latin Epitaphs in Early Modern England: The Funerary Inscriptions of Elizabeth Cooke Hoby Russell', *Sixteenth Century Journal*, 49/2 (2018), p. 346.

3. K.R. Bartlett, 'Barker, William (*fl.*1540–1576)', *ODNB* (Oxford, 2004).

4. W. Bercher [i.e., Barker], *The Nobility of Women by William Bercher, 1559. Now for the first time edited, with Introduction and Notes by R. Warwick Bond* (London, 1904). Barker's abridged translation of *La nobilita delle donne ... Ferrari* (1540) by Lodovico Domenichi, was based on a treatise by Henricus Cornelius Agrippa, *De nobilitate et praecellentia foemine sexus* (Antwerp, 1520).

5. McIntosh, 'Sir Anthony Cooke', p. 240, quoting W. Haddon, *Cantabrigienses: siue Exhortatio ad literas* (London, 1552).

6. Translated from the Latin epitaph on the tomb of Sir Anthony Cooke, parish church of St Edward the Confessor, Romford.

7. *Ibid.*

8. Lloyd, *Stateworthies*, pp. 252–3.

9. W. Camden, *The History of the Most Renowned and Victorious Princess Elizabeth late Queen of England* (London, 1688), p. 218.

10. From Lord Burghley's Latin epitaph to his wife Mildred, on her tomb in Westminster Abbey.

11. Allen, *Cooke Sisters*, p. 36.

12. J.A. Giles (ed.), *The Whole Works of Roger Ascham* (London, 1864–5), vol. i, pt. 1, pp. lxx–lxxi, quoted in P. Croft, 'Mildred Lady Burghley: The Matriarch', in P. Croft (ed.), *Patronage, Culture and Power: The Early Cecils* (New Haven and London, 2002), p. 284.

13. J. Clapham, *Certain Observations Concerning the Life and Reign of Queen Elizabeth*, eds E. Plummer Read and C. Read (1603; Philadelphia, 1951), quoted in Croft, 'Mildred Lady Burghley', p. 283.

14. J.L. Vives, 'Instruction of a Christian Woman', in F. Watson (ed.), *Vives and the Renascence Education of Women* (London, 1912), p. 48.

15. *Ibid.*, p. 56.

16. J. McConica, 'Erasmus, Desiderius (*c.*1467–1536)', *ODNB* (Oxford, 2004; online edn 2007).

17. C.R. Thompson (ed. and trans.), 'The Abbot and the Learned Lady', in *The Colloquies of Erasmus* (Chicago, 1965), pp. 83–4.

18. R.M. Verbrugge, 'Margaret More Roper's Personal Expression in the *Devout Treatise Upon the Pater Noster*', in Hannay (ed.), *Silent but for the Word*, pp. 30–1.

19. J. Coke, *The Debate between the Heralds of England and France* (1550; ed. L Pannier and P. Meyer, Paris, 1877), p. 109. Margaret Clement was Margaret More's foster sister and was educated with her.

20. E.F. Rogers (ed.), *St Thomas More, Selected Letters* (London and New Haven, 1961), pp. 103–5, quoted in E.E. Reynolds, *Thomas More and Erasmus* (New York, 1965), p. 135; J. Guy, *A Daughter's Love: Thomas and Margaret More* (London, 2009), p. 60.

21. Guy, *A Daughter's Love*, pp. 66–7.

22. Quoted in Guy, *A Daughter's Love*, pp. 64–5.

23. *Ibid.*, p. 64 and Notes, p. 288, quoting Rogers, *St Thomas More*.

24. *Ibid.*, p. 74., quoting Rogers, *St Thomas More*, p. 155.

25. *Ibid.*, p. 64, quoting Rogers, *St Thomas More*.

26. See J.D. Campbell, 'Humanism, Religion and Early Modern Englishwomen in their Transnational Contexts', in Philippy, *Early Modern Women's Writing*, pp. 153–69 and R. Bainton, 'Learned Women in the Sixteenth Century', in P. Labalme (ed.), *Beyond their Sex: Learned Women of the European Past* (New York and London, 1980), pp. 117–28.

27. Thompson, 'The Abbot and the Learned Lady', p. 223.

28. The history of the family, who lived and ran a printing business on the premises continuously from the 16th to the 19th century, is preserved in the Plantin-Moretus Museum, Antwerp.

29. M.K. Jones and M.G. Underwood, 'Beaufort, Margaret, countess of Richmond and Derby (1443–1509)', *ODNB* (Oxford, 2004; online edn 2004).

30. J. Hymers (ed.), *The Funeral Sermon of Margaret, Countess of Richmond and Derby ... preached by Bishop Fisher in 1509* (1522; London, 2018).

31. J. Harmer, 'Sir John Cheke's Greek Books', Centre for Material Texts, St John's College, University of Cambridge (2010), <https://www.english.cam.ac.uk/cmt/?p=878>, accessed 25 Oct 2017.

32. C. Tunstall, *De Arte Supputandi*, quoted in S. James, *Catherine Parr: Henry VIII's Last Love* (London, 2008), p. 29.

33. Quoted in James, *Catherine Parr*, p. 35.

34. *Ibid.*, p. 139.

35. Quoted in J.K. Sowards, 'Erasmus and the Education of Women', *The Sixteenth Century Journal*, 23/4 (1982), p. 81.

36. N. Udall, 'To the most virtuous … Quene Katherine', in *The First Tome or Volume of the Paraphrase of Erasmus upon the New Testamente* (London, 1548). The word 'nousled' is an archaic form of 'nuzzled'.

37. M. St Clare Byrne, *The Elizabethan Home Discovered in Two Dialogues by Claudius Hollyband and Peter Erondell* (London, 1930), p. 67, quoted in C. Merton, 'The Women who Served Queen Mary and Queen Elizabeth', PhD (Cambridge, 1991), p. 244.

38. R. Ascham, *The Scholemaster*, ed. E. Arber (1570; Westminster, 1897), p. 47.

39. G. Ballard, *Memoirs of Several Ladies of Great Britain who have been celebrated for their writings or skill in the learned languages arts and sciences* (Oxford, 1752), pp. 180–1.

40. J.L. Vives 'On the Learning of Women', in Watson, *Vives*, p. 200.

41. V. Wayne, 'Some Sad Sentence: Vives' *Instruction of a Christian Woman*', in Hannay, *Silent but for the Word*, p. 19.

42. Vives, 'On the Learning of Women', in Watson, *Vives*, p. 207.

43. J.L. Vives, *A very fruteful and pleasant boke called the Instruction of a christen woman … tourned out of latyne into Englishe by Rychard Hyrde* (London, 1557).

44. V. Wayne, 'Some Sad Sentence: Vives' *Instruction of a Christian Woman*', in Hannay, *Silent but for the Word*, p. 19.

45. Watson, *Vives*, pp. 61–2.

46. Smith, 'Humanist Education', p. 18.

47. Giles, *Whole Works of Roger Ascham*, vol. i, pt. 1, p. lxiii.

48. Allen, *Letters of Lady Anne Bacon*, p. 5; Allen, *Cooke Sisters*, p. 36.

49. E. McCutcheon, *Sir Nicholas Bacon's Great House Sententiae* (Amherst, 1977).

50. For a full account of evidence about the sisters' reading throughout their lives see Allen, *Cooke Sisters*, pp. 26–44.

51. C. Bowden, 'The Library of Mildred Cooke Cecil, Lady Burghley', *The Library*, 6/1 (2005), pp. 3–29; Croft, 'Mildred Lady Burghley', p. 283.

52. Allen, *Cooke Sisters*, p. 28.

53. F.G. Emmison, 'Sir Anthony Cooke of 'Guydyhall' [Gidea Hall] in [Romford in the parish of] Havering, knight, 22 May 1576', in *Elizabethan Life: Wills of Essex Gentry and Merchants proved in the Prerogative Court of Canterbury* (Chelmsford, 1978), p. 18.

54. S. Alford, *Burghley: William Cecil at the Court of Queen Elizabeth* (New Haven and London, 2011), p. 20.

55. Watson, *Vives*, p. 47.

Chapter 3

1. W.K. Jordan (ed.), *The Chronicle and Political Papers of King Edward VI* (New York, 1966), p. 4. Edward kept his *Chronicle*, a record of the events of his life, until 1552. The manuscript of the *Chronicle* is in the British Library, Cotton MS Nero C X.

2. *Ibid.*, p. 5.

3. C. Skidmore, *Edward VI: The Lost King of England* (London, 2007), p. 57.

4. B.L. Beer, 'Seymour, Edward, duke of Somerset [known as Protector Somerset] (c.1500–1552)', *ODNB* (Oxford, 2004; online edn 2004).

5. W.T. MacCaffrey, 'Cecil, William, first Baron Burghley (1520/21–1598), royal minister', *ODNB* (Oxford, 2004; online edn 2004).

6. The word Protestantism was initially little used outside Germany, where it was first coined by German princes and free cities who were protesting against the attack on Luther at the Diet of Speyer in 1529.

7. T. de Bèze, *Tractationes Theologiae* (1570–82), quoted in Demers, *Anne Cooke's Englishing of Bernardino Ochino*, p. 31.

8. N. Orme, *Tudor Children* (New Haven and London, 2023), p. 146.

9. 'Edward VI to Barnaby Fitzpatrick, 20 December 1551', in J.G. Nichols (ed.), *Literary remains of King Edward the Sixth: Edited from his autograph manuscripts, with historical notes and a biographical memoir* (London, 1857), pp. 70–1.

10. Lloyd, *Stateworthies*, p. 376.

11. Jordan, *Chronicle*, p. 3.

12. Skidmore, *Edward VI*, pp. 45–50.

13. Jordan, *Chronicle*, p. 5.

14. Bible reference: 2 Kings 22.

15. T. Cranmer, 'A Speech at the Coronation of Edward VI, Feb. 20 1547', in H. Jenkyns (ed.), *The Remains of Thomas Cranmer* (Oxford, 1833), p. 119.

16. J. Oxley, *The Reformation in Essex to the Death of Mary* (Manchester, 1965), p. 150.

17. C. Wriothesley, *A Chronicle of England during the Reign of the Tudors from AD 1485 to 1559*, vol. ii, Camden Society (1887), pp. 1–3.

18. *Ibid.*

19. T. Cranmer, 'Homily of Good Works', in Jenkyns (ed.) *The Remains of Thomas Cranmer*, p. 176.

20. *Ibid.*, p. 442, quoted in Duffy, *Stripping of the Altars*, p. 98.

21. D. Daniel, 'Coverdale, Miles (1488–1569), Bible translator and bishop of Exeter', *ODNB* (Oxford, 2004; online edn 2004).

22. Duffy, *Stripping of the Altars*, pp. 450–1

23. *Ibid.*, p. 452, see also pp. 37–40, 'Sacred Place, Sacred Time', for a detailed account of pre-Reformation worship in a Suffolk parish.

24. Alford, *Burghley*, p. 37.

Chapter 4

1. *The Capuchin Constitutions of 1536*, trans. P. Hanbridge (Rome, 2007), p. xi, quoted in Demers, *Anne Cooke's Englishing of Bernardino Ochino*, p. 6.

2. The remark is attributed to Emperor Charles V.G. Rosso, *Historia delle cose di Napoli sotto l'imperio Carlo Quinto* (Naples, 1760), quoted in A. Overell, *Italian Reform and English Reformations, c.1535–c.1585* (London, 2008), p. 45.

3. J.D. Campbell, 'Bernardino Ochino and the Women Who Made His Career Possible', Society for the Study of Early Modern Women and Gender, 2016, <https://ssemwg.org/campbell/>, accessed 3 Nov 2021.

4. Campbell, 'Humanism', pp. 160–1.

5. G. Primrose, *The Christian Mans Teares, and Christs Comforts* (1625), quoted in A. Ryrie, *Being Protestant in Reformation Britain* (Oxford, 2013), pp. 18–19.

6. Overell, *Italian Reform*, p. 1.

7. *Ibid.*, p. 46.

8. Allen, *Cooke Sisters*, p. 45, n.27, quoting 'G.B.', the anonymous editor of the 1551 edition of Anne Cooke's translation of Ochino's sermons.

9. Demers, *Anne Cooke's Englishing of Bernardino Ochino*, p. 13.

10. Overell, *Italian Reform*, p. 47.

11. B. Ochino, *Certayne sermons of the ryghte famous and excellente clerk master Barnardine Ochine … Faythfully translated into Englyshe*, trans A. Cooke, R. Argentine, (London, 1551).

12. Demers, *Anne Cooke's Englishing of Bernardino Ochino*.

13. *Ibid.*, p. 37.

14. 'How We Should Answer the Devil When He Tempteth Us…', in Demers, *Anne Cooke's Englishing of Bernardino Ochino*, pp. 42–8.

15. Ryrie, *Being Protestant*, p. 31.

16. The controversial introduction of the word 'alone', which was not in the original text, strengthened Luther's theological case for justification by faith not works. For a full discussion see C. Methuen, '"These four letters s o l a are not there": Language and Theology in Luther's Translation of the New Testament', *Studies in Church History*, 53 (2017), pp. 146–63.

17. P. Demers, 'Introduction', in *An Apology*, p. 11.

18. *Ibid.*

19. Demers, *Anne Cooke's Englishing of Bernardino Ochino*, p. 31.

20. *Ibid.*, p. 37.

21. *Ibid.*

22. 'Anne Cooke to Lady F, 1551', in Allen, *Letters of Lady Anne Bacon*, p. 53.

23. B. Ochino, *Fouretene sermons of Barnardine Ochyne, concernyng the predestinacion and eleccion of God: Translated out of Italian in to oure natyve tounge by A.C.*, trans A. Cooke (London, 1551).

24. Allen, *Cooke Sisters*, p. 59.

25. P. Marshall and A. Ryrie (eds), *The Beginnings of English Protestantism* (Cambridge, 2002), p. 188.

26. C. Parr, *Prayers Stirryng the Mynd unto Heavenlye Medytacions* (London, 1545), quoted in J. King, 'Patronage and Piety: The Influence of Catherine Parr', in Hannay, *Silent but for the Word*, p. 47.

27. King, 'Patronage and Piety', pp. 44–5 and 49–51.

28. Demers, *Anne Cooke's Englishing of Bernardino Ochino*, p. 15.

29. Richard Whalley to William Cecil, 26 June, 1s550, SP 10/10 ff. 21r –22v, quoted in Alford, *Burghley*, p. 41.

30. Duchess of Suffolk to William Cecil, 2 October 1550, SP 10/10 ff. 83r–84v, quoted in Alford, *Burghley*, p. 43.

31. H. Machyn, 'Diary: 1551', in J.G. Nichols (ed.), *The Diary of Henry Machyn, Citizen and Merchant-Taylor of London, 1550–1563* (London, 1848), pp. 3–13, British History Online <http://www.british-history.ac.uk/camden-record-soc/vol42/pp3-13>, accessed 27 September 2023.

32. D. Loades, *Mary Tudor* (Stroud, 2011), pp. 119–20.

33. G. Bray, 'Haddon, Walter (1514/15–1571), civil lawyer', *ODNB* (Oxford, 2004; online edn 2008).

34. Allen, *Letters of Lady Anne Bacon*, p. 57.

35. *Ibid.*, pp. 55–6.

36. J. Ingram, *Memorials of Oxford* (London, 1837), quoted in Bray, 'Haddon, Walter'.

37. Allen, *Cooke Sisters*, p. 205.

Chapter 5

1. R. Tittler, *Nicholas Bacon: The Making of a Tudor Statesman* (London, 1976), p. 41.

2. Redgrave Building Book, Bacon MSS (Chicago), f.132, quoted in A. Simpson, *The Wealth of the Gentry 1540–1660* (Cambridge, 1961), p. 40.

3. *Ibid.*, quoting f.207.

4. Tittler, *Nicholas Bacon*, p. 49.

5. N. Bacon, *The Recreations of his Age* (1903; Oxford, 1919). Bacon's poems were not published in his lifetime and only appeared in print in 1903. All are thought to postdate marriage to Anne in 1553. This poem's stylistic similarities to other verse published in the later 1550s indicates it could have been written in the early years of his marriage with Anne.

6. 'From the Lord Keeper's Book of his Lands, "An indenture between Sir Anthony Cooke knight and Nicholas Bacon esquire, concerning the Manor of Ingam xxvii die Januarii anno regnus Edward VI sexto" (1552)', Suffolk Archives HD526/79/2.

7. E. Sandeen, 'The Building of Redgrave Hall 1545–54', *Proceedings of the Suffolk Institute of Archaeology*, 29/1 (1964), p. 6.

8. *Ibid.*, p. 26.

9. Most prominent among the East Anglian men were Cardinal Thomas Wolsey, son of an Ipswich butcher, and Archbishop Stephen Gardiner, whose father was a clothmaker in Bury.

10. Sandeen, 'The Building of Redgrave Hall', p. 11.

11. W.R. Streitberger, *Court Revels 1485–1559* (Toronto, 1994), p. 293.

12. Skidmore, *Edward VI*, p. 246.

13. Hatfield House, Cecil Papers 151/103, quoted in Alford, *Edward VI*, p. 73.

14. J. Foxe, *Actes and Monuments of these Latter and Perillous Days, Touching Matters of the Church* (1563; London, 1570), Book 10, p. 1605, <https://www.dhi.ac.uk/foxe>.

15. Edward VI, 'My Devise for the Succession', Inner Temple, Petyt MS 538, vol. 47, fo. 317.

16. Skidmore, *Edward VI*, p. 250, quoting the contemporary account of John Bannister, a medical student whose father was a member of the royal household.

17. Alford, *Burghley*, p. 55.

18. *Ibid.*, quoting the letter from Cecil that survives as a copy in Lansdowne MS 104 ff 3r, 4v.

Chapter 6

1. See A. Whitelock and D. MacCulloch, 'Princess Mary's Household and the Succession Crisis, July 1553', *The Historical Journal*, 50/2 (2007), pp. 265–87.

2. This premise is put forward in J.L. McIntosh, *From Heads of Household to Heads of State: The Preaccession Households of Mary and Elizabeth Tudor, 1516–1558* (New York, 2009).

3. Alford, *Edward VI*, p. 81.

4. Calendar of State Papers Spanish, 14 July 1550, quoted in L. Porter, *Mary Tudor, The First Queen* (London, 2009), p. 166.

5. D. MacCulloch (ed. and trans.), 'The Vita Mariae Angliae Reginae of Robert Wingfield of Brantham', Camden Fourth Series, 29 (London, 1984), p. 251, translated from R. Wingfield, 'Vita Mariae Angliae Regine', British Library Add. MS 48093 (1554).

6. *Ibid.*, p. 252.

7. *Ibid.*, p. 253.

8. *Ibid.*, p. 270.

9. D. Loades, *Mary Tudor, a Life* (Oxford, 1989), p. 353.

10. 'From the Lord Keeper's Book of his Lands, "An indenture between Sir Anthony Cooke knight and Nicholas Bacon esquire, concerning the Manor of Ingam xxvii die Januarii anno regnus Edward VI sexto" (1552)', Suffolk Archives HD526/79/2.

11. McIntosh, *From Heads of Household to Heads of State*, p. 76.

12. British Library, Cotton MS Vespasian F XIII/2, f.207, published in M. Green (ed.), *Letters of royal and illustrious ladies of Great Britain: From the commencement of the twelfth century to the close of the reign of Queen Mary* (London, 1846), vol. ii, p. 320.

13. Loades, *Mary Tudor, a Life*, p. 353.

14. McIntosh, 'Some New Gentry in Early Tudor Essex', p. 132.

15. *Ibid.*, p. 135.

16. J. Stone, *The History of Mary I Queen of England* (London, 1901), pp. 170–1. Philip of Bavaria was an active suitor, travelling to England to meet Mary. Matters advanced as far as a draft marriage contract but progressed no further.

17. Loades, *Mary Tudor, a Life*, p. 117.

18. H. Clifford, *The Life of Jane Dormer, Duchess of Feria*, ed. J. Stevenson (London, 1887), p. 63.

19. The Kenninghall Inventory, The National Archives (LR 115, 116 and 117).

20. Alford, *Burghley*, p. 55, quoting the letter from Cecil that survives as a copy in Lansdowne MS 104 ff 3r, 4v.

Chapter 7

1. Foxe, *Actes and Monuments,* p. 1605, <https://www.dhi.ac.uk/foxe>.

2. MacCulloch, 'The Vita Mariae Angliae Reginae of Robert Wingfield of Brantham', p. 245.

3. E. Ives, *Lady Jane Grey: A Tudor Mystery* (Oxford, 2009), p. 185.

4. *Ibid.*, p. 187.

5. *Ibid.*, p.187, quoting R. De Vertot, *Ambassades de messieurs de Noailles en Angleterre* (1763), ii.211.

6. Machyn, 'Diary: 1553 (Jul–Dec)', in Nichols, *The Diary of Henry Machyn*, pp. 34–50.

7. *Ibid.*

8. A. Plowden, 'Grey [*married name* Dudley], Lady Jane (1537–1554)', *ODNB* (Oxford, 2004, online edn 2014).

9. F. Blomefield, *An Essay Towards a Topographical History of the County of Norfolk: Volume 1* (London, 1805; http://www.british-history.ac.uk/topographical-hist-norfolk/vol1), pp. 213–27.

10. Porter, *Mary Tudor*, p. 202.

11. MacCulloch, 'The Vita Mariae Angliae Reginae of Robert Wingfield of Brantham', p. 253.

12. Foxe, *Actes and Monuments,* p. 1605, <https://www.dhi.ac.uk/foxe>.

13. D. Loades, *John Dudley, Duke of Northumberland 1504–1553* (Oxford, 1996), p. 258.

14. Foxe, *Actes and Monuments,* p. 1606, <https://www.dhi.ac.uk/foxe>.

15. M. Drayton, *England's heroical epistles, written in imitation of the stile and manner of Ovid's Epistles with annotations of the chronicle history* (London, 1597; Early English Books Online <https://quod.lib. umich.edu/e/eebo2/A36526.0001.001/1:18? rgn=div1;view=fulltext>), p. 22.

16. Ives, *Lady Jane Grey*, pp. 203–12.

17. MacCulloch, 'The Vita Mariae Angliae Reginae of Robert Wingfield of Brantham', p. 270.

18. Alford, *Burghley*, p. 61.

19. MacCulloch, 'The Vita Mariae Angliae Reginae of Robert Wingfield of Brantham', p. 186.

20. *Ibid.*, p. 266.

21. H. Machyn, 'Diary: 1553 (Jul–Dec)', in Nichols, *The Diary of Henry Machyn*, pp. 34–50.

22. *Ibid.*

23. *Ibid.*

24. Plowden, 'Grey, Lady Jane', *ODNB*.

25. A. Bryson, 'Cheke, Sir John (1514–1557)', *ODNB* (Oxford, 2004; online edn 2008).

26. H. Machyn, 'Diary: 1553 (Jul–Dec)', in Nichols, *The Diary of Henry Machyn*.

27. Alford, *Burghley*, pp. 62–3.

28. *Ibid.*, p. 63.

29. R. Warnicke, 'Grey [*other married name* Stokes], Frances [*née* Lady Frances Brandon], duchess of Suffolk (1517–1559)', *ODNB* (Oxford, 2004).

30. C. Medici, 'Dudley [*née* Guildford], Jane, duchess of Northumberland (1508/9–1555)', *ODBN* (Oxford, 2004).

31. MacCulloch, 'The Vita Mariae Angliae Reginae of Robert Wingfield of Brantham', pp. 275–6.

32. *Ibid.*

33. Calendar of the Patent Rolls of Philip and Mary, vol. ii (AD 1554–55), 12.

Chapter 8

1. Alford, *Burghley*, p. 72.

2. Proclamation made at Richmond on 18 August 1553, 'Offering Freedom of Conscience; Prohibiting Religious Controversy, Unlicensed Plays, and Printing', in P. Hughes and J. Larkin (eds),

Tudor Royal Proclamations II (New Haven and London, 1969), p. 6.

3. Porter, *Mary Tudor*, p. 237.

4. Marshall and Ryrie, *Beginnings of English Protestantism*, p. 197.

5. R. Tittler, *The Reign of Mary I* (London and New York, 1983), p. 19.

6. Porter, *Mary Tudor*, pp. 320–1.

7. *Ibid.*, p. 322.

8. *Ibid.*, pp. 328–9.

9. Bryson, 'Cheke, Sir John (1514–1557)'.

10. D. MacCulloch, 'Cranmer, Thomas (1489–1556)', *ODNB* (Oxford, 2004; online edn 2015).

11. Marshall and Ryrie, *Beginnings of English Protestantism*, p. 198.

12. P. Marshall, *Heretics and Believers: A History of the English Reformation* (London and New Haven, 2017), p. 385.

13. Marshall and Ryrie, *Beginnings of English Protestantism*, pp. 198–9, quoting Nichols, *Diary of Henry Machyn*, p. 72.

14. Alford, *Burghley*, p. 73.

15. Tittler, *Nicholas Bacon*, pp. 48–9.

16. *Ibid.*, p. 54.

17. A. Pettegree, *Marian Protestantism: Six Studies* (Aldershot, 1996), pp. 88–9 and 102–4.

18. Merton, 'Women who served Queen Mary and Queen Elizabeth', Appendix 1.

19. Allen, *Letters of Lady Anne Bacon*, p. 58.

20. R. Houlbrooke, *The English Family 1450–1700* (London and New York, 1984), p. 136.

21. N. Bacon, 'Made at Wimbledon in His Lord's Great Sickness in the Last Year of Queen Mary', in *The Recreations of his Age*.

Chapter 9

1. B. Harris, 'The View from My Lady's Chamber: New Perspectives on the Early Tudor Monarchy', *Huntington Library Quarterly*, 60/3 (1997), p. 220, n. 31.

2. Starkey *et al.*, *The English Court*, pp. 82–3.

3. B. Harris, 'Women and Politics in Early Tudor England', *The Historical Journal*, 33/2 (1990), pp. 259–81.

4. Starkey *et al.*, *The English Court*, p. 83.

5. Porter, *Mary Tudor*, p. 250.

6. *Ibid.*, pp. 250–1.

7. Merton, 'The Women who served Queen Mary and Queen Elizabeth', p. 245.
8. Harris, 'Women and Politics in Early Tudor England', p. 281.
9. Merton, 'The Women who served Queen Mary and Queen Elizabeth', p. 155.
10. R. Beale, *Treatise of the Office of a Councillor and Secretary to Her Majesty* (1592), in C. Read, *Mr Secretary Walsingham and the Policy of Queen Elizabeth* (Cambridge, 1925), vol. i, pp. 423–43.
11. Merton, 'The Women who served Queen Mary and Queen Elizabeth', p. 149 and fn71.
12. Allen, *Cooke Sisters*, pp. 132–3.
13. Merton, 'The women who served Queen Mary and Queen Elizabeth', p. 31.
14. Allen, *Letters of Lady Anne Bacon*, pp. 229–31.
15. Orme, *Tudor Children*, p. 20.
16. Allen, *Letters of Lady Anne Bacon*, p. 32.
17. *Ibid.*, p. 36.
18. Harris, 'Women and Politics in Early Tudor England', p. 274.
19. Starkey *et al.*, *The English Court*, p. 149.
20. Merton, 'The Women who served Queen Mary and Queen Elizabeth', p. 13.
21. *Ibid.*, p. 80.
22. *Ibid.*, p. 32.
23. *Ibid.*, p. 261.
24. *Ibid.*, p. 10, p. 260 and n. 46, 47, 48.
25. B. Harris, *English Aristocratic Women, 1450–1550: Marriage and Family, Property and Careers* (Oxford, 2002), p. 103.
26. Porter, *Mary Tudor*, p. 338.
27. Calendar of the Patent Rolls of Philip and Mary, vol. ii (AD 1554–55), 12.
28. Tittler, *The Reign of Mary I*, p. 6.
29. Bacon, *The Recreations of his Age*.

Chapter 10

1. J. Hayward, *Annals of the First Four Years of the Reign of Queen Elizabeth,* edited from an MS in the Harleian Collection by J. Bruce (London, 1840), p. 6. Hayward's is not a first-hand account. He was born in 1560 and compiled his account of the early years of the queen's reign after her death, no doubt drawing on earlier sources.
2. *Ibid.*, p. 10.
3. *Ibid.*, p. 9. The parentheses in this quote were introduced by the nineteenth-century editor to indicate a slight variation between early versions of the work.
4. Alford, *Burghley*, pp. 85–6.
5. Tittler, *Nicholas Bacon*, p. 70.
6. Count de Feria to the King, 29 December 1558, Calendar of State Papers, Spain (Simancas), Volume 1, 1558–1567, <https://www.british-history.ac.uk/cal-state-papers/simancas/vol1>.
7. Tittler, *Nicholas Bacon*, pp. 70–1.
8. Marshall and Ryrie, *Beginnings of English Protestantism*, p. 206.
9. Pettegree, *Marian Protestantism*, p. 115.
10. Calendar of State Papers, Spain (Simancas), Volume 1, 1558–1567, pp. 7–21.
11. *Ibid.*
12. D. Crankshaw and A. Gillespie, 'Parker, Matthew (1504–1575)', *ODNB* (Oxford, 2004; online edn 2020).
13. Calendar of State Papers, Spain (Simancas), Volume 1, 1558–1567, pp. 7–21.
14. P. Collinson, *The Elizabethan Puritan Movement* (London, 1967), p. 30.
15. P. Collinson, 'Sir Nicholas Bacon and the Elizabethan Via Media', *The Historical Journal*, 23/2 (1980), pp. 255–73.
16. H. Robinson (ed.), *The Zurich Letters comprising the correspondence of several English bishops and others, with some of the Helvetian reformers, during the early part of the reign of Queen Elizabeth (Second Series), 1558–1602* (Cambridge, 1845), p. 13.
17. Collinson, *Elizabethan Puritan Movement*, p. 34.
18. Merton, 'The Women who served Queen Mary and Queen Elizabeth', p. 266.
19. Tittler, *Nicholas Bacon*, pp. 89–90.
20. N. Bacon, 'In Commendacion of the Meane Estate', in *The Recreations of his Age*.
21. B. Castiglione, *The Book of the Courtier, done into English by Sir Thomas Hoby, anno 1561* (London, 1900).
22. In 1559 the queen attended parliament to hear a petition that she 'would be pleased to dispose herself to marriage' (Hayward, *Annals*, pp. 32–3). The pressure on her to marry continued for many years.

Chapter 11

1. Wayne, 'Some Sad Sentences', in Hannay, *Silent but for the Word*, p. 27.
2. *An Apology or Answer in Defence of The Church Of England: Lady Anne Bacon's Translation of Bishop John Jewel's Apologia Ecclesiae Anglicanae*, ed. P. Demers, Tudor and Stuart Translations, 22 (Cambridge, 2016).
3. T. Becon, *The Catechism of Thomas Becon ... With Other Pieces Written by Him in the Reign of King Edward the Sixth*, ed. J. Ayre (Cambridge, 1884), p. 369.
4. Hannay, *Silent but for the Word*, pp. 4–7.
5. Watson, *Vives*, p. 55.
6. Hannay, *Silent but for the Word*, p. 9, quoting J. Florio, *The Essays…of Montaigne* (London, 1603).
7. R. Hyrde, preface to Margaret More Roper's *A Devout Treatise upon the 'Pater Noster'* (London, 1526).
8. Quoted in Hannay, *Silent but for the Word*, p. 9.
9. Demers, *An Apology*, p. 150.
10. Lamb, 'The Cooke Sisters', in Hannay, *Silent but for the Word*, p. 114.
11. Duffy, *Stripping of the Altars*, p. 571.
12. Demers, *An Apology*, p. 15.
13. *Ibid.*, p. 17.
14. *Ibid.*, p. 33.
15. I. Green, *Print and Protestantism in Early Modern England* (Oxford, 2000), p. 556.
16. *Ibid.*
17. C.S. Lewis, *English Literature in the Sixteenth Century Excluding Drama* (Oxford, 1954), p. 157.
18. His version of the Bible was nevertheless published and was the basis for the King James Bible.
19. Lewis, *English Literature*, p. 207.
20. Allen, *The Cooke Sisters*, p. 71.
21. Green, *Print and Protestantism*, Appendix 1: Sample of Best-sellers and Steady Sellers First Published in England c.1536–1700.
22. Demers, *An Apology*, pp. 24–5.
23. Allen, *Letters of Lady Anne Bacon*, p. 60.
24. R. Verstegan, *A Declaration of the True Causes of the Great Troubles* (Antwerp, 1592), p. 12, quoted in Goodrich, 'Reconsidering the Woman Writer', in Phillippy, *A History of Early Modern Women's Writing*, p. 57.
25. Lewis, *English Literature*, p. 307.
26. Allen, *Letters of Lady Anne Bacon*, pp. 61–2.
27. L. Magnusson, 'Imagining a National Church: Election and Education in the Works of Anne Cooke Bacon', in J. Harris and E. Scott-Baumann (eds), *The Intellectual Culture of Protestant Women* (Basingstoke, 2011), p. 43.
28. Demers, *An Apology*, p. 44.

Chapter 12

1. L. Jardine and A. Stewart, *Hostage to Fortune: The Troubled Life of Francis Bacon 1561–1626* (London, 1999), p. 442.
2. G.H. Gater and E.P. Wheeler (eds), 'York House', in *Survey of London: Volume 18, St Martin-in-the-Fields II: The Strand* (London, 1937), pp. 51–60.
3. *Ibid.*, quoting *Hist. MSS. Comm.*, MSS. of Marquess of Salisbury.
4. *Ibid.*
5. H. Lane, 'Gorhambury: 1561–1652', *Transactions of the St Albans and Hertfordshire Architectural and Archaeological Society* (1932), p. 184.
6. Tittler, *Nicholas Bacon*, pp. 124–5.
7. Letter from Cecil to Sir Thomas Smith, 26 November 1564, BL Lansdowne MS 102 (Burghley Papers), ff 103-4, quoted in Tittler, *Nicholas Bacon*, p. 125.
8. Tittler, *Nicholas Bacon*, p. 25.
9. J. Norden, *Speculi Britanniae Pars: II The Description of Hartfordshire* (London, 1598), p. 2.
10. J. Spedding, *Lives and Letters of Francis Bacon*, vol. i (London, 1861), p. 158.
11. A. Darr, 'Torrigiani [Torrigiano], Pietro (1472–1528)', *ODNB* (Oxford, 2004; online edn 2008).
12. Survey of Manor, HALS X1/2.
13. English Heritage, *History of Old Gorhambury House*, <https://www.english-heritage.org.uk/visit/places/old-gorhambury-house/history>.
14. A. Hassell Smith, 'The Gardens of Sir Nicholas and Sir Francis Bacon: An Enigma Resolved and a Mind Explored', in

A. Fletcher and P. Roberts (eds), *Religion, Culture and Society in Early Modern Britain* (Cambridge, 1994).

15. D. Spring, 'The London Connection', in D. Spring (ed.), *Hertfordshire Garden History*, vol. 2 (Hatfield, 2012), pp. 8–11.

16. BL Lansdowne (Burghley Papers, 1572), MS 14, f.176, Bacon to Burghley, July 12, 1572.

17. F. Bacon, *A Collection of Apophthegms, New and Old* (London, 1674; Early English Books Online Text Creation Partnership, <https://quod.lib.umich.edu/e/eebogroup/>, 2011).

18. McCutcheon, *Great House Sententiae*, p. 18.

19. *Ibid.* p. 29.

20. BM MS Royal 17A XXIII, quoted in McCutcheon, *Great House Sententiae*, p. 17.

21. S. Hodgson-Wright, 'Lumley [*née* Fitzalan], Jane, Lady Lumley (1537–1578)', *ODNB* (Oxford, 2004; online edn 2008).

22. McCutcheon, *Great House Sententiae*, p. 21.

23. Allen, *Letters of Lady Anne Bacon*, p. 78.

24. W. Urwick, *Nonconformity in Herts, Being Lectures Upon the Nonconforming Worthies of St Albans, and Memorials of Puritanism and Nonconformity in All the Parishes of the County of Hertford* (London, 1884), p. 83.

25. L. Scheiner, *Tudor and Stuart Women Writers* (Bloomington and Indianapolis, 1994), p. 39.

26. *Ibid.*, pp. 40–5, where the verses are translated and discussed in detail.

27. A. Hassell Smith, G.M. Baker and R.W. Kenny (eds), *The Papers of Nathaniel Bacon of Stiffkey*, vol. i, 1556–1577 (Norwich, 1979), p. 60.

28. Jardine and Stewart, *Hostage to Fortune*, pp. 36–7.

29. Hassell Smith *et al.*, *Papers of Nathaniel Bacon*, vol. i, pp. 173–4.

30. *Ibid.*, p. 43.

31. Allen, *Letters of Lady Anne Bacon*, p. 71.

32. Hassell Smith *et al.*, *Papers of Nathaniel Bacon*, vol. i, pp. 42 and 116.

33. *Ibid.*, pp. 173 and 269.

34. *Ibid.*, pp. 143–4.

35. *Ibid.*, pp. 22–3.

36. *Ibid.*, p. 60.

37. *Ibid.*, pp. 23–4.

38. *Ibid.*, pp. 81–2.

39. Orme, *Tudor Children*, p. 14.

40. Hassell Smith *et al.*, *Papers of Nathaniel Bacon*, vol. i, pp. 11–12.

41. *Ibid.*, pp. 10–11.

42. *Ibid.*, p. 23.

43. *Ibid.*, pp. 89–90.

44. *Ibid.*, p. 26.

45. *Ibid.*, p. 87.

46. *Ibid.*, p. 40.

47. I. Dunlop, *Palaces and Progresses of Elizabeth I* (London, 1962), p. 116.

48. Lambeth Palace Library MS 647 f9, reproduced as Appendix 2 in J. Rogers, 'The Manor and Houses of Gorhambury', *Transactions of the St Albans and Hertfordshire Architectural and Archaeological Society* (1933), pp. 109–10.

49. T. Twyne, *The garlande of godly flowers … Carefully collected, and diligently digested into ordre, by Tho. Twyne, Gentleman* (London, 1574).

50. J. Walsall, published dedicatory letter, *A sermon preached at Pauls Cross by John Walsall, one of the preachers of Christ his Church in Canterbury* (London, 1578), in Allen, *Letters of Lady Anne Bacon*, p. 76.

Chapter 13

1. Jardine and Stewart, *Hostage to Fortune*, p. 29.

2. *Ibid.*, p. 30.

3. *Ibid.*, pp. 42–3.

4. These details emerge in advice she later gave to Anthony when he suffered from the same conditions, see Chapter 15, p. 159.

5. Hassell Smith *et al.*, *Papers of Nathaniel Bacon*, vol. i, p. 269.

6. John Stowe, *The Annales or General Chronicle of England* (1580; London 1615), p. 685.

7. J. Spedding, R.L. Ellis and D.D. Heath (eds), *The Works of Francis Bacon* (London, 1862), vol. viii, p. 183.

8. A. Hassell Smith and G. Baker (eds), *The Papers of Nathaniel Bacon of Stiffkey*, vol. ii, 1578–85 (Norwich, 1983), p. 57. Dr Smythe was paid £6 13s 4d for his attendance, the equivalent of almost £3,000 today.

9. C. Gittings, *Death, Burial and the Individual in Early Modern England* (London, 1984), p. 166.

10. Hassell Smith and Baker (eds), *Papers of Nathaniel Bacon*, vol. ii, p. 59.

11. *Ibid.*, p. 62.

12. Quoted in Jardine and Stewart, *Hostage to Fortune*, p. 66.

13. Hassell Smith and Baker (eds), *Papers of Nathaniel Bacon*, vol. ii, pp. 58–9.

14. Simpson, *Wealth of the Gentry*, p. 25; Tittler, *Nicholas Bacon*, p. 193.

15. Hassell Smith and Baker (eds), *Papers of Nathaniel Bacon*, vol. ii, p. 57.

16. British Library Egerton MS2642, fol. 168, quoted in J. Woodward, *The Theatre of Death: The Ritual Management of Royal Funerals in Renaissance England 1570–1625* (Woodbridge, 1997), p. 17.

17. W. Camden, 'The funeral procession of Elizabeth I', British Library Add. MS 5408 (1603).

18. Hassell Smith and Baker (eds), *Papers of Nathaniel Bacon*, vol. ii, p. 70.

19. One of the principal thoroughfares of Tudor London, the Strand was paved, unlike most other streets.

20. Tittler, *Nicolas Bacon*, p. 22.

21. Simpson, *Wealth of the Gentry*, pp. 22–6, with reference to detailed accounts in 'The whole charges of the funeralles of Sir Nicholas Bacon Knight a.d.1578', MS. Ashhm. 836, Bodleian Library.

22. Woodward, *Theatre of Death*, p. 17.

23. *Ibid.*, p. 15.

24. It has been estimated that between 63% and 89% of married men in early modern England named their wives as either sole or joint executrix. See A.L. Erickson, *Women and Property in Early Modern England* (London, 1993), pp. 157–8.

25. *Ibid.*

26. 'Will of Sir Nicholas Bacon, Lord Keeper', in Hassell Smith and Baker, *Papers of Nathaniel Bacon*, vol. ii, pp. 25–9.

27. R. Tittler, 'Bacon, Sir Nicholas (1510–1579), lawyer and administrator', *ODNB* (Oxford, 2004; online edn 2004).

28. Simpson, *Wealth of the Gentry*, p. 89.

29. The total estimated cost of the funeral, £900, is the equivalent of around £320,000 today.

30. Hassell Smith and Baker, *Papers of Nathaniel Bacon*, vol. ii, p. 82.

Chapter 14

1. 'T.E.', *The Lawes Resolutions of Womens Rights…* (London, 1632), p. 232.

2. B. Harris, 'Property, Power and Personal Relations: Elite Mothers and Sons in Yorkist and Early Tudor England', *Signs*, 15/3 (1990), pp. 606–32.

3. The terms 'feme sole' and 'feme covert' are English spellings of medieval Norman phrases that became incorporated into the legal language of England.

4. W. Blackstone, 'Of husband and wife', *Commentaries on the Laws of England, Vol 1* (Oxford, 1765), pp. 442–5.

5. L.A. Greenberg (ed.), *Legal Treatises: Essential Works for the Study of Early Modern Women: Series III, Part One* (London, 2005), vol. iii, p. xxiv.

6. Greenberg, *Essential Works*, vol. i, p. xxiii.

7. P. Hogrefe, 'Legal Rights of Tudor Women and the Circumvention by Men and Women', *The Sixteenth Century Journal*, 3/1 (1972), p. 98.

8. Hassell Smith *et al.*, *Papers of Nathaniel Bacon*, vol. i, pp. 76–7.

9. Hogrefe, 'Legal Rights of Tudor Women', p. 25.

10. Greenberg, *Essential Works*, vol. i, p. xxv.

11. 'Out of his shadow: The long struggle of wives under English Law', The High Sheriff of Oxfordshire's Annual Law Lecture, given by Lord Wilson on 9 October 2012, <https://www.supremecourt.uk/docs/speech-121009.pdf>.

12. J.L. Vives, *The Education of a Christen Woman*, 1541, f136, quoted in T. Stretton, *Women Waging Law in Elizabethan England* (Cambridge, 1998), p. 49.

13. Greenberg, *Essential Works*, vol. i, p. xix.

14. *Ibid.*, p. xxx.

15. T. Stretton, *Women Waging Law*, p. 27.

16. 'From the Lord Keeper's Book of his Lands, "An indenture between Sir Anthony

Cooke knight and Nicholas Bacon esquire, concerning the Manor of Ingam xxvii die Januarii anno regnus Edward VI sexto" (1552)', Suffolk Archives HD526/79/2.

17. *Ibid.* A mark was worth two-thirds of a pound. According to the Bank of England inflation calculator 400 marks would buy the equivalent in goods and services of around £100,000 today.

18. The University of Chicago Sir Nicholas Bacon Collection of English Court and Manorial Documents. Final payment recorded 26 March 1610, MS reference 3858.

19. *Ibid.*, pp. 26–7.

20. Hassell Smith and Baker, *Papers of Nathaniel Bacon*, vol. ii, p. 28.

21. *Ibid.*, pp. 119–20.

22. Thomas Cotheram to Anthony Bacon, 3 March 1580, Lambeth Palace Library MS 647, ff 556r, 54r, quoted in Jardine and Stewart, *Hostage to Fortune*, p. 77.

23. Hassell Smith and Baker, *Papers of Nathaniel Bacon*, vol. ii, p. 77.

24. *Ibid.*, pp. 77–8.

25. *Ibid.*, p. 102.

26. *Ibid.*, p. 93.

27. D. MacCulloch (ed.), *Letters from Redgrave Hall: The Bacon Family 1340–1744* (Woodbridge, 2007), p. 33.

28. *Ibid.*, pp. 57–8.

29. Hassell Smith and Baker, *Papers of Nathaniel Bacon*, vol. ii, pp. 93–5.

30. *Ibid.*, pp. 101–4.

31. Hassell Smith *et al.*, *Papers of Nathaniel Bacon*, vol. i, p. 107.

32. *Ibid.*, p. 120.

33. Allen, *Letters of Lady Anne Bacon*, p. 152.

34. Hassell Smith and Baker, *Papers of Nathaniel Bacon*, vol. ii, pp. 31–77.

35. *Ibid.*, p. 68.

36. Allen, *Letters of Lady Anne Bacon*, p. 82.

37. Jardine and Stewart, *Hostage to Fortune*, pp. 72–3.

Chapter 15

1. Jardine and Stewart, *Hostage to Fortune*, p. 72.

2. *Ibid.*, pp. 80–1.

3. *Ibid.*, p. 73.

4. *Ibid.*, p. 74.

5. *Ibid.*, p. 75, quoting letters from Francis Walsingham of 1 and 19 August 1580, LPL MS 647, ff 56r, 54r.

6. *Ibid.*, p. 86.

7. *Ibid.*, pp. 81–2.

8. *Ibid.*, p. 84.

9. *Ibid.*, pp. 85–6.

10. Jardine and Stewart, *Hostage to Fortune*, p. 79; for a full explanation of the significance of the public fast see Ryrie, *Being Protestant in Reformation Britain,* pp. 195–9.

11. Thomas Cotheram to Anne Bacon, 3 March 1580, LPL MS 647, ff 89-90, quoted in Jardine and Stewart, *Hostage to Fortune*, p. 76.

12. Jardine and Stewart, *Hostage to Fortune*, pp. 77–8.

13. *Ibid.*

14. Quoted in D. du Maurier, *Golden Lads: A Study of Anthony Bacon, Francis and their Friends* (1975; London, 2007), pp. 48–9.

15. *Ibid.*, p. 53.

16. Further details of Anthony Bacon's time in France can be found in Jardine and Stewart, *Hostage to Fortune*, Chapter 4 and in W. Tosh, *Male Friendship and Testimonies of Love in Shakespeare's England* (London, 2016).

17. T. Birch, *Memoirs of the Reign of Queen Elizabeth*, vol. i (London, 1754), p. 54.

18. du Maurier, *Golden Lads*, pp. 89–90.

19. Tosh, *Male Friendship and Testimonies of Love*, pp. 1 and 5.

20. *Ibid.*, p. 280.

21. Birch, *Memoirs*, vol. ii p. 134.

22. Allen, *Letters of Lady Anne Bacon*, p. 100.

23. Birch, *Memoirs*, vol. i, p. 56.

24. Jardine and Stewart, *Hostage to Fortune*, pp. 113–14.

25. Birch, *Memoirs*, vol. i, p. 56.

26. *Ibid.*, p. 68.

27. LPL, MS 648, art. 51 quoted in A. Stewart, 'Bacon, Anthony (1558–1601)', *ODNB* (Oxford, 2004; online edn 2008).

28. Allen, *Letters of Lady Anne Bacon*, p. 137.

29. Birch, *Memoirs*, vol. i, p. 116.

30. Allen, *Letters of Lady Anne Bacon,* pp. 99–100.

31. *Ibid.*, p. 103.

32. *Ibid.*, p. 119.

33. LPL, MS 648, fols. 23r–26v quoted in Stewart, 'Bacon, Anthony (1558–1601)'.

34. Allen, *Letters of Lady Anne Bacon*, p. 249.

35. *Ibid.*, pp. 146–7.

36. Jardine and Stewart, *Hostage to Fortune*, pp. 161–2.

37. H. Wotton, *The characters of the Earl of Essex and George Villiers, Duke of Buckingham compared and contrasted*, ed. E. Brydges (Kent, 1814), p. 14.

38. Allen, *Letters of Lady Anne Bacon*, p. 128.

39. *Ibid.*

40. Allen, *Letters of Lady Anne Bacon*, pp. 125–6.

41. *Ibid.*, p. 124.

42. *Ibid.*, p. 124, fn329.

43. *Ibid.*, p. 188.

44. *Ibid.*, pp. 123–4.

45. *Ibid.*, p. 101.

46. For a full discussion of this episode see Allen, *The Cooke Sisters*, pp. 149–57.

47. Allen, *Letters of Lady Anne Bacon*, p. 194.

48. *Ibid.*, p. 135.

49. Jardine and Stewart, *Hostage to Fortune*, pp. 464–6.

50. Tosh, *Male Friendship and Testimonies of Love*, pp. 6–7.

51. Allen, *Letters of Lady Anne Bacon*, p. 249.

52. *Ibid.*, p. 287.

53. Jardine and Stewart, *Hostage to Fortune*, pp. 203–8.

54. Allen, *Letters of Lady Anne Bacon*, p. 210.

55. *Ibid.*, p. 162.

56. *Ibid.*, p. 194.

57. *Ibid.*, p. 217.

58. *Ibid.*, p. 117.

59. *Ibid.*, p. 231 fn927.

60. *Ibid.*, pp. 232–3.

Chapter 16

1. Allen, *Letters of Lady Anne Bacon*, pp. 127 and 136.

2. *Ibid.*, p. 223.

3. *Ibid.*, p. 270.

4. *Ibid.*, p. 136.

5. *Ibid.*, p. 176.

6. *Ibid.*, pp. 212–13.

7. *Ibid.*, p. 156.

8. *Ibid.*, p. 128.

9. *Ibid.*, p. 212.

10. Edward Spencer to Anthony Bacon ?late July 1594, LPL MS 650, art.151; Spedding (ed.), *Letters and Life of Francis Bacon*, vol. i, p. 310, quoted in Jardine and Stewart, *Hostage to Fortune*, p. 167.

11. G. Goodman, *The Court of James the First* (London, 1839).

12. Allen, *Cooke Sisters*, pp. 217–23.

13. Allen, *Letters of Lady Anne Bacon*, p. 159.

14. *Ibid.*, p. 270.

15. See C. Laoutaris, *Shakespeare and the Countess: The Battle that gave Birth to the Globe* (London, 2014).

16. National Archives, C3/222/84.

17. National Archives, E 134/43 Eliz/Hi16 43 Eliz, 1601.

18. Harris, *English Aristocratic Women*, pp. 145–6.

19. The Bank of England inflation calculator shows that goods and services bought for £200 in 1578 would have cost £280 by 1600, with inflation averaging 1.6% per year, <https://www.bankofengland.co.uk/monetary-policy/inflation/inflation-calculator>.

20. Allen, *Letters of Lady Anne Bacon*, p. 150.

21. C. Bowden, 'Killigrew (nee Cooke), Katherine (c.1542–1583)', *ODNB* (Oxford, 2004; online edn 2008).

22. Jardine and Stewart, *Hostage to Fortune*, pp. 96 and 539n.

23. Hatfield Cecil MSS 203.88.

24. P. Priestland, 'Russell (nee Cooke), Elizabeth, Lady Russell (other married name Elizabeth Hoby, Lady Hoby) (c.1540–1609)', *ODNB* (Oxford, 2004).

25. Allen, *Letters of Lady Anne Bacon*, p. 242.

26. *Ibid.*, pp. 166–70.

27. G. Paule, *Life of Whitgift* (1612), quoted in Collinson, *Elizabethan Puritan Movement*, p. 243.

28. Allen, *Letters of Lady Anne Bacon*, pp. 87–8.

29. *Ibid.*, p. 212.

30. Record of Quitclaim, National Archives, Kew, reference WARD 2/57C/212/26.

31. Collinson, *Elizabethan Puritan Movement*, p. 440.

32. Allen, *Letters of Lady Anne Bacon*, p. 181.

33. *Ibid.*, p. 104.

34. Collinson, *Elizabethan Puritan Movement*, pp. 439–40.

35. Allen, *Letters of Lady Anne Bacon*, p. 104n.

36. *Ibid.*, pp. 280–2.

37. See Allen, *Letters of Lady Anne Bacon*, p. 19, for an explanation of the biblical origin of this role for widows.

38. *Ibid.*, p. 236.

39. *Ibid.*, pp. 262–8.

40. P. Collinson, 'Field [Feilde], John (1544/5?–1588)', *ODNB* (Oxford, 2004; online edn 2008).

41. Allen, *Letters of Lady Anne Bacon*, pp. 287–8.

42. *Ibid.*, p. 288.

43. Jardine and Stewart, *Hostage to Fortune*, p. 247.

44. N.E. McClure (ed.), *The Letters of John Chamberlain* (London, 1939), vol. i, p. 123.

45. Stewart, 'Bacon, Anthony (1558–1601)'.

46. Jardine and Stewart, *Hostage to Fortune*, pp. 290 and 564n.

47. Spring, *Hertfordshire Garden History*, vol. 2, pp. 13–14.

48. J. Aubrey, 'Francis Bacon', in *Brief Lives: A selection based upon existing contemporary portraits*, ed. R. Barber (1680; London, 1975), p. 36.

49. BL Lansdowne MS 91, f.183, quoted in Jardine and Stewart, *Hostage to Fortune*, p. 321.

Conclusion

1. Demers, *An Apology*, pp. xi–xii.

Bibliography

Primary sources
Hertfordshire Archives and Local Studies
Gorhambury estate papers. Map of the manor of Gorhambury 1634, by Benjamin
    Hare. HALS, D/EV P1.
Survey of Manor. HALS, X1/2.
Deed surrendering Lady Bacon's interest in four manors. HALS, IX.D.3.

The National Archives
C3/222/84.
E 134/43 Eliz/Hi16 43 Eliz, 1601.
The Kenninghall Inventory, LR 115, 116 and 117.
Record of Quitclaim, WARD 2/57C/212/26.
Calendar of the Patent Rolls of Philip and Mary, Volume II (AD 1554–55), 12.
Calendar of State Papers, Spain (Simancas), Volume 1, 1558–1567 <https://www.
    british-history.ac.uk/cal-state-papers/simancas/vol1>.

British Library
Camden, W., 'The funeral procession of Elizabeth I', British Library Add. MS 5408
    (1603).

Lambeth Palace Library
Correspondence between Lady Anne Bacon and Anthony Bacon. MS 651.

Inner Temple
Edward VI, 'My Devise for the Succession', Inner Temple, Petyt MS 538, vol. 47, fo. 317.

Suffolk Archives
'From the Lord Keeper's Book of his Lands, "An indenture between Sir Anthony
    Cooke knight and Nicholas Bacon esquire, concerning the Manor of Ingam
    xxvii die Januarii anno regnus Edward VI sexto" (1552)', Suffolk Archives
    HD526/79/2.

Hatfield House
Cecil MSS 203.88.

The University of Chicago
Sir Nicholas Bacon Collection of English Court and Manorial Documents, MS
  reference 3858.

Published primary sources

Allen, G. (ed.), *The Letters of Lady Anne Bacon*, Camden Fifth Series, vol. xliv
  (Cambridge, 2014).

Ascham, R., *The Scholemaster*, ed. E. Arber (1570; Westminster, 1897).

Aubrey, J., *Brief Lives: A selection based upon existing contemporary portraits*, ed.
  R. Barber, (1680; London, 1975).

Bacon, F., *A Collection of Apophthegms, New and Old* (London, 1674; Early English
  Books Online Text Creation Partnership, <https://quod.lib.umich.edu/e/
  eebogroup/>, 2011).

Bacon, N., *The Recreations of his Age* (1903; Oxford, 1919).

Ballard, G., *Memoirs of Several Ladies of Great Britain who have been celebrated for
  their writings or skill in the learned languages arts and sciences* (Oxford, 1752).

Becon, T., *The Catechism of Thomas Becon ... With Other Pieces Written by Him in
  the Reign of King Edward the Sixth*, ed. J. Ayre (Cambridge, 1884).

Bercher [i.e., Barker], W. *The Nobility of Women by William Bercher, 1559. Now for the
  first time edited, with Introduction and Notes by R. Warwick Bond* (London, 1904).

Birch, T., *Memoirs of the Reign of Queen Elizabeth* (London, 1754), 2 vols.

Camden, W., *The History of the Most Renowned and Victorious Princess Elizabeth
  late Queen of England* (London, 1688).

Castiglione, B., *The Book of the Courtier, done into English by Sir Thomas Hoby,
  anno 1561* (London, 1900).

Clapham, J., *Certain Observations Concerning the Life and Reign of Queen
  Elizabeth*, eds E. Plummer Read and C. Read (1603; Philadelphia, 1951).

Clifford, H., *The Life of Jane Dormer, Duchess of Feria*, ed. J. Stevenson
  (London, 1887).

Coke, J. *The Debate between the Heraldes of Englande and Fraunce* (London, 1550),
  in L. Pannier and P. Meyer (eds), *Le Débat des Hérauts d'Armes de France et
  d'Angleterre suivi de The Debate Between the Heralds of England and France*
  (Paris, 1877).

Demers, P. (ed.), *An Apology or Answer in Defence of The Church of England: Lady
  Anne Bacon's Translation of Bishop John Jewel's Apologia Ecclesiae Anglicanae*,
  Tudor and Stuart Translations, 22 (Cambridge, 2016).

Demers, P. (ed.), *Anne Cooke's Englishing of Bernardino Ochino* (Cambridge, 2023).

Drayton, M., *England's heroical epistles, written in imitation of the stile and manner
  of Ovid's Epistles with annotations of the chronicle history* (London, 1597;
  online edn, Early English Books Online <https://quod.lib.umich.edu/e/eebo2/
  A36526.0001.001/1:18?rgn=div1;view=fulltext>).

Emmison, F.G., *Elizabethan Life: Wills of Essex Gentry and Merchants proved in the Prerogative Court of Canterbury* (Chelmsford, 1978).

Foxe, J., *Actes and Monuments of these Latter and Perillous Days, Touching Matters of the Church* (1563; London, 1570, online edn <https://www.dhi.ac.uk/foxe>).

Giles, J.A. (ed.), *The Whole Works of Roger Ascham Now First Collected and Revised, with a Life of the Author*, 4 vols (London, 1864–5).

Green, M. (ed.), *Letters of royal and illustrious ladies of Great Britain: From the commencement of the twelfth century to the close of the reign of Queen Mary*, 3 vols (London, 1846).

de Guaras, A., ed. and trans R. Garnett, *The Accession of Queen Mary: being the contemporary narrative of Antonio de Guaras, a Spanish Merchant resident in London* (1553; London, 1892).

Hassell Smith, A., Baker, G.M. and Kenny, R.W. (eds), *The Papers of Nathaniel Bacon of Stiffkey*, vol. i, 1556–1577 (Norwich, 1979).

Hassell Smith, A. and Baker, G. (eds), *The Papers of Nathaniel Bacon of Stiffkey*, vol. ii 1578–1585 (Norwich, 1983).

Hayward, J., *Annals of the First Four Years of the Reign of Queen Elizabeth*, ed. J. Bruce (London, 1840).

Henry VIII, King of England, *Assertio Septem Sacramentorum adversus Martinum Lutherum* (London, 1521).

Hughes, P. and Larkin, J. (eds), *Tudor Royal Proclamations II* (New Haven and London, 1969).

Hymers, J. (ed.), *The Funeral Sermon of Margaret, Countess of Richmond and Derby, Mother of King Henry VII, and Foundress of Christ's and St John's College in Cambridge, preached by Bishop Fisher in 1509* (1522; London, 2018).

Jenkyns, H. (ed.), *The Remains of Thomas Cranmer*, 4 vols (Oxford, 1833).

Jewel, J., *The apology of the Church of England: with a briefe and plaine declaration of the true religion professed and vsed in the same. Published by the most Reverend Father in God John Jewel, Bishop of Salisbury*, trans A. Bacon (1564; London, 1635).

Jordan, W.K. (ed.), *The Chronicle and Political Papers of King Edward VI* (London, 1966).

Lloyd, D., *Stateworthies: or the Statesmen and Favourites of England since the reformation their prudence and policies, successes and miscarriages, advancements and falls during the reigns of King Henry VIII. King Edward VI. Queen Mary. Queen Elizabeth King James. King Charles*, ed. C. Whitworth (1670; London, 1766).

MacCulloch, D. (ed. and trans), 'The Vita Mariae Angliae Reginae of Robert Wingfield of Brantham', Camden Fourth Series, 29 (London, 1984).

MacCulloch, D. (ed.), *Letters from Redgrave Hall: The Bacon Family 1340–1744* (Woodbridge, 2007).

McClure, N.E. (ed.), *The Letters of John Chamberlain* (London, 1939).

Nichols, J.G. (ed.), *The Diary of Henry Machyn, Citizen and Merchant-Taylor of London, 1550–1563* (London, 1848; British History Online <http://www.british-history.ac.uk>).

Nichols, J.G. (ed.), *Literary remains of King Edward the Sixth: Edited from his autograph manuscripts, with historical notes and a biographical memoir* (London, 1857).

Norden J., *Speculi Britanniae Pars: An Historical and Chorographical Description of the County of Essex, 1594*, ed. H. Ellis (London, 1840).

Norden, J., *Speculi Britanniae Pars: II The Description of Hartfordshire* (London, 1598).

Ochino, B., *Sermons of Barnardine Ochine of Sena*, trans A. Cooke (London, 1548).

Ochino, B., *Certayne sermons of the ryghte famous and excellente clerk master Barnardine Ochine, borne within the famous vniuersitie of Siena in Italy, now also an exyle in this lyfe, for the faithful testimony of Iesus Christe. Faythfully translated into Englyshe*, trans A. Cooke, R. Argentine (London, 1551).

Ochino, B., *Fouretene sermons of Barnardine Ochyne, concernyng the predestinacion and eleccion of God: Translated out of Italian in to oure natyve tounge by A.C.*, trans A. Cooke (London, 1551).

Robinson, H. (ed.), *The Zurich Letters comprising the correspondence of several English bishops and others, with some of the Helvetian reformers, during the early part of the reign of Queen Elizabeth (Second Series), 1558–1602* (Cambridge, 1845).

Rogers, E.F. (ed.), *St Thomas More, Selected Letters* (London and New Haven, 1961).

Roper, M. More, *A Devout Treatise upon the 'Pater Noster'* (London, 1526).

Spedding, J. (ed.), *The Letters and the Life of Francis Bacon*, 7 vols (London, 1861–74).

Spedding, J., Ellis, R.L. and Heath, D.D. (eds), *The Works of Francis Bacon*, 14 vols (London, 1857–61).

Stowe, J., *The Annales or General Chronicle of England* (1580; London, 1615).

Strype, J., *Annals of the Reformation and Establishment of Religion and Other Various Occurrences in the Church of England during Queen Elizabeth's Happy Reign*, 4 vols (1709–31; Oxford, 1824).

Summerson, J. (ed.), *The Book of Architecture of John Thorpe in Sir John Soane's Museum* (Walpole Society, 1966), vol. xl.

'T.E.', *The Lawes Resolutions of Womens Rights: or, the Lawes Provision for Woemen: a Methodicall Collection of such Statutes and Customes, with the Cases, Opinions, Arguments and Points of Learning in the Law, as doe properly concerne Women: Together with a Compendious Table, whereby the Chiefe Matters in this Booke contained, may be more readily Found The Lawes Resolution* (London, 1632).

Thompson, C.R., (ed. and trans.), 'The Abbot and the Learned Lady', in *The Colloquies of Erasmus* (Chicago, 1965).

Twyne, T., *The garlande of godly flowers bewtifully adorned as most freshly they flourish in the gardeins of right faithfull Christian writers. Yéeldyng foorth a very comfortable sauour to the afflicted soule, wherby hée is salfly [sic] transported vnto the mercifull throne of the most glorious God. Carefully collected, and diligently digested into ordre, by Tho. Twyne, Gentleman* (London, 1574).

Udall, N., 'To the most virtuous … Quene Katherine', in *The First Tome or Volume of the Paraphrase of Erasmus upon the New Testamente* (London, 1548).

Vives, J.L., *A very fruteful and pleasant boke called the Instruction of a christen woman ... tourned out of latyne into Englishe by Rychard Hyrde* (London, 1557).

Vives, J.L., *The Education of a Christen Woman*, trans R. Hyde (London, 1541).

Wotton, H., *The characters of the Earl of Essex and George Villiers, Duke of Buckingham compared and contrasted*, ed. E. Brydges (Kent, 1814).

Wriothesley, C., *A Chronicle of England during the Reign of the Tudors from AD 1485 to 1559*, vol. ii, Camden Society (1887).

Secondary sources

Alford, S., *Burghley: William Cecil at the Court of Elizabeth I* (New Haven and London, 2011).

Alford, S., *Edward VI* (London, 2014).

Allen, G., *The Cooke Sisters: Education, Piety and Politics in Early Modern England* (Manchester, 2013).

Bainton, R., 'Learned Women in the Europe of the Sixteenth Century', in P. Labalme (ed.), *Beyond Their Sex: Learned Women of the European Past* (New York and London, 1980), pp. 117–28.

Bartlett, K.R., 'Barker, William (*fl.*1540–1576)', *ODNB* (Oxford, 2004).

Beer, B.L., 'Seymour, Edward, duke of Somerset [*known as* Protector Somerset] (*c.*1500–1552)', *ODNB* (Oxford, 2004; online edn 2004).

Bernard, G.W., 'The Making of Religious Policy, 1533–1546: Henry VIII and the Search for the Middle Way', *The Historical Journal*, 41/2 (1998), pp. 321–49.

Blackstone, W., *Commentaries on the Laws of England, Vol. 1* (Oxford, 1765).

Blomefield, F., *An Essay Towards a Topographical History of the County of Norfolk: Volume 1* (London, 1805; online edn <http://www.british-history.ac.uk/topographical-hist-norfolk/vol1>).

Bowden, C., 'Killigrew (nee Cooke), Katherine (c.1542–1583)', *ODNB* (Oxford, 2004; online edn 2008).

Bowden, C., 'The Library of Mildred Cooke Cecil, Lady Burghley', *The Library*, 6/1 (2005), pp. 3–29.

Bray, G. 'Haddon, Walter (1514/15–1571)', *ODNB* (Oxford, 2004; online edn 2008).

Bryson, A., 'Cheke, Sir John (1514–1557)', *ODNB* (Oxford, 2004; online edn 2008).

Byrne, M. St Clare, *The Elizabethan Home Discovered in Two Dialogues by Claudius Hollyband and Peter Erondell* (London, 1930).

Byrne, M. St Clare, 'The Mother of Francis Bacon', *Blackwood's Magazine*, 234 (1934), pp. 758–71.

Calkins, D., 'Cooke, Sir Anthony (1505/6–1576), educator and humanist', *ODNB* (Oxford, 2004; online edn 2019).

Campbell, J.D., 'Humanism, Religion and Early Modern Englishwomen in their Transnational Contexts', in P. Phillippy (ed.), *A History of Early Modern Women's Writing* (London, 2018), pp. 153–69.

Coast, D., 'William Tyndale, Henry VIII, and The Obedience of a Christian Man', *The Historical Journal* 64/4 (2021), pp. 823–43.

Collinson, P., *The Elizabethan Puritan Movement* (London, 1967).

Collinson, P., 'Sir Nicholas Bacon and the Elizabethan Via Media', *The Historical Journal*, 23/2 (1980), pp. 255–73.

Collinson, P., 'Field [Feilde], John (1544/5?–1588)', *ODNB* (Oxford, 2004; online edn 2008).

Crankshaw, D. and Gillespie, A., 'Parker, Matthew (1504–1575)', *ODNB* (Oxford, 2004; online edn 2020).

Croft, P. (ed.), *Patronage, Culture and Power: The Early Cecils* (New Haven and London, 2002).

Daniel, D., 'Coverdale, Miles (1488–1569), Bible translator and bishop of Exeter', *ODNB* (Oxford, 2004; online edn 2004).

Darr, A., 'Torrigiani [Torrigiano], Pietro (1472–1528)', *ODNB* (Oxford, 2004, online edn 2008).

Duffy, E., *The Stripping of the Altars: Traditional Religion in England 1400–1580* (New Haven and London, 1992).

Dunlop, I., *Palaces and Progresses of Elizabeth I* (London, 1962).

Erickson, A.L., *Women and Property in Early Modern England* (London, 1993).

Fletcher, A. and Roberts, P. (eds), *Religion, Culture and Society in Early Modern Britain* (Cambridge, 1994).

Gater, G.H. and Wheeler E.P. (eds), *Survey of London: Volume 18, St Martin-in-the-Fields II: The Strand* (London, 1937).

Gittings, C., *Death, Burial and the Individual in Early Modern England* (London, 1984).

Goodman, G., *The Court of James the First* (London, 1839).

Goodrich, J., 'Class, Humanism, and Neo-Latin Epitaphs in Early Modern England: The Funerary Inscriptions of Elizabeth Cooke Hoby Russell', *Sixteenth Century Journal*, 49/2 (2018), pp. 339–68.

Goodrich, J., 'Reconsidering the Woman Writer', in P. Phillippy (ed.), *A History of Early Modern Women's Writing* (London, 2018), pp. 46–65.

Green, I., *Print and Protestantism in Early Modern England* (Oxford, 2000).

Greenberg, L.A. (ed.), *Legal Treatises: Essential Works for the Study of Early Modern Women: Series III, Part One*, 3 vols (London, 2005).

Guy, J., *A Daughter's Love: Thomas and Margaret More* (London, 2009).

Hannay, M. (ed.), *Silent but for the Word: Tudor Women as Patrons, Translators, and Writers of Religious Works* (Kent, Ohio, 1985).

Harris, B., 'Property, Power and Personal Relations: Elite Mothers and Sons in Yorkist and Early Tudor England', *Signs*, 15/3 (1990), pp. 606–32.

Harris, B., 'Women and Politics in Early Tudor England', *The Historical Journal*, 33/2 (1990), pp. 259–81.

Harris, B., 'The View from My Lady's Chamber: New Perspectives on the Early Tudor Monarchy', *Huntington Library Quarterly*, 60/3 (1997), pp. 215–47.

Harris, B., *English Aristocratic Women, 1450–1550: Marriage and Family, Property and Careers* (Oxford, 2002).

Harris, J. and Scott-Baumann, E. (eds), *The Intellectual Culture of Protestant Women* (Basingstoke, 2011).

Hasler, P.W. (ed.), 'Cooke, Sir Anthony (c.1505–76), of Gidea Hall, Essex and Abergenny Place, Warwick Lane, London', in *The History of Parliament: The House of Commons 1558–1603* (Woodbridge, 1981).

Hassell Smith, A., 'The Gardens of Sir Nicholas and Sir Francis Bacon: An Enigma Resolved and a Mind Explored', in A. Fletcher and P. Roberts (eds), *Religion, Culture and Society in Early Modern Britain* (Cambridge, 1994).

Hassell Smith, A., 'Bacon, Sir Nathaniel (1546?–1622)', *ODNB* (Oxford, 2004; online edn 2015).

Hodgson-Wright, S., 'Lumley [*née* Fitzalan], Jane, Lady Lumley (1537–1578)', *ODNB* (Oxford, 2004; online edn 2008).

Hogrefe, P., 'Legal Rights of Tudor Women and the Circumvention by Men and Women', *The Sixteenth Century Journal*, 3/1 (1972), pp. 97–105.

Houlbrooke, R., *The English Family 1450–1700* (London and New York, 1984).

Ives, E., *Lady Jane Grey: A Tudor Mystery* (Oxford, 2009).

James, S., *Catherine Parr: Henry VIII's Last Love* (London, 2008).

Jardine, L. and Stewart, A., *Hostage to Fortune: The Troubled Life of Francis Bacon 1561–1626* (London, 1999).

Jones, M.K. and Underwood, M.G., 'Beaufort, Margaret, countess of Richmond and Derby (1443–1509)', *ODNB* (Oxford, 2004; online edn 2004).

Jordan, W.K. (ed.), *The Chronicle and Political Papers of King Edward VI* (New York, 1966).

Kelso, R., *Doctrine for the Lady of the Renaissance* (Urbana, 1956).

King, J., 'Patronage and Piety: The Influence of Catherine Parr', in M. Hannay (ed.), *Silent but for the Word: Tudor Women as Patrons, Translators, and Writers of Religious Works* (Kent, Ohio, 1985), pp. 43–90.

Labalme, P.H. (ed.), *Beyond their Sex: Learned Women of the European Past* (New York and London, 1980).

Lamb, M.E., 'The Cooke Sisters: Attitudes toward Learned Women in the Renaissance', in M. Hannay (ed.), *Silent but for the Word: Tudor Women as Patrons, Translators, and Writers of Religious Works* (Kent, Ohio, 1985), pp. 107–25.

Lane, H., 'Gorhambury: 1561–1652', *Transactions of the St Albans and Hertfordshire Architectural and Archaeological Society* (1932), pp. 183–211.

Laoutaris, C., *Shakespeare and the Countess: The Battle that gave Birth to the Globe* (London, 2014).

Lewis, C.S., *English Literature in the Sixteenth Century Excluding Drama.* The completion of the Clark Lectures, Trinity College Cambridge, 1944 (Oxford, 1954).

Loades, D., *Mary Tudor, a Life* (Oxford, 1989).

Loades, D., *John Dudley, Duke of Northumberland 1504–1553* (Oxford, 1996).

Loades, D., *Mary Tudor* (Stroud, 2011).

MacCaffrey, W.T., 'Cecil, William, first Baron Burghley (1520/21–1598), royal minister', *ODNB* (Oxford, 2004; online edn 2004).

McConica, J., 'Erasmus, Desiderius (*c.*1467–1536)', *ODNB* (Oxford, 2004; online edn 2007).

MacCulloch, D., *Suffolk and the Tudors: Politics and Religion in an English County 1500–1600* (Oxford, 1986).

MacCulloch, D., 'Cranmer, Thomas (1489–1556)', *ODNB* (Oxford, 2004; online edn 2015).

MacCulloch, D., *All Things Made New: Writings on the Reformation* (London, 2016).

McCutcheon, E., *Sir Nicholas Bacon's Great House Sententiae* (Amherst, 1977).

McIntosh, J.L., *From Heads of Household to Heads of State: The Preaccession Households of Mary and Elizabeth Tudor, 1516–1558* (New York, 2009).

McIntosh, M.K., 'Sir Anthony Cooke; Tudor humanist, educator and religious reformer', *Proceedings of the American Philosophical Society*, 119/3 (1975), pp. 233–50.

McIntosh, M.K., 'Some New Gentry in Early Tudor Essex: The Cookes of Gidea Hall 1480–1550', *Essex Archaeology and History*, 9 (1977), pp. 129–37.

Magnusson, L., 'Imagining a National Church: Election and Education in the Works of Anne Cooke Bacon', in J. Harris and E. Scott-Baumann (eds), *The Intellectual Culture of Protestant Women* (Basingstoke, 2011).

Marshall, P., *Heretics and Believers: A History of the English Reformation* (London and New Haven, 2017).

Marshall, P. and Ryrie, A. (eds), *The Beginnings of English Protestantism* (Cambridge, 2002).

du Maurier, D., *Golden Lads: A Study of Anthony Bacon, Francis and their Friends* (1975; London, 2007).

Medici, C., 'Dudley [*née* Guildford], Jane, duchess of Northumberland (1508/9–1555)', *ODNB* (Oxford, 2004).

Merton, C., 'The Women who served Queen Mary and Queen Elizabeth: Ladies, Gentlewomen and Maids of the Privy Chamber 1553–1603', PhD (Cambridge, 1991).

Methuen, C., '"These four letters *s o l a* are not there": Language and Theology in Luther's Translation of the New Testament', *Studies in Church History*, 53 (2017), pp. 146–63.

Morant, P., *The History and Antiquities of the County of Essex*, 2 vols (1763–68; republished 1978 in collaboration with Essex County Library).

Orme, N., *Tudor Children* (New Haven and London, 2023).

Overell, A., *Italian Reform and English Reformations, c.1535–c.1585* (London, 2008).

Oxley, J., *The Reformation in Essex to the Death of Mary* (Manchester, 1965).

Pettegree, A., *Marian Protestantism: Six Studies* (Aldershot, 1996).

Phillippy, P. (ed.), *A History of Early Modern Women's Writing* (Cambridge, 2018).

Plowden, A., 'Grey [*married name* Dudley], Lady Jane (1537–1554)', *ODNB* (Oxford, 2004; online edn 2014).

Porter, L., *Mary Tudor, The First Queen* (London, 2009).

Powell, W.R. (ed.), *VCH Essex,* vol. 7 (London, 1978).

Prest, W. R., 'Law and Women's Rights in Early Modern England', *The Seventeenth Century*, 6/2 (1991), pp. 169–87.

Priestland, P., 'Russell (nee Cooke), Elizabeth, Lady Russell (other married name Elizabeth Hoby, Lady Hoby) (c.1540–1609)', *ODNB* (Oxford, 2004).

Read, C., *Mr Secretary Walsingham and the Policy of Queen Elizabeth* (Cambridge, 1925).

Reynolds, E.E., *Thomas More and Erasmus* (New York, 1965).

Rogers, J., 'The Manor and Houses of Gorhambury', *Transactions of the St Albans and Hertfordshire Architectural and Archaeological Society* (1933), pp. 35–112.

Ryrie, A., *Being Protestant in Reformation Britain* (Oxford, 2013).

Sandeen, E.R., 'The Building of Redgrave Hall 1545–1554', *Proceedings of the Suffolk Institute of Archaeology*, 29/1 (1964), pp. 1–33.

Scheiner, L., *Tudor and Stuart Women Writers* (Bloomington and Indianapolis, 1994).

Simpson, A., *The Wealth of the Gentry 1540–1660* (Cambridge, 1961).

Skidmore, C., *Edward VI: The Lost King of England* (London, 2007).

Smith, H.L., 'Humanist Education and the Renaissance Concept of Woman', in H. Wilcox (ed.), *Women and Literature in Britain 1500–1700* (Cambridge, 1996), pp. 9–29.

Sowards, J.K., 'Erasmus and the Education of Women', *The Sixteenth Century Journal*, 23/4 (1982), pp. 77–89.

Spring, D. (ed.), *Hertfordshire Garden History*, vol. 2 (Hatfield, 2012).

Starkey, D. *et al.*, *The English Court: From the Wars of the Roses to the Civil War* (London, 1987).

Stewart, A., 'The Voices of Anne Cooke, Lady Anne and Lady Bacon', in D. Clarke and E. Clarke (eds), *This Double Voice: Gendered Writing in Early Modern England* (Basingstoke, 2000), pp. 88–102.

Stewart, A., 'Bacon, Anthony (1558–1601)', *ODNB* (Oxford, 2004; online edn 2008).

Stone, J., *The History of Mary I Queen of England as found in the public records, despatches of ambassadors in original private letters, and other contemporary documents* (London, 1901).

Streitberger, W.R., *Court Revels 1485–1559* (Toronto, 1994).

Stretton, T., *Women Waging Law in Elizabethan England* (Cambridge, 1998).

Sutton, A., 'Cook, Sir Thomas (c.1410–1478), draper and mayor of London', in H.C.G. Matthew and B. Harrison (eds), *ODNB* (Oxford, 2004; online edn 2004).

Taplin, M., 'Ochino, Bernardino (c.1487–1564/5) Capuchin friar and evangelical reformer', *ODNB* (Oxford, 2004; online edn 2004).

Thomas, D., 'Reconstructing Broadsheet Production in Reformation Wittenberg', in A. Pettegree (ed.), *Broadsheets: Single-sheet Publishing in the First Age of Print* (Leiden, 2017), pp. 114–38.

Tittler, R., *Nicholas Bacon: The Making of a Tudor Statesman* (London, 1976).

Tittler, R. *The Reign of Mary I* (London and New York, 1983).

Tittler, R., 'Bacon, Sir Nicholas (1510–1579), lawyer and administrator', *ODNB* (Oxford, 2004; online edn 2004).

Tosh, W., *Male Friendship and Testimonies of Love in Shakespeare's England* (London, 2016).

Urwick, W., *Nonconformity in Herts, Being Lectures Upon the Nonconforming Worthies of St Albans, and Memorials of Puritanism and Nonconformity in All the Parishes of the County of Hertford* (London, 1884).

Verbrugge, R.M., 'Margaret More Roper's Personal Expression in the *Devout Treatise Upon the Pater Noster*', in M. Hannay (ed.), *Silent but for the Word: Tudor Women as Patrons, Translators, and Writers of Religious Works* (Kent, Ohio, 1985), pp. 30–42.

Virgoe, R., 'Walter Haddon', *History of Parliament online* <http://www.historyofparliamentonline.org>, 1982.

Wales, R.J.W., 'Cooke, Sir Anthony (1505/6–76) of Gidea Hall, Essex', *History of Parliament online* <http://www.historyofparliamentonline.org>, 1982.

Warnicke, R., 'Grey [other married name Stokes], Frances [*née* Lady Frances Brandon], duchess of Suffolk (1517–1559)', *ODNB* (Oxford, 2004).

Watson, F. (ed.), *Vives and the Renascence Education of Women* (London, 1912).

Wayne, V., 'Some Sad Sentences: Vives' *Instruction of a Christian Woman*', in M. Hannay (ed.), *Silent but for the Word: Tudor Women as Patrons, Translators, and Writers of Religious Works* (Kent, Ohio, 1985), pp. 15–29.

Whitelock, A. and MacCulloch, D., 'Princess Mary's Household and the Succession Crisis, July 1553', *The Historical Journal*, 50/2 (2007), pp. 265–87.

Whiting, M.B., 'The Learned and Virtuous Lady Bacon', *The Hibbert Journal*, 29 (1931), pp. 270–83.

Wilcox, H. (ed.), *Women and Literature in Britain 1500–1700* (Cambridge, 1996).

Woodward, J., *The Theatre of Death: The Ritual Management of Royal Funerals in Renaissance England 1570–1625* (Woodbridge, 1997).

Electronic

The Acts and Monuments Online <http://www.dhi.ac.uk/foxe>.

British History Online <http://www.british-history.ac.uk>.

Campbell, J.D., 'Bernardino Ochino and the Women Who Made His Career Possible', Society for the Study of Early Modern Women and Gender, 2016 <https://ssemwg.org/campbell/>, accessed 3 Nov 2021.

Early English Books Text Creation Partnership <https://quod.lib.umich.edu/e/eebogroup/>.

St Edward the Confessor, the Parish Church of Romford <https://www.stedwardsromford.com/history>, accessed 15 February 2022.

English Heritage, *History of Old Gorhambury House* <https://www.english-heritage.org.uk/visit/places/old-gorhambury-house/history>.

Harmer, J., Sir John Cheke's Greek Books', Centre for Material Texts, St John's College, University of Cambridge (2010), <https://www.english.cam.ac.uk/cmt/?p=878>, accessed 25 Oct 2017.

Mantel, H., First Reith Lecture (2017) <http://downloads.bbc.co.uk/radio4/reith2017/reith_2017_hilary_mantel_lecture1.pdf>.

'Out of his shadow: The long struggle of wives under English Law', The High Sheriff of Oxfordshire's Annual Law Lecture, given by Lord Wilson on 9 October 2012, <https://www.supremecourt.uk/docs/speech-121009.pdf>.

Oxford Dictionary of National Biography Online (ODNB) <https://www.oxforddnb.com>.

Index

Note: *italicised* page references indicate illustrations; the suffix 'n' indicates a note